"Mothering is just about the hardest job around. Denise's material puts powerful tools into the hands of mothers to navigate the journey victoriously."

JOSH MCDOWELL
SPEAKER AND AUTHOR

"Are you a mom who needs encouragement, hope, energy? WISE up! Let Denise show you the way to life and freedom in Christ through her teaching and heartwarming stories."

DR. KEVIN LEMAN
PARENTING EXPERT AND AUTHOR OF *THE BIRTH ORDER BOOK*,
BECOMING THE PARENT GOD WANTS YOU TO BE, AND *MAKING CHILDREN MIND WITHOUT LOSING YOURS*

"This study treats motherhood as the divine calling God intends it to be. If your heart's cry is to know Him and the power of His resurrection, read this book."

JENNIFER KENNEDY DEAN
EXECUTIVE DIRECTOR, THE PRAYING LIFE FOUNDATION
AUTHOR OF *HE RESTORES MY SOUL*

"*Freedom for Mothers* leads us to the author and perfecter of motherhood, the person who can change us and our homes from the inside out. I appreciate Denise's personal and practical approach, and the emphasis on a personal discovery of these truths. A must for mothers!"

BONNIE BARROWS THOMAS
SPEAKER, DAUGHTER OF CLIFF BARROWS, DAUGHTER-IN-LAW OF MAJOR IAN THOMAS

"Denise Glenn invites you to have a cup of tea with her as she shares from her heart the wisdom God has given her. This is a personal book. You feel as if she is having a one-on-one conversation with you as she shares an in-depth Bible study, a guided time of prayer, and tips on being a parent. A must-read for all mothers!"

JOBETH YOUNG
WIFE OF PASTOR ED YOUNG, SECOND BAPTIST CHURCH, HOUSTON

"This book and these videos give us so much of God's wisdom in parenting and provide us with His love and direction. What an awesome God! I think Denise Glenn has captured that very thing in this book!

MARGE CALDWELL
AUTHOR, NATIONAL CONFERENCE SPEAKER, COUNSELOR,
WIFE, MOTHER OF THREE, GRANDMOTHER, AND GREAT GRANDMOTHER

"*Freedom for Mothers* is not only a captivating title, but also an invaluable resource for mothers (and grandmothers) of all ages! Denise Glenn's wise and godly life and experiences are mirrored in every single page. The book is definitely a 'must' for Christian homes and church libraries."

BEVERLY TERRELL
NATIONAL CONCERT ARTIST AND SEMINAR SPEAKER

MOTHERWISE

Freedom for Mothers

FIVE LIBERATING PRINCIPLES FOR VICTORIOUS MOTHERING

Multnomah Publishers® *Sisters, Oregon*

DENISE GLENN

FREEDOM FOR MOTHERS
published by Multnomah Publishers, Inc.

© 1999 by Denise Glenn
International Standard Book Number: 1-57673-594-X

Design by Christopher Gilbert
Cover photograph by Laurence Monneret/Tony Stone Images
Interior illustrations of flesh pictures, octopus, and butterfly by Paige S. Holsapple

Scripture quotations are from
New American Standard Bible © 1960, 1977 by the Lockman Foundation.
Used by permission.

Multnomah is a trademark of Multnomah Publishers, Inc. and is registered in the U.S. Patent and Trademark Office.
The colophon is a trademark of Multnomah Publishers, Inc.

For information:
MOTHERWISE MINISTRIES
11875 W. LITTLE YORK, SUITE 1104
HOUSTON, TEXAS 77041

99 00 01 02 03 04 05   10 9 8 7 6 5 4 3 2 1

TO DAVID

I want to commemorate
our journey in parenting by sharing with others the powerful
way God has worked to teach us the truths contained in this book.
You are my love, my mentor, my dearest friend, and
my partner in ministry.

and

TO DANIELLE

You had the courage to do the will
of God when no one understood.
Not even me.

Acknowledgments

I wish to thank:

Danielle Young, my firstborn, for allowing me to share both our painful and victorious moments in the pages of this book. Thank you for your encouragement, sweetheart.

Stephanie Ottosen, my precious, organized daughter, who serves as our operations manager, and Phyllis Sullivan, our faithful ministry coordinator. Without them the MotherWise ministry could not have managed its recent tremendous growth.

Brittany, the "baby" of our family, for encouraging me to do what God has called me to do even when it is inconvenient for you.

Carrie Overby, my talented sister, for helping create the mothering skills discussions.

Paige Holsapple for her beautiful illustrations.

Cindy Blades and her children, Joe, Travis, Christiana, and Jason; Katie and Maggie Schneider; and Stephanie Ottosen and Brittany Glenn for performing so beautifully in the mothering skills skits on the video. Thanks, guys!

Kathy and Tommy Orr for the loan of their beautiful home for the filming of the skits. Thanks for letting us invade for a long afternoon.

Liza Brown, for cooking meals and running errands and making phone calls so I could write this book.

Cliff Young, my creative son-in-law, for ideas on getting this message out in unique ways.

Charlie Davis, Shirita and Paul Schneider, and the entire Winning Walk family for all the support and love they give to me and this ministry.

David, my husband and soul mate, for being in constant prayer and enabling me to follow the Cross.

From the Author

As a tiny girl, I wanted to be a mother. Baby dolls were my constant companions. The Christmas I was fourteen, my mother told me that it was the last Christmas I would get a doll—it was getting embarrassing!

My love of babies never left me. After David Glenn and I married while attending Texas Tech University in Lubbock, Texas, I impatiently waited through graduation (his from Texas Tech and mine from the University of Houston) and the purchase of our first little house to begin a family. However, God had other plans.

Infertility plagued us, and I finally consulted a Christian counselor for help in dealing with the pain. My counselor suggested what sounded like a simple solution: "Tell God it's okay if you never have a child; what you want is Him." Thinking I could complete any "Christian" assignment, I walked out of the office and tried to pray that prayer. However, it occurred to me that God might take me up on it! For three days and nights I wrestled with the Lord. I finally got on my face on my shag carpet (this was 1975 and you could literally hang on to your carpet!) and told God it was okay if I never had a child, what I wanted was Him—and I wasn't even sure what that meant! I was immediately at peace and assumed that meant God had heard my prayer and that we would not have children.

God must have been smiling. Soon those little dolls of my childhood were replaced with three little girls—all born within four years—being a mother had finally become a reality. But it wasn't quite the fantasy world I had imagined. Overwhelmed with three preschoolers, I began a diligent search to discover how to be a better mom.

I have been a Christian since the age of five and was reared in the loving home of a Baptist minister of music and education. Both my mother and my grandmother were excellent role models in the nurturing, supportive part mothers play in their children's lives. In addition to their godly counsel, God brought five godly older women into my life who also began practicing what Titus 2 teaches. The Bible studies contained in this book are the result of twenty-one years of prayer and sharing with those precious women.

Our three girls are Danielle, Stephanie, and Brittany. Danielle is married to Cliff Young, and they are in full-time ministry in the Christian folk band, Caedmon's Call. Stephanie is married to Micah Ottosen. Micah manages Caedmon's Call along with other Christian bands, and Stephanie is busy finishing her college education and working in the MotherWise office. Brittany is a busy high schooler who sings in a Christian praise-and-worship band, is looking forward to attending college, and keeps us on our toes! David works as a geophysicist with a Houston-based oil company, is involved in lay counseling, and is an active deacon at our church.

MOTHERWISE VISION

Never in America's history have her children been more in need of strong parenting. Never have mothers been more desperate for answers…

Our objective is to inspire mothers to profess faith in Jesus Christ, to pass on the blessing of effective communication about her faith to her children, to deepen her walk with Jesus Christ through in-depth Bible study, and to provide her with information about mothering skills that will give her the tools to empower, not impair, her children. We believe the time has come to launch a major outreach program to the mothers of America. "For if you remain silent at this time, relief and deliverance will arise...from another place… And who knows whether you have not attained royalty for such a time as this?" (Esther 4:14)

MotherWise, a multifaceted training and support ministry to mothers, is a program of Winning Walk Family, Dr. Ed Young, and Second Baptist Church, Houston, Texas. The components include Bible study, prayer, and instruction in mothering skills. The program ministers to a mother's body, mind, and spirit (1 Thessalonians 5:23).

PERSONAL NOTE FROM DENISE

My prayer for you is that you will open your heart to hear from God on the subject of mothering. No human source of wisdom can even approach what God specifically wants to say to you. So listen to Him speak to you through His Word, in your prayers, and through His servants. He alone can show you the path to being the mother He desires you to be.

Contents

Contents continued

Introduction

Hi! Get a cup of tea and sit down with me. Are you searching for answers to good mothering? That's exactly where I was when I began this journey. I believe there is no challenge in your life that will equal the demands and joys of motherhood. And I believe God has something He wants to say to you on that very subject.

God's Word is your main resource for this course. I use the New American Standard version of the Bible throughout the text. Although we have printed some of the Scripture for you, you will need to keep your Bible handy as you study.

THE MOTHERWISE PROGRAM

Although a mother may use this workbook for personal Bible study, a mom benefits the most from being a part of a MotherWise group that participates in the full MotherWise program. In the MotherWise program, a group meets for two hours once a week for ten weeks. The meetings consist of four thirty-minute segments:

- Bible Study
- Prayer
- Mothering Skills
- Exercise

MotherWise Groups

The best way to study this material is with a group of five to twenty other mothers to form a support group. These groups can meet in homes, churches, office buildings—anywhere mothers can gather to encourage one another.

1. The support group will want to purchase the video set for the Bible study teaching segment. Each member of the group will need her own workbook.

2. If the group of moms is over ten, it should be divided into smaller groups of four or five. A Mentoring Mom will lead prayer time and discussion of the mothering skills each week. The questions at the end of each unit and the leader's guide will enable her to facilitate the discussions.

A Mentoring Mom is an experienced mother who will support and encourage the mothers in her group. In Titus 2:3–4, older women are told to encourage younger women to love their husbands and children. We want to encourage the development of these mentoring relationships between Titus 2 "mothers" and "daughters" through the use of this program.

3. We suggest that you exercise for thirty minutes together as a group to warm-up physically and spiritually before you watch the Bible study video. You may want to have someone lead the exercises, or you can purchase a Christian exercise video for your use at home or in your group setting. If space is limited, you might want to walk outside as a group for your exercise segment.

4. Mothers who work outside the home can meet in an office building conference room during the noon hour to have a support group. Brown bag lunches work best for these groups to conserve time. The regular two-hour program is condensed to a one-hour format by eliminating exercise and by shortening the prayer and mothering skills time to fifteen minutes each, instead of thirty.

Products Available

WORKBOOK AND LEADER'S GUIDE

This workbook is divided into ten units. Each unit represents one week of study. Each weekly unit is then divided into five daily lessons. One day's assignment should take approximately twenty to thirty minutes to complete. These studies were purposely designed to take a short amount of time because mothers are constantly "on call"!

The leader's guide is a resource for Mentoring Moms and directors of MotherWise groups.

AUDIO TAPES

Audio cassette tapes of this study are available from the MotherWise headquarters at Winning Walk. On the tapes, Denise Glenn teaches each lesson for thirty minutes. These tapes contain the audio portion of the video tapes.

VIDEO TAPES

The video set includes videotapes of Denise Glenn teaching each Bible study. The lessons are approximately thirty minutes in length. An introductory video is included in which Denise shares her personal testimony, explains how MotherWise got started, and gives an overview of the Bible studies.

To Contact MotherWise

Write to: MotherWise   Call: 1-888-272-6972 or 1-713-849-9335
11875 W. Little York, Suite 1104
Houston, TX 77041
www.motherwise.org

UNIT 1

FUEL FOR MOTHERS

INTRODUCTION

DAY 1
RUNNING ON EMPTY

DAY 2
HUNGER PANGS

DAY 3
THIRST QUENCHER

DAY 4
FRESH BREAD

DAY 5
FILL IT UP

———⊰⊱———

There has never been a time in our history when we have needed stronger mothers. And as we enter this new millennium, we know parenting has never been more complex. But moms are stretched in every way. They are physically, emotionally, and spiritually drained. How can a mom give what she doesn't have? Are there any real answers?

———⊰⊱———

Introductory Session

Welcome to MotherWise and the *Freedom for Mothers* Bible study! If you are participating in a MotherWise group, today will be a time to get acquainted with the women in your small discussion group and to familiarize yourself with the course and how it works.

These materials were prepared with group study in mind. However, if you are working in the workbook alone, here are a few suggestions to help you make the most of each component of the *Freedom for Mothers* Bible study.

Use the Bible study listening guide to take notes while listening to the audio or while viewing the video for each session. Or simply use the guide when you finish each unit as a way to review the concepts covered in the study.

The MotherWise group prayer requests form is a wonderful place for you to record the names of those for whom you would like to remember to pray. Read the guidelines for prayer in this introductory session for ideas on how to pray and consider praying as you start each unit. Guidelines are also given for prayer in each homework session.

Each unit also contains a mothering skills discussion guide. Read through this and think about the questions posed. Consult the resources listed under "Tools to Meet the Challenge" for additional information.

Days 1 through 5 are home study sessions designed to thoroughly familiarize you with the concepts covered in each unit. Consider setting aside five days each week to complete the homework. This would have you finishing the course in ten weeks, much the same as those in a MotherWise group.

Introductions

As each person in the group shares personal data about herself, fill in the chart below. Writing it down will help you remember.

MENTORING MOM

Name: _____

Husband's name: _____

Children's names and ages: _____

_____

Address: _____

Phone: (_____) _____-_____   Hometown: _____

EXERCISE LEADER

Name: _____

Husband's name: _____

Children's names and ages: _____

_____

Address: _____

Phone: (_____) _____-_____Hometown: _____

DISCUSSION GROUP MEMBERS

Name: _____

Husband's name: _____

Children's names and ages: _____

_____

Address: _____

Phone: (_____) _____-_____ Hometown: _____

Name: _____

Husband's name: _____

Children's names and ages: _____

_____

Address: _____

Phone: (_____) _____-_____ Hometown: _____

Name: _____

Husband's name: _____

Children's names and ages: _____

_____

Address: _____

Phone: (_____) _____-_____ Hometown: _____

Name: _____

Husband's name: _____

Children's names and ages: _____

_____

Address: _____

Phone: (_____) _____-_____ Hometown: _____

Name: _____

Husband's name: _____

Children's names and ages: _____

_____

Address: _____

Phone: (_____) _____-_____ Hometown: _____

Name: _____

Husband's name: _____

Children's names and ages: _____

_____

Address: _____

Phone: (_____) _____-_____ Hometown: _____

Name: _____

Husband's name: _____

Children's names and ages: _____

_____

Address: _____

UNIT 1
Bible Study Listening Guide

As you are watching the video or listening to the audio, watch interactively by filling in the answers to the following questions.

1. What do you consider the most memorable event about the beginning of MotherWise?

   _____

2. In the overview of the Bible study, the five principles we will study are:

   Principle #1:

   _____

   Principle #2:

   _____

   Principle #3:

   _____

   Principle #4:

   _____

   Principle #5:

   _____

3. In this workbook, the homework _____ the lesson instead of precedes the lesson.

4. The things I need to remember about prayer time are:

   _____

   _____

5. How will you create community among the women in your MotherWise group?

   _____

   _____

   _____

Group Prayer Guidelines

1. If your MotherWise ministry has mothers of children of various age groups, break into small groups of five to six for prayer and discussion time together each week according to the age of the children. Because the children are somewhat at the same stage of development, these mothers will have many common mothering issues.

2. We recommend that prayer time be observed *before* the mothering skills discussion time. Experience has taught us that it is difficult to stop discussion and begin prayer time. Please keep prayer requests limited to yourself and your immediate family (husband and children). While we realize that prayer for our extended family and friends is very important, MotherWise time with your group is limited and is precious.

3. Please remember that what you discuss in prayer time is very personal. We ask that the requests lifted up in class be kept confidential within the group.

4. We hope that you feel comfortable in sharing your heart with the group. In MotherWise, we always have an imaginary sign written above the door of our meeting place, "Here you are loved and accepted just as you are!"

5. In general, we will try to follow the "Six S's for Prayer Time" as outlined by Evelyn Christensen in her book, *What Happens When Women Pray*. They are:

    (1) Subject by subject

    (2) Short Prayers

    (3) Simple Prayers

    (4) Specific Prayer Requests

    (5) Silent Periods

    (6) Small Groups

6. Prayer time together is a vital part of MotherWise. We look forward to all that God will do in it and through it!

MotherWise Group Prayer Requests

The first person in the group will share a one-sentence prayer request about her husband or children. Each person in the group will pray a one-sentence prayer over that request before moving on to the next person's request. The group will continue in this way until everyone has prayed over each request.

    1._____

    2._____

    3._____

4._____

5._____

6._____

7._____

8._____

9._____

10._____

UNIT 1
MOTHERING SKILLS DISCUSSION:

Introductory Session

1. During MotherWise, I hope to

_____

_____

_____

2. The thing I like best about motherhood is

_____

_____

_____

3. My greatest problem with my mothering is

_____

_____

4. My experience with God and spiritual things so far has been

_____

_____

_____

DAY 1

Running on Empty

BEGIN WITH PRAYER

Ask the Lord to do all the work in your heart that He wants to do.
Give Him complete freedom to work on any area that He desires.
Ask Him to make you the mother for your children that He wants you to be.

Motherhood may baffle you. Marriage may bewilder you. You may feel overwhelmed by trying to be super-woman to all the people around you. Sometimes you may feel like a total failure in the very roles where you want to succeed the most. Perhaps your life isn't the way you imagined it would be.

You may have begun your journey in mothering thinking that it would be a bed of roses. You may have envisioned cherublike little children cuddled in your arms sleeping peacefully while their siblings played quietly by. The reality may be a two-year-old who won't potty train, a third grader with ADHD, a sassy fourteen-year-old, a high school senior you can't let go of, or a twenty-five-year-old prodigal. You may feel like you are operating on an empty tank.

Do you want to be a mother who exhibits love, joy, peace, patience, kindness, goodness, faithfulness, gentleness, and self-control with her children on a consistent basis? Of course you do. But reality is sometimes disappointing, right?

Mom, there is help and there is hope. The Lord Jesus wants to take you in His everlasting arms and soothe away the frustrations and hurts. He wants to give you the answers you need. What your heart so desires is exactly what He wants to give you.

You see, Jesus did not come just to help you be a mom. He came to do the work *for* you, *in* you, and *through* you. That is totally different from pulling yourself up by the bootstraps, trying very hard, and then asking Jesus to bless you. Jesus wants to bless you by filling your life with His life so He can accomplish His purposes on the earth through you.

In the next ten weeks, we're going to begin a journey with God. We will ask Him to remove the roadblocks and open the channels in our hearts so we can receive all of the life of Jesus that He desires to pour in. When that occurs, we will begin to experience the freedom of being the women, wives, and mothers God intended.

We have a God who doesn't just love us. He *is* love. We have hearts that are desperately in need of His unconditional, never-changing, always-available love. The trouble is, there is blockage in our hearts that keeps us from receiving the love of God. And when we as wives and mothers don't receive the love of God, we can't give love. We're supposed to give unconditional love to our husbands, our children, our neighbors, our friends and extended family, our co-workers, and the lost world around us. That's the way God planned for it to work.

PROBLEMS WITH A SOLUTION

Let's begin our study by reading Psalm 107:1–9.

What are the problems encountered in verses 4–5?

_____

Read Psalm 107:10–16.

What is the problem in verses 10–12?

_____

Read Psalm 107:17–22.

What is the problem in verses 17–18?

_____

Read Psalm 107:23–32.

What is the problem in verses 23–27?

_____

Can you relate to any of these problem situations? Does mothering make you feel like the situation in verses 4–5? Are you a traveler in distress not knowing which way to go? Do you have a child who can't find his way?

Does your home situation feel like a prison as the scenario in verses 10–12 expresses? Do you have children who are imprisoned in "darkness and misery"?

Does the sickness of verses 17–18 look familiar? Are you sometimes so upset about your children that you can't eat? Do you have a daughter suffering from anorexia or bulimia? Are you?

Is your mothering experience like a stormy sea as in verses 23–27? Are you tossed about on the waves—up one minute and down the next? Are you fearful about a child who is being tossed about on the seas of peer pressure? Are you afraid they'll go down like the Titanic?

Most of us who've been mothers more than a few weeks have had some of those feelings to some degree or another. Maybe your problem situations are very serious. Perhaps they are only minor and temporary. But we all have experienced times when we need help. We've seen the problems. Now let's look at the solutions.

What is the prayer in verse 6?

_____

_____

What is the prayer in verse 13?

_____

_____

What is the prayer in verse 19?

_____

_____

_____

What is the prayer in verse 28?

_____

_____

In each case, the people in distress cried out to the Lord and He delivered them. Our first step in becoming free as mothers is to cry out to the Lord. In the form of a prayer, write out your main concerns about your children or other areas of your life. Pour out your heart to Him.

_____

_____

What is the provision of God in verses 6–7?

_____

What is the provision of God in verses 13–14?

_____

What is the provision of God in verses 19–20?

_____

_____

What is the provision of God in verses 28–30?

_____

_____

When we come to God with our heart's cry and if we are willing to listen to Him and obey Him, He will "lead us by a straight way." He will "bring us out of the darkness." He will send His Word and bring "healing" to our situation. He will cause our "storms to be still."

What is the praise in verses 8–9?

_____

_____

What is the praise in verses 15–16?

_____

_____

What is the praise in verses 21–22?

_____

_____

What is the praise in verses 31–32?

_____

_____

Compare verse 9 with Psalm 22:26; 34:10; 63:5; 146:7. Summarize the message of these verses.

_____

_____

FULLNESS AND FREEDOM FOR MOTHERS

In the next ten weeks, we are going to be taking a journey in God's Word to discover the fullness and freedom we can experience as mothers. This journey begins with a look inside our own hearts and ends at the foot of the cross. You may have never experienced Jesus the way you will during the next few weeks. During this study you will learn:

- **The Principle of the Vine: Why Jesus Can Fill Your "Love Bucket"**

   To be a fulfilled wife and mother, you must first get your personal needs met from Jesus, the only one who can truly meet those needs. In unit 2 we will cover this vital first step to being a complete woman, wife, and mother.

- **The Principle of the Branch: How to Get Empty So He Can Fill You**

   Most of us go to all the wrong places to try to get our needs met for love, acceptance, and security. We end up discouraged, depressed, and distraught. In units 3 and 4 of this workbook, we will examine what the Bible has to say about the "fleshy" ways we set up roadblocks to receiving the love of God.

- **The Principle of the Shears: The Ultimate Solution to Being Filled and Free**

   The answer to our heart's cry is more simple than most of us think. God's plan for our freedom and fulfillment is not complicated, but it is costly. Units 5 and 6 will take us on a journey to the cross—the only place where troubles can end and life can begin.

- **The Principle of the Bud: Living Life with a New Heart and a New Mind**

   Most of us want to be mothers who exhibit love, joy, peace, patience, kindness, goodness, gentleness, faithfulness, and self-control in every situation and relationship. But reality is sometimes disappointing. We know we can't accomplish that. It would require someone else to do it for us—someone whose love is always pure and whose thoughts are always wise. In units 7 and 8, we will discover how to begin the process of allowing Jesus to renew our hearts and minds and to live His life _in_ us, _through_ us, and _for_ us. This is how fulfillment and freedom can finally be ours.

- **The Principle of the Fruit: Keeping the Bucket Full**

   Now that I am filled up, I want to stay that way! I want to continuously express love, joy, and peace. That's a tall order! It requires setting our minds on Christ and being equipped to engage in spiritual warfare. Those are the topics of units 9 and 10—the powerful conclusion to our study. Mom, are you ready to have those empty places in your heart filled up? Are you ready to experience freedom in every relationship? Are you ready to be whole and clean and pure? I must tell you there is a cost. The process is simple but expensive. In fact, it will cost you your very life. But in return, you will experience life as it was meant to be lived—with all the love and joy and peace you can possibly contain. You will "run and not grow weary, you will walk and not grow faint."

If you will come to God hungry and ready to be filled up with what He can give you, you'll be amazed at what He will do. He will do more for you than you can imagine. I cannot promise that your children will immediately straighten up and that your marriage will be perfectly in tune after this *Freedom for Mothers* study, but I can tell you that if you allow God access to your heart during the next ten weeks and ask Him to fill you with all that you need for your situation, He will do it.

I can't wait to show you the liberating truths in the next lessons. Hang on to your seats because you're in for a journey with Jesus—and that's always exciting!

Prayer

Father, I am ready for You to work in my life. I want You to do whatever it takes to make me the woman, wife, and mother You want me to be. I love you, Lord. I pray all this in the name of Jesus. Amen.

Mothering Tip

Set aside a specific time each day to be alone with God. Use your workbook as a guide to get started. Get out your Bible and answer the questions in this workbook. Try praying aloud on your knees. If you consistently spend a few minutes each day, you'll be surprised at how much you will learn!

DAY 2

BEGIN WITH PRAYER

Tell the Lord you want to open your heart to receive His love and tender care.

Tell Him that sometimes you have trouble receiving His love.

Ask Him to take the next ten weeks to show you how to let His love into your heart.

The tantalizing aromas of a bakery or chocolate factory create desires in us. All of a sudden we "need" some pastries or some chocolate candy. The smart merchant uses the aroma to lead buyers to his source.

Our restless hunger is not a bad thing but a good thing that drives us to find a way our need can be met.

Read Matthew 5:6.

Who is satisfied?

_____

What are they hungry and thirsty for?

_____

Do you sense a restless longing for something and you aren't sure what would satisfy? Could it be that you are restless for a deep relationship with God?

Read Psalm 143.

Write out phrases from the following verses that describe the psalmist's longing for God.

Verse 1:   _____

Verse 6:   _____

Verse 7:   _____

Verse 8:   _____

Verse 9:   _____

Verse 10:   _____

Verse 11:   _____

Write out verse 6:

_____

_____

Take a few moments to stretch out your hands heavenward. Raise your arms to the Father as your little children would raise their arms for you to pick them up. Read Psalm 143:6 to God as a prayer.

Prayer

Lord Jesus, open my eyes that I might see You. Let me begin to get Your heart and Your mind concerning me.

Take me on this journey to discover who I am and who You are. I give my life into Your hands.

And I pray this in Your precious Name. Amen.

Mothering Tip

Listen to praise and worship CDs or cassette tapes in your car, in the house, and even when you are outside. Christian bookstores have many selections in different musical styles. Some are just instrumental and some are sing-alongs. Some are new choruses and others are old hymns. Choose several that fit your style and listen continuously throughout the day. You will be amazed at how it helps you to focus on the Lord and brings peace to your household.

Day 3
Thirst Quencher

BEGIN WITH PRAYER

Open your heart to the love of God.
Settle yourself, be still and quiet, and get ready to hear from Him.

COME TO ME

Jesus really does understand your situation. No one else really can understand what you are feeling and experiencing, but He does, and He has a message for you today.

Read Matthew 11:28–30.

Who does Jesus welcome to come to Him?

_____

What does He promise when we come to Him?

_____

What do you think He means by "take My yoke upon you"?

_____

Which "yoke" or "load" in your life is heavy and hard and weighing you down?

_____

What does Jesus say about His yoke?

_____

Jesus offers rest for our souls. Your soul is made up of your mind, your emotions, and your will. Dr. Bill Gillham from Fort Worth, Texas, says we have a "thinker," a "feeler," and a "chooser." Jesus tells us we can come to Him to find rest for all three, but there is a condition to this promise.

The command in these gentle verses is to take the yoke of Jesus and to learn from Him. To get into a yoke or harness, one must submit to being harnessed. The one harnessed must submit to the master.

Are you willing to let Jesus put you into His harness and teach you so you can find rest for your soul? Will you allow Him to lead you down His path? Record your thoughts.

_____

_____

SOUL REST

Read Psalm 116:1–9.

Find the verse that contains the word *rest* and copy it here.

_____

_____

Why can the psalmist enter into God's rest?

_____

_____

The psalmist can rest because he trusts God to take care of his problems. He has seen God rescue him in the past. He reminds himself that he has a compassionate and gracious Lord who hears his voice.

Now read all nine verses again. In verses 1 and 2, why does the psalmist say he loves the Lord?

_____

_____

Copy Psalm 116:5–7 here.

_____

_____

_____

_____

Now repeat it back to God as a prayer. Direct the words right to Him. Instead of saying, "the Lord," say, "You." Take your time on this activity. Use it to praise and worship your gracious and righteous and compassionate heavenly Father in whom you can find rest.

Gracious are You, Lord, and righteous; yes, You are compassionate.
You preserve the simple; I was brought low, and You saved me. Return to your rest,
O my soul, for the Lord has dealt bountifully with you.

MOTHERING TIP

Feelings are fickle. We can't live our lives based on our feelings. You may feel like a failure one minute or like superwoman of the century the next. But it's not our changeable feelings that should govern our lives. We must live our lives on the truth of God's Word.

Repeat this sentence out loud to yourself several times today: "God loves me and I choose today to rest in Him."

DAY 4

Fresh Bread

BEGIN WITH PRAYER

If you know the song, "Open My Eyes, Lord, I Want to See Jesus,"
sing it as a prayer. Sit in silence for a few moments to collect
your thoughts and focus on Jesus Christ.

Read John 6:22–31.

Why were the people seeking Jesus?

_____

What did they want Him to do for them?

_____

Copy verse 27.

_____

_____

_____

_____

Summarize this verse in your own words.

_____

_____

Jesus had fed five thousand hungry people with five loaves and two fish. (See John 6:4-14.) The people wanted Him to again meet their physical needs. Jesus had become instantly famous and popular with the people because they saw Him as a "Sugar Daddy" to be exploited. Jesus would have no part of it. He continued to direct them to their real source of hunger—their real need which He came to fulfill.

Read John 6:32–35, 47–48, 51.

What is the true bread of heaven according to John 6:35?

_____

In John 6:35, Jesus makes an amazing promise. What is that promise?

_____

_____

What do you think the promise means in your life?

_____

Why are you seeking Jesus? Is it to get Him to do your will? Do you want Him to solve your problems according to your plan? Do you want a few "loaves of bread" from Him to satisfy your immediate need, or are you ready to ask Him to feed you the "true bread of heaven"? The true bread of heaven is Jesus Himself. It is not what He can do for us; it is His life in us. Are you ready for the True Bread?

During the next ten weeks, I want to challenge you to open your heart fully to the Lord Jesus Christ and ask Him to fill you with all of His life and power. If you do, you will begin to experience the flow of His love and joy and peace like you never dreamed possible. You will see dramatic changes in your heart that will enable you to give your children the strong mothering they so desperately need. Will you join me in this adventure?

Lord Jesus, I open my heart to You today. I want to know You, Lord, like I have never known You before.

Fill me with Yourself as I give myself to You. I pray this in Jesus' holy name. Amen.

Encourage your young children to read by:

1. Reading to them at bedtime, naptime

2. Listening to them read their early readers

3. Buying books for them

4. Turning off the television

5. Letting them see you reading for pleasure

Encourage your older kids to read by:

1. Buying books they like to read

2. Taking them to the library or bookstore

3. Asking them to tell you about their books…and then really listen and ask questions

4. Turning off the television

5. Letting them see you reading for pleasure

DAY 5

BEGIN WITH PRAYER

Enter into your prayer time thanking God for all His blessings.

Really take the time to "count your blessings and name them one by one."

THE PLACE OF PEACE

Read Psalm 23.

What is the setting and scenery described in this psalm?

_____

The Lord is described as a _____

What do people in that occupation do?

_____

List every reference in the psalm to the words "my," "I," and "me." After each reference write out what the Lord does for us in each case.

For example, Verse 1: "My shepherd"—the Lord takes care of me like I'm His lamb. "I shall not want"—God gives me everything I need.

Verse 2:

_____

_____

_____

Verse 3:

_____

_____

_____

Verse 4:

_____

_____

_____

Verse 5:

_____

_____

_____

Verse 6:

_____

_____

_____

What do you think God wants you to know about your relationship with Him through this psalm?

_____

_____

The pastoral setting of this psalm takes us to a quiet stream and a green meadow where our heavenly Shepherd cares for us. Our souls can find rest here. Here we are safe. The beginning of opening our hearts to receiving God's love is getting quiet and beginning to hear His sweet voice.

He longs to shepherd us. He wants to lead us to feed where we can grow and become fully mature and strong. That is what shepherds do. They protect the sheep from harm, all the while leading them to wonderful, rich feeding grounds. That is what Jesus wants to do for you. Your job is to follow the Shepherd.

Did you discover all the ways He wants to care for you? He makes you lie down in green pastures, leads you beside quiet waters, restores your soul, guides you in the paths of righteousness for His name's sake, is with you in trouble, comforts you, feeds you in the presence of your enemies, anoints you with the oil of His Spirit, fills the cup of your heart, and allows you to stay at His house. Moms, it just doesn't get any better than that! Spend a few quiet moments allowing the truths of Psalm 23 to soak into your heart and mind today.

Do you sometimes have trouble feeling God's love? Ask Him to speak to you in a way you can hear Him and understand Him. Tell Him that you are going to choose to believe that His love is real and true even when you can't feel it. Now spend the rest of the day listening to God, allowing Him to express His love to you.

Journal your experience.

_____

_____

_____

_____

_____

_____

Prayer

Lord, I thank You that You care for me in big and small ways.

Today let me see Your tender, loving care. I choose to rest in the place where You have led me.

I pray this in Your precious name. Amen.

Mothering Tip

A big part of a mother's job is taking care of sick children. One idea many moms have shared is how important it is to have over-the-counter drugs in the house *before* anyone gets sick. Invariably the onset of illness comes in the middle of the night or when you are alone in the house with a sick child and don't want to take him out.

Ask your doctor which medicines he recommends for your medicine cabinet. Keep an up-to-date supply on hand for those times when you hear, "Mom, I don't feel good...."

UNIT 2

THE PRINCIPLES OF THE VINE: THE LIFE

MOTHERING SKILL: ENCOURAGING YOUR CHILD'S NEXT STEP TOWARD GOD

DAY 1
LOVE BUCKET

DAY 2
LOVE FOUNTAIN

DAY 3
LOVE LINE

DAY 4
LOVE MESSAGES

DAY 5
LOVE LIFE

For a mother to give love and acceptance and security to her children, she must have her own needs met. Many women try to get those needs met from relationships, achievements, and appearance. Are these the answers?

UNIT 2
Bible Study Listening Guide

1. The visual aids used to help me remember the lesson were:

_____

2. The key Bible verse is:

_____

3. The principle we are studying is:

_____

4. What I personally need to remember from this lesson is:

_____

MotherWise Group Prayer Requests

1._____

2._____

3._____

4._____

5._____

6._____

7._____

8._____

9._____

10._____

UNIT 2
MOTHERING SKILLS DISCUSSION:

Encouraging Your Child's Next Step toward God

Challenge: To say the words, pray the prayers, provide the materials and activities that will encourage our children to seek God on their own.

During this discussion time, you will get practical help in leading your child to Christ and in encouraging his spiritual growth.

What is your child's next step toward God? That is, what do you perceive to be the next step in your child's journey in walking with God? Is it to be exposed to godly influences? Understand the plan of salvation? Accept Christ? Read the Bible? Pray? Be obedient? Relate common daily occurrences to God? Stand firm under peer pressure? Follow God's direction for his life?

_____

What scares you most about your role in leading your children?

_____

_____

_____

What progress in the past six months have you seen in your child's walk with God?

_____

_____

_____

What is your greatest concern about your child's walk with God?

_____

_____

_____

Tools to Meet the Challenge:

How to Lead a Child to Christ, Daniel H. Smith (Chicago: Moody Press, 1987).

When Mothers Pray, Cheri Fuller (Sisters, Ore.: Multnomah Publishers, Inc., 1998).

Teaching Your Child How to Pray, Rick Osborne (Chicago: Moody Press, 1997). Rick Osborne's web site for parents and kids: www.lightwavepublishing.com

Live a Praying Life (Independence, Mo.: The Master's Touch Publishing Co., 1998). *Power Praying* (Mukilteo, Wash.: WinePress Publishing, 1997); and *Heart's Cry* (Birmingham, Ala.: New Hope Publishing, 1997) all by Jennifer Kennedy Dean.

Praying God's Will for My Son/Daughter, Lee Roberts (Nashville, Tenn.: Thomas Nelson Publishers, 1998).

- **Words to Encourage Your Child's Next Step toward God**

  Tell the truth…about heaven, hell, death, and other topics that concern them.

  Take advantage of opportunities as they arise.

  Don't use force or manipulation.

- **Prayers to Encourage Your Child's Next Step toward God**

  Pray Scripture prayers over your children. This means to take a passage out of the Bible and read it to God as a prayer. Personalize it by directing it to God:

  Ephesians 1:16–23

  Ephesians 3:14–21

  Colossians 1:9–14

- **Materials to Encourage Your Child's Next Step toward God**

  Your child should have his own Bible.

  Use devotional books.

  Read Christian biographies and fiction.

  Listen to Christian music.

- **Activities to Encourage Your Child's Next Step toward God**

  Children's and youth activities at church

  Vacation Bible School

  Christian summer camps

  Christian music concerts

  Christian retreats

  Consider Christian schools or homeschooling

- **Your Life Can Encourage Your Child's Next Step toward God**

  The single most important thing you can do is to live in absolute surrender to God. They are watching you, imitating you, scrutinizing your motives and behaviors. If God is real in your life, they can't miss it!

LEADING YOUR CHILD TO CHRIST

The most awesome privilege for parents is to introduce their children to Jesus Christ and to give them an opportunity to accept Jesus as Savior. While we cannot make the decision for the child, neither should we have a "hands off" attitude. I strongly encourage you to read the little book, *How to Lead a Child to Christ*, Daniel H. Smith (Chicago: Moody Press, 1987).

1. From the day you find out you are pregnant, begin praying for the salvation of your child or grandchild. (I have begun to pray for my "grandchildren-to-be"!)

2. Teach your child how very much God loves him and also that He has a plan for his life.

3. Help your child have an awareness of sin—that is, teach your child that when anyone (including you) deliberately chooses to disobey God, they have sinned. But be careful here, Mom. Don't use this as an opportunity to use guilt and scare tactics to force your child to "make a decision for Christ" before he is ready.

4. Answer your child's questions about God in simple, straightforward language.

5. When he is old enough to understand, explain how Jesus died on the cross to pay the cost of his sin. Then tell him that if he asks Jesus to forgive him of his sin and to come into his heart, Jesus will immediately come to live inside him. Also, he will live with Jesus in heaven someday. Continue to answer his questions and pray for him.

6. Wait on your child to respond in his own time. Do not hurry your child to "make a decision for Christ." You are not your child's Holy Spirit. Let the Spirit do the work of convicting your child. Simply be available to the Lord to be used as a vessel in God's hand to speak at the right time and to be silent at the right time.

Little children want to please. Don't use "making a commitment to Christ" as a way for your child to please you. When children know the truth about sin, heaven, hell, death, Christ's love, and His plan to pay for our sins, they can, and many do, respond on their own to Christ. I am seeing children who are very young understand and respond to the gospel.

7. When he is ready to make the decision to become a Christian, don't put it off. Don't wait to talk to a minister. Lead him to Christ in that moment when his heart is tender and ready.

Pray a simple prayer, letting him repeat your prayer. You might have him pray,

> *Lord Jesus, thank You for loving me.*
> *I know I am a sinner and I need You.*
> *Thank You for paying for my sins by dying on the cross.*
> *Please come into my heart now.*
> *I want to be Your child. I give You my whole life.*
> *In Jesus' holy name I pray. Amen.*

Then have him pray whatever is on his heart. Don't help him with the second part of the prayer. It is very important that he pray on his own, expressing himself to God. Then tell him the angels are rejoicing in heaven because now he is God's child!

ENCOURAGING YOUR BELIEVING CHILD

If your child is a born-again believer in Jesus Christ, you have the awesome privilege of helping him throughout his life in taking his next step in walking with God.

While They Are Living at Home:

You have direct influence over:

a. church attendance

b. Bible training

c. encouraging their prayer life

d. relating daily life occurrences to God and His Word

When They Leave Your Home:

You still have a big job, Mom.

a. Your work is to pray continuously for your child.

b. Invite your children to events that will inspire them.

c. Occasionally provide materials to stimulate their spiritual growth.

d. If your relationship allows, ask them questions about what God is currently teaching them.

e. Keep your mouth shut most of the time, and pray, pray, pray, pray….

These are questions to ask yourself if your children are still at home.

How often does my child attend church? Why?

_____

_____

What sort of Bible training is my child receiving?

_____

_____

When does my child hear me pray? When do I pray with my child? Do I ever hear or know that my child is praying?

_____

_____

At our house, some of the most important times of encouraging our children's spiritual growth have come in the everyday occurrences of life. When our children are in a crisis—like losing a friend, doing poorly in school, not making the team, being rejected by peers, or making a foolish mistake—we try to listen, talk it through, and ask ourselves and our child what God is trying to communicate to us through this event. Then we pray with our child right then as openly and honestly as we know how. During these times, we learn more about our kids and more about God. It is a "next step toward God" for all of us.

DAY 1

Love Bucket

BEGIN WITH PRAYER

Ask Jesus to let you see yourself as you really are. Ask that all
the blinders be removed from your eyes.
Ask Him to give you spiritual insight this week by flooding
the eyes of your heart with light.

Just about every mother I know desires to be a good one. In fact, most of us want to be the kind of mom our children will want to write poetry and music about! But when we stop daydreaming, we have to admit that we all struggle in some area of mothering.

All of us have mothering issues that are currently causing us stress. Our teenagers may be giving us trouble. Or our middle schooler is being rejected, and we're the one who's really hurting. Training our preschoolers may be overwhelming to us. Or our issues may concern our marriage. We may have financial burdens or work related difficulties. Or our aging parents may be the cause of our distress.

The message of this workbook is that Jesus wants to set you free to be the mother He is calling you to be. As you allow Him full access to your heart through Bible study and prayer, and as you respond in obedience, you will begin to see emerging from your life the godly, fulfilled mother you long to be.

God has something planned for your life that will astound you. If you allow Him to work in your life during these weeks we spend together, you will see in the mirror a changed woman. Do you want to see love and joy and peace coming out of your life? Isn't that the kind of mother you want to be? One who is loving, joyous, peaceful, patient, kind, good, faithful, gentle, and self-controlled? Then dive into this study with your whole heart. And God will do, as it says in the Greek, "super super-abundantly" far over and above all you could dare to ask or think.

To begin our study in how to become free as moms—free of past hurts, present stresses, and fear of the future—let's go to the book of John.

LIFE IN THE VINE

Just before He was crucified, Jesus taught His disciples many important things. Starting in John 13 and continuing through John 17, He told them some of the most profound teachings He had ever shared.

When someone knows he is going to die, he doesn't waste words. Everything that person says becomes vital. The following were Jesus' last words to His disciples. Can you imagine how Jesus felt as He articulated these words?

Read John 15:5.

What plant is Jesus using for illustration? Which part of the plant does Jesus use to describe Himself? What part of the plant does Jesus use to describe you?

_____

When are you able to bear fruit?

_____

Finish the phrase, He says, "apart from Me…"

_____

"Apart from Him you can do nothing." As we say in Texas, "That's a zero with the rim knocked off." I cannot do my job as a mother or as a wife or as a worker apart from His vine life in me.

Jesus says He is the vine and we are His branches. The only way to have life is to be attached to the vine. To bear fruit, we have to have the vine life flowing through us. The sap of the vine is where the life of the vine resides.

The grapes that are formed are a result of the energy that has filled the vine. That's how your life will be. You will be so full of Jesus' vine life that the fruit of love, joy, peace, patience, kindness, goodness, faithfulness, gentleness, and self-control will come flowing out of your life. It won't require self-effort, it will happen naturally as a result of abiding in the vine.

But first, we must ask a basic question. Are you connected to the vine life of Jesus? Have you ever made a personal commitment to Him by asking Him to be Lord of your life? If not, this is where you need to begin.

CONNECTED TO THE VINE

If you want to connect yourself to Jesus for the first time in your life, start by reading Acts 16:31.

To trust God fully you must trust Him through Jesus Christ, His Son.

In John 14:6, Jesus says of Himself, *"I am the way, and the truth, and the life; no one comes to the Father, but through Me."*

Turning your life over to Jesus is the only way to have a relationship with God. You must go through Jesus to get to God.

Ask God to speak to you as you explore this truth in the book of Romans.

The Roman Road to Salvation:

Romans 3:23	*For all have sinned and fall short of the glory of God.*
Romans 5:8	*But God demonstrates His own love toward us, in that while we were yet sinners, Christ died for us.*
Romans 6:23	*For the wages of sin is death, but the free gift of God is eternal life in Christ Jesus our Lord.*

Romans 10:9–10	*That if you confess with your mouth Jesus as Lord, and believe in your heart that God raised Him from the dead, you shall be saved; for with the heart man believes, resulting in righteousness, and with the mouth he confesses, resulting in salvation.*
Romans 10:13	*For "Whoever will call on the name of the Lord will be saved."*

To have a relationship with God—to become "born again"—you must:

Acknowledge that you are a sinner and that you need a relationship with Jesus Christ to save you from everlasting hell.

Admit and *confess* your sins.

About face, turning from sin to God.

Ask Jesus to save you by His grace.

Allow Jesus Christ to rule your life.[1]

If you are ready, pray a prayer like this: *Lord Jesus, I am a sinner and I admit it. I am confessing this to You today. Forgive me of my sins. I want Your death on the cross to pay the penalty for my sins. I turn now from my sin and I turn to You. Save me and have mercy on me, Lord. Be my Master and my Lord. You alone are my God. In Jesus' name I pray. Amen.*

If you prayed that prayer from your heart, the angels are rejoicing! You are now God's child! You've just been born into a new family! *Now* you have the power source to become the kind of mother your children can call "blessed"!

Write today's date or the date of your own experience of trusting God for the first time.

_____/ _____/ _____

Call on your pastor or MotherWise group leader or a Christian friend and share this important decision. You need to tell someone about your new faith! Read Matthew 10:32.

If you have already made this crucial initial step in receiving God's love—if you are already a branch on the vine—then you may be asking the next important questions: *How do I draw life from the vine? What does it mean to abide? How does my attachment to the vine life of Jesus affect my mothering? My marriage?* We'll discover the answers to those questions in this unit and in the units to follow by taking it step by step.

First, let's talk about you and me. There will be no hiding behind a mask or façade. It's just us girls, so let's get personal.

THE LOVE BUCKET

Imagine a large bucket. This is your love bucket. It represents the place inside us that needs to be filled with love. You were created with a big empty love bucket. There is an empty place in me and an empty place in you. What would fill your love bucket?

What are the things that would make you feel satisfied and happy right now?

_____

_____

In that empty place in our hearts, we need to have our basic needs met. Compare your list of desires with the following three illustrations.

Blanket of Unconditional Love

In our "love buckets," we need to have the blanket of unconditional love. We need love, acceptance, and security. We want someone to love us without having to change. We want to be loved unconditionally just as we are. We want acceptance among our peers. We want the security of knowing there is someone in our lives who will always be there for us.

Blue Ribbon of Worth

We also need to know that we have value and worth. We need to receive a "blue ribbon" in some area that is important to us. We want to know that our lives count for something important. We want to do something valuable.

Letter Jacket

In the South, we have a tradition. It's not as popular as it was when I was growing up, but in many high schools, kids still participate in this ritual. When a couple is going together steadily and exclusively, the girl wears her boyfriend's letter jacket. What does that say about them? It says they belong to each other.

Every one of us has a need to belong. We need to have a relationship with someone we hold dear. We want to wear the "letter jacket" of being in an identifiable relationship.

These needs are not optional. We don't just want these needs to be met, we *must* have them met, and we will find a way. One way or another, we will find a way to stop the aching emptiness. We will do anything in the world to get our love buckets filled.

Read Philippians 4:19.

Where should you go to get your needs met?

_____

How many of your personal needs will be met if you go to this source? What does the verse say?

_____

What resource is tapped to supply your needs?

_____

Jesus is the vine. All life is in Him. We will find that the solution to our love needs, acceptance needs, security needs, significance needs, and identity needs are met in Him. Only He can meet the needs of our hearts. Only He will do so without ever letting us down and disappointing us.

Reread John 15:5. Copy it here.

_____

_____

_____

Lord Jesus, I want Your vine life to flow through me. Fill me with Your love.
Fill me with Your joy. Fill me with Your peace. You alone are God. You alone can meet the needs of my heart.
I acknowledge this in the name of Jesus, my Lord. Amen.

ℳOTHERING 𝒯ip

Purchase a small amount of flannel baby blanket fabric. Cut a small square with pinking shears and put it in your Bible at John 15. You have just made a "receiving blanket" for yourself. Every time you read this passage, concentrate on receiving Jesus' vine life, asking Him to let His life flow through yours.

If you have older children or teens, give them a square of the fabric and share what you learned today.

DAY 2

Love Fountain

BEGIN WITH PRAYER

Ask Jesus to fill you with His vine life.
Ask Him to open your heart fully to Him.
Put yourself in His hands today.

Read Psalm 81:8–10.

Rewrite verse 10 as a prayer. It might begin something like this:

Lord, You are my God, who delivered me. I now open _____

_____

_____

_____

The word *fill* in verse 10 is the Hebrew word *mala*. One of the meanings of that word is "to satisfy." If we open our hearts to the Lord, He promises to satisfy our longings. As mothers, we may have big gaping holes in our love buckets.

You may have gotten married thinking that your husband would supply all of your love needs. Surely here was a person who really understood you and really loved you unconditionally. He made you feel accepted and secure. You felt valuable and significant. You finally belonged.

But in reality, no matter how wonderful (or horrible) the man you chose to marry turned out to be, he is not God. He cannot meet all the needs of your heart. He will eventually disappoint you and let you down.

Or maybe you thought that children would solve the ache in your heart. Don't kids love their moms? You could just envision your children "rising up to call you blessed."

But crying babies or defiant toddlers or stubborn grade schoolers or rebellious teens have taught you that your children expect you to fill their buckets. It's not the other way around.

THE TRUE SOURCE

Read John 15:1–5.

How does Jesus describe Himself in verse 1?

_____

How does He describe God?

_____

What does Jesus do to branches that do not bear fruit at all?

_____

What does He do to branches that do bear fruit?

_____

What do you think "pruning" means?

_____

When Jesus says to His disciples that they are already "clean," He is referring to a gardening term. That means those branches have already been pruned of extraneous twigs that take the sap away from the main branch. How does Jesus tell them He has accomplished this pruning?

_____

What is Jesus' command in verse 4?

_____

How does the first part of John 15:5 fly in the face of those who claim that man is God?

_____

When have you recently tried to be the "vine" instead of the "branch"?

_____

What was the result?

_____

Apart from Jesus Christ we can do…

_____

How does that statement affect your mothering?

_____

Your marriage?

_____

The first lesson I must learn is that He is the Vine, I am not. He is God and I am not. Let that sink in for a moment. Are you tempted to play God in your own life?

Jesus did not come to help you with your life. He came to *be* your life and that is very different. He did not just come to be your Savior. He did not just come to be your Lord. He came to be your life!

Jesus said, "Every branch in me that does not bear fruit He [the Father] takes away." In verse 6, He is even more descriptive of what happens to branches that don't abide and bear fruit. They are gathered and cast into the fire and are burned. Hell is a real place reserved for judgment of those who choose to reject Jesus Christ.

Every branch that bears fruit, He prunes. Pruning is the process that fruit growers use to keep the trees bearing fruit. Branches and limbs must be trimmed away so that the healthy strong limbs of a tree will produce the best fruit. We all know that. But this is a principle in the Christian life that many of us find a bit shocking. "You mean God intentionally comes into my life and removes things so that I will bear more fruit?! Whatever happened to God as a God of love?"

We want to bear fruit. We want the Galatians 5 fruit to come flowing unhindered out of our lives. Read Galatians 5:22–23 to discover what fruit is possible for moms to bear. List them here:

_____

_____

We want our mothering to be characterized by love, joy, peace, and patience. But we don't want to endure the sometimes painful process to get there.

"There is no other way to be happy in Jesus, but to trust and obey," as the song reminds us. And sometimes that means trusting God when the plan includes pruning.

Jesus told us the secret to bearing fruit. We must abide in Him and He must abide in us. Look at the picture of your union with your husband. It is when you abide in each other that you bear the fruit of your womb. Bearing a child is only a shadow of our spirit relationship with our Lord. To abide in Him is to be grafted into His vine life.

Grafting involves cutting both the rootstock and the stem to be grafted in. Then the life-giving centers of each, called the cambium, must be matched perfectly. When those centers are perfectly matched so that the flow of life can go from the root to the stem, they are tied together securely. The nutrients the root takes up are sent up into the new branch producing new shoots and the new branch sends down energy gathered from the sun through photosynthesis into the rootstock. The life begins to flow and fruit is formed. The vine and the branch have become one. During that delicate process of growth, the plants must not be moved. They must remain firmly in place.[2]

Read Romans 11:16–18.

According to verse 16, how does the root affect the branches?

_____

Does a grafted branch receive something different from the root than a natural branch?

_____

What supports the branch?

_____

Here, Paul describes the grafting in of the Gentiles, the "wild olive branch" into the rich root of the olive tree, the life of the Lord Jesus. We partake of His life because in His mercy He allowed us to be grafted in.

The cambium of our hearts, our inmost being, must touch His heart. My heart and His heart must be one. We must be tied together firmly. Nothing must separate me from my Lord. And in the process of growth, I must remain very still in Him so that my roots can go deep into Him and He can abide deeply in me.

How does one abide? You begin with your prayer life. Your words to God are the way you reach up into Him to draw life down into yourself. His Word dwelling in you is the way He reaches down into you to pour out His life. As you begin to take in more of His Word, not just by reading and studying, but by obeying, you will begin to see His fruit born out in you.

Acknowledging that you can't do everything and that only He can is the first step to really being free, Mom. Write out a prayer of commitment to Christ. You might want to include your confession that you recognize that He is God and that you are not God. In your prayer, humble yourself before Him and submit your will to Him.

Write it out to seal it in your heart and mind.

_____

_____

_____

Father, I offer my emptiness to You and I ask You to fill it with Yourself.

Lord, I truly desire to abide in You and I want You to abide in me. Open my heart today and pour Yourself in.

Enable me to receive Your life in all of its fullness. Lord, I admit I have used other things and people to try to get my needs met. But today I am turning to You. I love you, Lord. In Jesus' name. Amen.

Let Jesus use your hands and feet to fill someone's love bucket today. For your husband, try a back rub after work or his favorite meal for dinner. Maybe a clean house would mean the most to him.

For adolescents why don't you put a note on his/her bed or mirror reminding them how much you love them? Tell them you're praying for them today. Then go to their bed when they aren't home and kneel down and pray for them.

Most little children love a good rock in the rocking chair or going outside to swing.

DAY 3

Love Line

BEGIN WITH PRAYER

Enter into God's presence with thanksgiving.
Thank Him for being in control of the universe and in control of your life.
Acknowledge to Him that He alone is your source of life.
Commit yourself to abiding in Him today
by keeping His commandment of love.

I am terrible at math. I am more right-brained than left, and that means I love language but am not too thrilled with linear thinking in mathematics. However, in his book *Handbook to Happiness,* Dr. Charles Solomon designed a mathematical illustration that really made sense to me.[3] It has helped me to understand something about Jesus' vine life in me. It enabled me to see how Jesus could undertake the mission of my marriage and the mothering of my children for me and through me.

A RAY

THE RAY

Adam

Romans 5:12, 18 & 19

Hell

That ray represents Adam's life. God created Adam at a definite point in time. Adam sinned, so his life's "ray" is pointing down toward hell. All people born on the earth are born into his family, the family of man. Before I became a Christian, I was like a dot on that ray.

Read 1 Corinthians 15:21–22.

As a member of Adam's family, we are doomed to die and spend eternity in hell. But there is good news.

A LINE

Now think about a line. A line in math is a string of points along a plane that goes for infinity in both directions. That line represents the life of Jesus Christ. His life goes forever in the past and forever in the future.

Read Hebrews 1:6–12.

Which verse speaks of Jesus existing before the world was created?

_____

Copy that verse here:

_____

_____

_____

Which verse speaks of Jesus living forever into the future?

_____

Copy that verse here:

_____

_____

Read John 17:24.

Which phrase in this verse proves that Jesus lived in eternity past?

_____

That lifeline of Jesus intersects the line of Adam. When we recognize that we are doomed to hell because our sins deserve it and choose to repent of our sins and ask Jesus Christ to be our indwelling Lord and master, we "jump" from the line of Adam to the lifeline of the Lord Jesus. We now share His life. His life is our life.

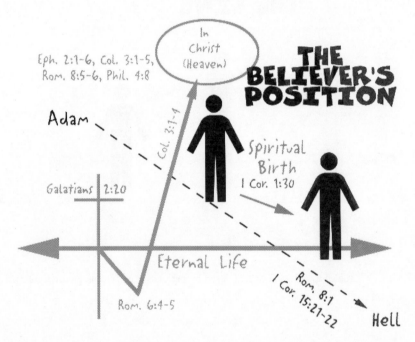

Taken from *Handbook to Happiness*, by Charles R. Solomon © 1971. Used by permission of Tyndale House Publishers, Inc. All rights reserved.

Read Ephesians 1:3–13.

How many times do you find the phrase "in Him" or "in Christ"?

_____

What do you have as a result of being "in Him" according to verse 3?

_____

Verse 5?

_____

Verse 7?

_____

Verse 9?

_____

Verse 11?

_____

Verse 13?

_____

Do you see all the incredible riches that belong to you when you are "in Him" on that eternal lifeline? You share His life. You are in a covenant relationship with Him, so that all He has, He gives to you. He has given you every spiritual blessing in the heavenly places, adoption as His child, redemption through His blood, the forgiveness of your sins, and we've been sealed with the Holy Spirit. All this and more we receive because our lives are "in" Him. Wow! You have absolutely everything you need. This is the truth! It does not depend on how you feel about it to be the truth. It is true because God said it. I may feel empty or stressed in my "feeler." But with my "chooser," I choose to believe the truth from God's Word that I have everything I need for this day. I have every spiritual blessing. I have love enough for my bucket because I have God and He is love. I have joy because His life is in me and His life is joyous in all circumstances. I have peace because He is my peace. My peace does not depend on my circumstances. My peace depends on His life flowing though me. I can choose as an act of my will to live by His life in me, not by the swirling circumstances around me.

Your "feeler" takes input from the circumstances and then panics. Your "thinker" takes input from the circumstances and begins to try to solve the problem—even if it's unsolvable! Your "chooser" must decide whether life will be lived from the input of the "feeler" or the "thinker," or it may take the third option. It can decide to submit to the life of Jesus operating within. (Colossians 3:3–4)

LIVING "IN" HIM

Read 1 John 3:23–24.

John explains what it means to abide in Christ in this passage. How does one abide in Him?

_____

According to verse 23, what two commandments are we to keep?

_____

Obedience is critical to abiding. We cannot go our own way and still abide. We cannot have it both ways. We must connect to the Vine. And what are we to obey? The law of love. We are to love the Lord with all our hearts and minds and souls and love our neighbors the same as we love ourselves.

Read 2 Peter 1:2–3.

What has Jesus' divine power granted to us?

_____

How do we obtain that?

_____

Jesus has called us by His own glory and excellence to have everything that we need that pertains to this life and to living it in a godly lifestyle. It is through the true knowledge of Him that we will have His life operating in us.

Now let's make this very practical. Could Jesus manage your children? Could He discipline them firmly and fairly with perfect consistency? Could He relate to your husband with constant unconditional love and acceptance without being passive or aggressive or selfish but totally giving while retaining a perfect balance of His own worth? Yes, of course He could. Can you do all those things all the time? No, of course you cannot.

If you are a believer, you have the life of the resurrected Lord Jesus Christ operating inside of you. He is able to do whatever He has called you to do. He has not asked you to do it. He knows you cannot. What He wants is to accomplish His purpose and His will in you and through you. That is very different from "helping" you do it. Do you see?

The task of mothering is over your head. I don't care how many degrees in childhood development and certifications in teaching children you have. Mothering is bigger than you are. If you don't know that, you probably haven't had your second child yet....

The only person who is accomplished at the awesome task of mothering is Jesus Christ Himself. He can do it. He can do it all for you.

Prayer

Lord, I want You to take over the controls of mothering for me. I cannot do it.
It is too hard and too complicated for me. I know that You are able to accomplish every mothering task for me
and through me. I now trust You to do that. I pray this in the name of Jesus Christ. Amen.

MOTHERING TIP

When our children get angry and frustrated and direct that anger at us, it's very easy as a mom to lash out and escalate the situation. Begin practicing what you learned today about Jesus being your life. When you find yourself in the middle of turmoil with your children, call a "time out." Let them know you need to collect your thoughts and pray before you talk to them because you don't want to say something you will regret. Take a few moments to ask Jesus to be your wisdom and discernment in that circumstance. Ask Him to direct your attitudes and your actions toward your children.

If it's time to mete out firm discipline, you'll know it. If it's time to just sit on the couch and listen to your child express all of what's on his mind, you'll know that, too. I have often been amazed at the insight the Lord gives me when I need Him "on the spot."

DAY 4

Love Messages

BEGIN WITH PRAYER

Ask the Father to speak clearly through His word to you today.
Ask Him to communicate with you in a way you can hear and understand.
Tell Him how very much you love Him and trust Him with the control of your life.

When I was a young girl, my parents really filled up my love bucket. They smothered me in love and acceptance. They often told me how much they believed in me. I believed I was smart enough and cute enough to do anything I wanted to accomplish. I look back at the pictures of myself in junior and senior high school and I'm horrified at the ugly little string bean in the pictures. But Mom and Dad told me I was cute and smart and I believed them! So the first set of messages I received about myself were positive. I even signed letters using my nickname, "Nicy the Great!" I really thought I was great! So prideful attitudes and patterns of thinking began forming in me at an early age.

But when I went to school it was a different story. Of course, who wants to befriend "Nicy the Great?"

Nobody! And we moved all the time, so I was always the "new kid" and in most little towns where I lived, you had to be born there to really be in the "in" group. Since my dad was in the ministry, the combination of not too much money and a lot of strict boundaries didn't make me too popular either. So the set of messages I got from my peers gave me plenty of rejection and negative feedback. Believing that I was inferior socially somehow became a part of my thinking.

Then I met David. He was so handsome and intelligent and he was president of a Christian organization at our university. He wore cute clothes, and he drove a great car. What more could you want? While we were dating, he made me feel great because he was definitely "cool," and I guess he was the first "cool" person who ever thought I was "cool," too. I was swept off my feet. We married after my sophomore and his senior year in college at ages 19 and 22. I was finally going to get my need for approval met from someone besides Mom and Dad. What a shock marriage turned out to be.

When we had been married three days, I cried myself to sleep. All of a sudden, my knight in shining armor fell off his horse. He didn't think everything I did was great. In fact, he began correcting and criticizing my every flaw. I had thought that marriage was the way to get my love bucket filled on a continual basis. I thought David would reinforce those messages of my parents that I was "great." Boy, was I wrong! David's messages made it feel like holes were being drilled in the bottom of my bucket. We limped through the first few months and years of marriage as I finished my degree.

Do you see how we begin to form an image of ourselves in our minds? We believe that the messages we hear are the truth. If our parents, peers, and partners tell us we are wonderful, we believe them. If they say we are awful, we believe them.

I had always wanted to be a mom, so the day after my graduation from college I was ready to have a baby. That gnawing emptiness would surely be filled with a baby. Don't babies love their mothers? Doesn't every child look up dreamily at his mother letting her know how special she is? I'm sure you can see it coming….

By now you know my story of infertility. We tried to have a baby, but no baby would come. I became really desperate. I had such aching needs in my heart for love, acceptance, and security. I really believed a child would solve those problems.

I was so anxious over our infertility that David sent me to a Christian counselor. She encouraged me to pray, "Lord, it's okay if I never have a child, what I want is You." I left her office thinking, "No problem. I can do any Christian assignment." But I got to the parking lot and thought, "No way! I'm not going to pray that. If I tell God it's okay if I never have a child, He'll take me up on it. And it's not okay with me!"

For three days and nights I struggled, feeling the strong pressure of God's hand on my life. Finally, I got down on my shag carpet (this was 1975 and everyone, including me, had orange shag carpet). I prayed the prayer I had been encouraged to pray and released my children to God. For me, it was also letting go of a possible source of approval and acceptance.

When I prayed that prayer and confessed to God that I wanted Him and Him alone, He began to work a miracle. I ran into a fertility specialist who thought a simple procedure might help. I had that and God did give us a child. Our little Danielle was in my arms 16 months after that prayer. I thought, "This is it! Now my heart has found a source for love. Danielle will meet my needs!" And I felt that way until we got home from the hospital!

That baby cried and screamed and threw up every meal and never slept and had diarrhea and drove us crazy. Hmm, maybe babies don't fill your love bucket after all. When Danielle was a year old, I went to the doctor for my one year check-up. "Mrs. Glenn, congratulations. You're pregnant!" I was incredulous! This wasn't supposed to happen to us. The earlier procedure had offered no guarantees, so we still considered ourselves infertile. However, our sweet little Stephanie joined us when Danielle was 21 months old. And I got pregnant with Brittany when Stephanie reached 21 months....

Now I was drowning in babies. They were drilling holes in the bottom of my bucket just as fast as they could. They didn't wake up in the morning and say, "Mom, how can I make you feel loved and accepted and secure." They were dipping out of the bucket just as fast as they could. I became pretty desperate.

I reached out to a friend who needed mentoring as a mom and wanted a prayer partner. I knew I needed prayer. I needed Jesus. I had been a Christian since I was five years old, but I had never been so desperate for Him as I was now. My friend, Deanne Knowles, and I began to pray, and that was the beginning of MotherWise. We were the first MotherWise group. We were just two moms searching for a source of love and security for ourselves and wisdom to rear our children. And we found it in Christ.

We discovered that we were created with these desperate needs for love and acceptance and security for one purpose and one reason. Jesus created us with empty love buckets so He could fill us with Himself.

Read Ephesians 3:14–21.

When referring to God in this passage, what name does Paul use for God? (See verse 14.)

_____

According to verse 16, what does Paul pray for the Ephesians so they can receive the love of Christ?

_____

This first part of Paul's prayer establishes that before we can receive Christ's love, we have to be a part of God's family. He is our Father and gives us His name. As my Father, God sends me true messages. What He communicates to me through His written Word and through His Spirit is accurate and true. I don't have to rely on my parents' messages to know the truth about myself in my inner being. I don't have to get strokes from my peers, my spouse, or my kids. I can rely on the source of truth that is absolutely always true—my heavenly Father.

What do I want to know in my inner being? What are the questions in my heart?

Am I loved?

Am I accepted?

Am I secure?

Am I worthy and significant?

Do I belong to someone?

We will continue to study God's Word to see if our Father communicates to us the answer to these important questions.

What does Christ provide for our "inner man" according to verse 16?

_____

How does He provide it?

_____

Jesus provides the strength I need in my inner man. He plugs the "holes" in my love bucket by the power of His Holy Spirit.

Why do we need to be "strengthened in our inner man," according to verse 17?

_____

In the first part of verse 17, there is Christ's part and your part. Describe each.

Christ's Part:

_____

My part:

_____

My inner man may feel weak because of the messages I have received and believed. My love bucket may be so full of holes I couldn't contain Christ's love even if He poured it in. So, the first thing Jesus does is use His power to strengthen my inner man.

The word *power* in verse 16 is the Greek word, *dunamis. Dunamis* means "miraculous power," "strength," "violence," "mighty [wonderful] work."[4] Jesus strengthens me with His mighty, dynamic, dynamite-like power to do two things. First, that He may dwell—or live permanently in residence—in my heart. He comes in to fill up all the holes and gaps. When He comes in to abide in me (or live in me), He brings with Him what my heart so desperately needs.

What does the last half of verse 17 say that He provides?

_____

What two words—taken from gardening and building—does Paul use to describe what Christ's love does for me?

_____

What I need is "love sweet love." I don't just want it, I need it. Christ knows me so well that He knows I must be both rooted and grounded in it. These two words give us graphic pictures of the process.

ROOTED AND GROUNDED

We recently had an incident at home that helped me understand the concept of being "rooted" and being "grounded." We discovered that our Houston home, like almost every other house in our bayou city, needed foundation repair. The roots of one of our trees became an object of concern. For the foundation, it would have been best to cut some of the large exposed roots on the surface of the ground. However, if we did that, the tree—even though it is a large oak—would topple over in the wind. You see, those roots hold the tree steady and firm in adversity. There are holding roots and feeding roots. Both are necessary for the survival of the tree.

Rooted means made stable.[5] Think back to John 15:4. We are to abide in him with our branches firmly rooted in His vine life. When Jesus said you need to be rooted in His love, He means that you need those abiding roots going deep into His love holding you steady in life's circumstances and you need constant feeding from that same source of unending love.

The word *grounded* means to lay a foundation.[6] In Houston, our soil is so full of gumbo-type clay that it expands and contracts according to the amount of moisture in the soil. That's not good news for foundations under houses. When the soil begins to shift, so does the foundation, and the homeowner begins to notice doors that stick and cracks in the walls.

The foundation of our house needed solid ground underneath it. So we hired some men to put pillars under our house that rested far beneath the surface on solid rock. This is exactly what Jesus intends for your life. You are not only rooted in His love, but also founded on the solid, never changing, never shifting rock of His great love. This is the whole purpose for His "dwelling in your heart by faith." He is there to provide what your empty heart needs. He is there to supply your love needs. His message to you is LOVE.

How big is the love of Christ as explained in Ephesians 3:18–19?

_____

The last half of verse 19 says, "that you may be…"

_____

Jesus has come to dwell in your heart so you will be rooted and grounded in His love, and according to verses 18 and 19, that you will *comprehend* and *know* His love. *Comprehend* means "to take eagerly, seize and possess."[7] *Know* means "to be sure, to understand, to be resolved."[8] Verses 18 and 19 could be rewritten, "[That you] may be able to eagerly grasp with all Christians what is the breadth and length and height and depth and to know for sure in your 'knower' the love of Christ.…" This is the love message Jesus is sending to you. You are loved. You are accepted. You are secure. You don't have to wait for someone to tell you that. If you believe the Bible is true, then you have to believe these messages God is sending to your heart are true.

And it gets even better.

In verses 19 and 20, Paul has a hard time using language big and expansive enough to describe the love that Christ has for us. He says it surpasses knowledge. We can't even think that big. This love Jesus has for you is so big and vast your little brain just can't take it all in. And if that weren't enough, he says this big love of God is for a reason.

What is the reason for God's love for you?

_____

I love the definition of the Greek word for "filled up." It means "to cram, level up, satisfy."[9] Jesus' love is designed to top off your love tank. There is enough love to fill every crack and crevice of your heart. You do not have a bottomless pit in your heart that cannot be filled with the love of Christ. However deep your despair, His love goes deeper still. However great your needs, His love is greater still.

Reread verse 20. How well do you think Jesus can meet your need for love?

_____

He will meet your love needs beyond your wildest imagination. Verse 20 says He will do far and above all we could even ask Him to do.

Why does this issue of love matter to mothers? How does knowing that God loves you make you a better mom?

Here's how. You cannot give away what you do not possess. Your children need your unconditional love. If they don't get it, they will be emotionally damaged. But to give your children love, you must first receive love yourself. You must take it in all the way to the bottom of your heart. You need a full tank of love to be a mom. And it is available to you.

Picture your love bucket. What did you learn today about the true source of love to fill it? Tell God how you feel about His true messages to you.

_____

_____

_____

_____

Lord, I have a lot to learn about the great depth of Your love for me. I
want You to open up my capacity to receive Your love. I want to know in my "knower" that Your love is enough
when my husband and my children and my friends let me down.
I'm ready to grow and I'm ready to learn. Teach me in my inner man. I pray this in Jesus' name. Amen.

Mothering Tip

Your role as a mother is defined by the name Adam gave his wife. "Eve" means "life-giver." You are to be a life-giver for your children and this goes beyond their physical life. Your children need three gifts from you. They need unconditional love, firm and fair discipline, and the "bread of life,"—which is the blessing of being exposed to the gospel truth of Jesus Christ. Today, practice "receiving" your love from Christ and giving your love to your children. Let each of your children know, in a way they can receive, how deep your love is for them.

DAY 5

Love Life

BEGIN WITH PRAYER

Ask the Lord Jesus to root and ground you in His love.
Ask Him to allow you to comprehend and know
His love that goes beyond what you can understand with your mind.
Ask Him to reveal His love to your heart.

Imagine a scarecrow in a garden. He is full of straw and lifelessly stands in the garden day after day. But imagine now that the farmer takes down the scarecrow, removes all the straw and puts on the scarecrow's clothing. He walks out into the garden shooing away the birds before they can light.

Do you sometimes feel as lifeless and helpless as that scarecrow when you start to tackle all of your mothering tasks? When you try to discipline firmly, make each child feel loved, attend every school event, get them to all their lessons, help with homework, cook, clean, wash, be a nurse, counselor, teacher, and drill sergeant, do you sometimes feel "full of straw"? Do you feel like the "birds of prey" are after your children and you can do nothing about it?

Jesus' purpose is to remove all your dead "straw," fill you with His life, and accomplish the work of mothering through you. His purpose is to fill you with His life to satisfy your aching heart. His purpose is to fill you with Himself so that He will be mothering your children through you. You are not to gear up and try harder to accomplish these things independently from Him.

Read John 11:25.

How did Jesus describe Himself?

_____

Read Colossians 3:4.

Who is our life, according to this verse?

_____

Jesus did not come to help me be a mom. He came to do it for me. I don't just need a "mothering instruction manual," I need the one who has mastered parenting to do the job for me!

CHRIST IN ME

Read John 14:20.

Where is Jesus in relation to where you are?

_____

Draw a diagram of John 14:20. Draw four concentric circles and label each one according to this verse. Label the largest circle "God," the next circle "Jesus," the next circle "me" and the smallest circle "Jesus."

Do you see that Jesus is "in" God, you are "in" Jesus (if you have received Jesus into your heart and have become His child) and Jesus is "in" you? So now answer that first question:

Do you see the liberating truth of this verse? You are not alone!

Miss Bertha Smith, a missionary to China in the1950s, used baskets to teach this illustration to the new Chinese converts. Each basket nested inside the other. She would say, "Jesus is on the inside of you and He is on the outside of you and that's the only two sides you have!"

Jesus is filling the inside of us so He can handle our lives for us! And nothing can get to us that hasn't been filtered by His love. So if He allows a circumstance to come to us, our job is to trust Him. His job is to do the work. There is nothing He cannot do. *"For nothing will be impossible with God"* (Luke 1:37).

Jesus said that He is in His Father. His life here on earth and His life in heaven consists of abiding in His Father. He says that we are in Him and He is in us. He's on the inside of us and the outside of us! Can you think of a better way to live your life?

Read 1 Corinthians 1:30.

This verse was written to believers. If you are a believer, where are you according to the first part of this verse?

_____

What four things does this verse state that you have from Jesus now that you are "in" Him?

1. _____   3. _____

2. _____   4. _____

Jesus supplies us with wisdom, with righteousness to cover our past sins, with sanctification for present cleansing and renewal, and with redemption for our eternal future in Him. He has provided your past, your present, and your future. That about covers it!

THE RELIABLE SOURCE

Jesus is a reliable source for meeting our personal needs of love, acceptance, security, and identity. Our husbands cannot always meet them. Our children cannot fill us. Our own appearance or achievements cannot satisfy us. The only reliable source for us is the life of the Lord Jesus Christ. This is not a heavenly "pie in the sky by and by" ditty. It is not for later, it is for now. The vine life of the Lord Jesus Christ is available to you on a continual basis.

He did not come to help you with your life. He came to be your life. Let that sink in. There is a radical difference between the two. According to His own Word in John 15:5, without His indwelling life flowing through you, you are completely incapable of being the wife, the mother, or the worker you know you should be. It is impossible. But with His life in you doing the work through you, nothing is impossible.

Have you noticed that you are incapable of keeping God's laws all on your own? If you're trying really hard, you might do well for a while, but you don't have the staying power on your own to do what you know to do. God never intended for you to keep His commandments independent of His life in you. That was the whole point of Jesus coming to earth. You couldn't keep His covenant, so He came and died and rose again to live in you to do it for you. That is why the New Testament is such good news.

Jesus didn't come just to be your Savior. He didn't come just to be your Lord. He came to be your life. Now that is good news for every mom.

Read the following verses and look for one word that is common to all three.

John 1:16

Ephesians 1:22–23

Ephesians 3:19

What key word is common to these verses?

_____

Did the word "fullness" jump out at you? Jesus is the fullness that fills us up to all the fullness of God. He fills our all with His all. Are you picturing your love bucket now? Is it full or empty? Will you base that answer on your feelings or on the truth of God's Word?

Reread John 15:1–5.

Rewrite these verses in the form of a prayer. You might begin, "Lord, You are the vine and our Father is the vinedresser. I release myself into Your hands for pruning so that I will bear more fruit.…"

_____

_____

_____

_____

_____

_____

Lord, I want You to be my power source.

I'm asking You now to be my life.

Reveal Yourself to me day by day so I can fully understand the truth.

I love You, Lord. Amen.

MOTHERING TIP

If you are in a difficult mothering situation—for example, if your child has ADHD, learning problems, or a physical disability—share it with your MotherWise group and find another mom as a prayer partner to walk through it with you. Jesus meets our personal heart needs, but He has called the body of Christ to be His hands and feet. We all need someone with skin on when we are hurting and having difficulty. Don't try to manage alone. The worst thing you can do is stay isolated out of pride.

UNIT

THE PRINCIPLE OF THE BRANCH: THE ROOT OF THE PROBLEM

MOTHERING SKILL: TOYS AND TECHNOLOGY

DAY 1
THE BIG "I"

DAY 2
F-L-E-S-H

DAY 3
THE ANATOMY OF FLESH

DAY 4
THE NATURE OF FLESH

DAY 5
I GOTTA HAVE IT: BEAUTY, BRAINS, AND CASH

If we are Christians and Jesus is living inside of us, why aren't we always mothering and parenting just like Jesus would on a continual basis? What is the tourniquet on my heart that keeps me from giving my children consistent, godly mothering?

UNIT 3

Bible Study Listening Guide

1. The principle used to help me remember the lesson was:

_____

2. The song used to help me remember the principle was:

_____

3. The key Bible verses are:

_____

4. Flesh profits _____.

5. The illustration used to help me remember the lesson was:

_____

6. What I personally need to remember from this lesson is:

_____

MotherWise Group Prayer Requests

1._____

2._____

3._____

4._____

5._____

6._____

7._____

8._____

MOTHERING SKILLS DISCUSSION:

Toys and Technology: Tots to Teens

Challenge: To provide safe, age-appropriate fun for our children, balanced with age-appropriate work.

The fact that the topic of discussion for today is toys and technology says a lot about our society. Most of us can afford luxuries for our children that would have amazed our grandparents. But do all these gizmos and gadgets really deliver the promised "goods" to our kids?

Name the top five "toys" your child uses to entertain himself/herself. (Older children and teens have "toys"—just as adults do—like stereos, CDs, etc.)

1._____

2._____

3._____

4._____

5._____

What is the one thing your child uses for entertainment the most?

_____

What is your knowledge of the Internet? How computer-literate are you?

_____

How much time does your child spend on the computer unsupervised?

_____

Tools to Meet the Challenge:

Kids Online—Protecting Your Children in Cyberspace, Donna Rice Hughes (Grand Rapids, Mich.: Fleming H. Revell, 1998).

Safety Net, Zachary Britton (Eugene, Ore.: Harvest House Publishers, 1998).

50 Practical Ways to Take Our Kids Back from the World, Michael J. McManus (Wheaton, Ill.: Tyndale House Publishers, 1993).

To provide your children with fun, consider some of the following forms of entertainment:

For Young Children:

More unstructured toys than structured toys—dolls, balls, blocks, boxes, blankets, tents, sand shovels, pails, water, clean paint brushes, crayons, paper, scissors.

For School-Aged Kids:

Outdoor toys: bikes, skates, trampolines, jump ropes, sidewalk chalk, frisbees, balls, hoops, musical instruments.

For Preteens and Teens:

Technological toys—if it is possible for you to do so, provide computer access. Computers are actually not just "toys." Knowledge of computers and access to the Internet are now an integral part of our children's education. In most high schools, many courses require papers that are written on computers and most research is done via the Internet.

Sports equipment—balls, bats, gloves, knee pads, etc.

Supplies for hobbies—art, photography, hiking, cooking, etc.

Fitness equipment—weights, workout shoes, etc.

Musical instruments—guitars, keyboards

Toys to avoid: Cultic toys—ouija boards, etc.

STRUCTURED AND UNSTRUCTURED TOYS

Toys can be divided into two main categories: structured and unstructured. Structured toys can only be used one or maybe two ways. A jack-in-the-box is an example of a structured toy. It doesn't use the imagination. You can only play with it in one way. Some structured toys are good and can teach important prereading and premathematical skills.

For instance, toys that require a child to do things in a certain order teach "sequencing." This is an important prereading skill because in reading comprehension you must be able to keep up with a story's sequence of events to understand it. Toys that help a child to understand one-to-one ratio (you only count to one when you have only one apple) teach a premath skill that is necessary to understanding addition. Puzzles that provide these two experiences create great exercises for little brains.

Too many structured toys, however, inhibit the spontaneous, free, imaginative play we want to see in our children. Therefore, I recommend that children play with as many unstructured toys as possible.

Unstructured toys are different from structured toys in that they can be enjoyed in a variety of ways. They usually encourage the use of the imagination and/or the intellect. A ball is probably the most classic example of a good unstructured toy. Every age and stage of child/adult can enjoy playing with a ball. Even tiny children can roll balls. The ball can be used in a variety of games that can be made up by the players.

EXAMPLES

Most dolls are unstructured toys. Baby dolls, in particular, are a good example of unstructured toys because they engage the imagination and can be played with by little girls in every culture.

Although teen dolls are an unstructured toy, I am not fond of giving little girls teen dolls. I think it promotes teen behaviors—like dating, driving, wearing make-up, etc.—in little girls who grow up too fast in our society.

Blocks are another wonderful example of unstructured toys. They stir the imagination and the intellect (it takes elementary engineering to play with them) and can be played with in many ways. Even an old blanket, some folding chairs, and some "costumes" made of your old high heels and beads and your husband's old ties, hats, and shoes can serve as great unstructured toys.

Older children and teens often turn to structured "toys" like stereos, TV, movies, and computers for their entertainment. But when encouraged, some enjoy more creative forms of leisure. Girls may want to get involved in crafts, and guys might enjoy making model planes or cars. Some teens are artistic and just need to be supplied with good materials to work with.

I've known some kids who took up photography and became really good at it. Some play musical instruments. Brittany has spent most of her leisure time as a teen playing the piano. All three of my kids especially enjoyed puttering in the kitchen experimenting with recipes during their teen years.

When purchasing forms of entertainment for our children, we need to stop and ask ourselves some questions:

1. Will my child use his/her imagination with this toy?
2. Will my child use his/her intellect with this toy?
3. For young children: Will my child learn to "sequence" with this toy?
4. Will he/she learn one-to-one ratio?
5. Does this toy promote family unity or disharmony?
6. Will this toy encourage physical fitness?
7. Is this going to provide "good clean fun"?

The most appealing "toy" to hit the market in recent years has been the home computer and the Internet. Although most of us know the advantages of the vast knowledge now available on the Internet, many moms have learned too late that it is a "toy" that needs much supervision.

Much is being written about the dangers of the Internet. If your children are old enough to sit at a computer, you must inform yourself about how to protect your child from the pedophiles and pornographers that lurk there.

Two helpful books that I found in the Christian bookstore are: *Kids Online—Protecting Your Children in Cyberspace,* by Donna Rice Hughes, and *Safety Net,* by Zachary Britton. They are both excellent resources for mothers seeking to arm themselves with information about this important subject.

These "beginner safety tips" come from *Kids Online*. Immediately teach your children that they must:

- Never give out personal information or use a credit card online without your permission.
- Never share their password, even with friends.
- Never arrange a face-to-face meeting with someone they met online unless you are present.
- Never respond to messages that leave them feeling confused or uncomfortable. Encourage them to ignore the sender, end the communication, and tell you or another trusted adult immediately.
- Be cautious in assuming that the people they meet online are who they say they are.[1]

Even if your computer skills are in the beginning stages, most of your children are proficient in cyberspace. We must educate ourselves in order to make the Internet a friend of the family instead of its foe.

Day 1

The Big "I"

BEGIN WITH PRAYER

Ask the Father to search you and try you and see if there is any hurtful way in you and lead you in the way everlasting.

PSALM 139:23–24

NEW WINESKINS

I do not want to tell you how to patch up your mothering. I don't want to give you a few little tips that will solve all your parenting problems in "three easy steps." I don't want to pour new information into your old thought processes. If I did that, you'd be right back to your old mistakes and habits a few weeks after you put down this book. No, I have something much better and more effective to offer you.

Read Matthew 9:16–17.

In these words, Jesus was giving us the secret to successful mothering. It's not a quick fix, "instant tea" approach. It is a complete new way of thinking and living. Let's do some study to discover it.

In verse 16, the illustration Jesus uses is:

_____

In verse 17, His illustration is:

_____

What is the common key word in the two verses?

_____

What two things are contrasted in verse 17?

_____

What does the new wine represent?

_____

Jesus used an old garment and an old wineskin to illustrate our minds and hearts. Even if we get a "patch" of His Word and "sew" it onto our old thought patterns, it will "tear" when "washed" in the swirling waters of life's difficult circumstances. The new and the old can't work together. We need an entirely new garment.

If we take the old wineskin of our attitudes, behaviors, and thought patterns as a mother and pour in God's Word, the old thinking patterns won't be able to contain the new powerful truths. The old will be shattered by the new. No, we must have new wineskins—new ways of thinking and new attitudes—to contain the new wine of Jesus' powerful life within us.

If you have a domineering, controlling pattern of thought and behavior toward your children, and you sew on a patch of God's Word from Proverbs that instructs us to discipline, you might be too harsh and authoritarian. The domineering, controlling-to-get-your-needs-met patterns need to be transformed into new patterns of thought that come from Jesus, who carefully disciplines us for the glory of God and for our good.

If you have passive, permissive, people-pleasing patterns of thought toward your children, and you fill that old wineskin with the new wine of God's Word from 1 John that instructs us to love one another, you might be fearful of setting boundaries for your children and withhold godly discipline from them.

Do you see what you need to be a great mom? You not only need the new wine of God's Word, you need a new wineskin to contain it. You don't need a patch of God's Word to sew onto your tattered old ideas, you need a new garment to wear. You must be transformed by the renewing of your mind (Romans 12:2).

So this week we're going to allow the Holy Spirit to work through God's Word to reveal the "old garments" and the "old wineskins" that need to be replaced. Let's begin by asking a question.

WHAT IS THE OLD WINESKIN?

If Jesus has made His fullness available to fill our love buckets, why don't our lives continually flow with love and joy and peace? Why are we sometimes domineering and sometimes permissive with our children? Why do we get angry and frustrated and lose our tempers? Why are we impatient with our children and unforgiving of our husbands? Why do we cave in just when we should stand up?

I want to be a great mother. I want to behave in just the right way in every mothering situation. I want to discipline firmly and fairly. I want to love unconditionally when my children least deserve it. I want my children to continually see Jesus shining through me with unmistakable clarity.

But something keeps me from it. What is it?

God explains the problem and the solution in His Word, but it is not a very popular Bible study topic. In fact, a lot of Christians would like to cut it out of their Bibles. Many of us have adopted just enough of the Christian life to keep us from going to hell. We tip our hats toward God and then go on about our business until we get into trouble. And then like little children, we go running to God to hurry up and "fix" it. Just ease our pain and we'll be back on our way.

We have missed the whole point. Life was meant to be lived on a much higher plane. We have settled for mediocrity at best and failure at worst. God has called us to something far above that! Life was designed to be lived in victory and joy and confidence and love. We are destined to be free. We shouldn't accept anything less!

To take hold of this grand and glorious life that belongs to us, however, we will have to pay a price. It is going to cost us something. Do we really want to be free enough to pay for it?

In this unit and the next, we will be confronted with a choice: to live life on our own terms or to live life on God's terms, to live life in the "flesh" or in the "Spirit." The choice is yours, but so are the consequences of that choice.

FLESH VERSUS SPIRIT

As mothers, we are in a unique position: our choices affect the lives of our children in a profound way. Our decision to live "according to the flesh" or "according to the Spirit" will affect not only our lives and our children's lives, but also the lives of our descendants for generations to come…to the third and fourth generations.

Are you ready to take this adventure to get in on God's great design for your life? Do you want to be a blessing to your children, your grandchildren, and to the lives of generations to come? Then let's begin the study of life in the "flesh" contrasted with life in the "Spirit."

Read Judges 21:25.

What did "everyone" do?

_____

This is the last verse in this sad book about Israel during a particularly black period of their history. It is a definition of life in the "flesh." "Everyone did what was right in his own eyes." Everyone was living according to his own "flesh" instead of in the "Spirit."

Read Isaiah 53:6.

The first part of this verse says, "Each of us has _____."

Frank Sinatra sang a song that epitomized what it's like to live in the "flesh." He sang, "I did it my way…." When I choose to live according to what pleases me, satisfies me, exalts me, I am living in the "flesh."

In her wonderful book, *Heart's Cry,* Jennifer Kennedy Dean describes "flesh" as a tourniquet.[2] A tourniquet cuts off the flow. If you have a tourniquet on your spirit quenching the life-giving flow of Christ's life in you, you are in trouble. Your love bucket cannot be filled from the source designed to fill it. And you cannot be a channel of His life to others. Unless you abide in Him, you can do absolutely nothing.

Prayer

Lord Jesus, forgive me when I have chosen to live "my way" instead of Your way.

Teach me to know the difference.

Give me wisdom and discernment, Lord.

I pray this sincerely in Your name. Amen.

Mothering Tip

Since this week we're going to be doing a little heart-housecleaning, why not take the same concept to your house. Clean out one refrigerator shelf and one kitchen drawer each day this week. As you work, ask the Lord to work on cleaning out the junk drawers of your heart. You'll be amazed at the peace cleanliness of heart and home brings!

DAY 2

FLESH

Sit quietly for a moment.

Ask the Father to work in a powerful way in your heart all through this week.

Ask Him to keep working even when you get uncomfortable!

Read John 6:63.

What does the "Spirit" do for us?

_____

What does the "flesh" do for us?

_____

The flesh profits absolutely nothing! My mom recently shared an acrostic with me that describes flesh:

F—following

L—long

E—established

S—self-centered

H—habits

In contrast with the flesh, the Spirit gives life. Walking in the flesh brings about death. Death to relationships, death to peace, death to love, death to joy. It's just not worth it!

Read Galatians 6:8.

What do we reap from flesh?

_____

What do we reap from the Spirit?

_____

I used to read these passages of Scripture and think that the references to *flesh* must mean murder, stealing, lying, gossiping—that kind of thing. My eyes began to open to my own flesh when our girls were teenagers. My gross inadequacies as a mother began to prove to me that I had lots of "fleshy" attitudes that were not Spirit-filled. My flesh stuck out all over me and I had to face it. It was a tough time as I fell off my own pedestal.

David often says, "Self-revelation has to come before God-revelation." That's what happened in my case.

When God began to reveal my fleshy areas, then I began to see what He was doing and wanted to do in my life. I could finally cooperate with Him, allowing Him to do the surgery in my heart that was necessary to get rid of flesh so the Spirit could work through me.

FLESH: "GETTING WHAT I WANT"

One of the best working descriptions of flesh I have read is "getting what I want, when I want it, the way I want it!" Notice the key word *I*. A great one-word description of *flesh* is *self*. It is "I," "my," "me," and "mine." Flesh exhibits self-gratification—it pulls in to satisfy, and it exhibits self-legislation—it reaches out to control.

If I mother my children in the flesh instead of in the Spirit, my mothering will be defective. I will be grasping to satisfy my personal needs in my own way at the expense of others—including my children. I will be concentrating on controlling people and situations to get my needs met. When fleshy attitudes are the primary motivators for my behavior as a wife and mother, my husband and my children suffer.

Our daughter, Stephanie, had only been married eight weeks when she told me the sad story of one of her friends who was also a newlywed. The couple was already in big trouble. Stephanie said, "Mom, you can't be selfish and be married. It just doesn't work." I thought those were insightful words coming from one who had just gotten married. (And inside I was saying, "Yes! She's got it!")

Stephanie is right. You can't be selfish and have a good marriage. And you can't be selfish and be a good mom. There is just no way around it.

If you are brave, take the following test:

MOM'S ATTITUDE CHECK TEST

Are you exercising self-gratification (pulling in to satisfy) or self-legislation (reaching out to control) in:

Disciplining your child?

Example: Are you disciplining your child too harshly in an effort to protect your reputation? Are you over-controlling him so he won't embarrass you at church, at school, or in front of your family and friends? Do you see how that can be a form of self-legislation? Are you reaching out to control him to satisfy your personal need for acceptance?

Or are you gratifying yourself by being overly permissive, allowing your child to disobey your directives because you are trying to get your personal need for acceptance met from him?

_____

Your child's school situation?

Example: Are you reaching out to control your child's teacher? Have you gone beyond being concerned to being controlling?

_____

Your work/recreation schedule?

Example: Is your work/play schedule designed to honor God, to submit to your husband, to minister to your children, and to build your home? Or is it causing you to go on a "flesh trip" of gratifying self to the exclusion of all others?

_____

Your child's eating/sleeping/exercising habits?

Example: Have you set your child's schedule to meet your personal needs or is it set because it is what is best for that child and the whole family? Are you permissive with your child's eating habits, desiring to get your need for acceptance met?

_____

Your eating/sleeping/exercising habits?

_____

Your marriage?

_____

Your media intake habits?

_____

Now copy Galatians 6:8.

_____

_____

_____

Prayer

Lord, I see where I have been trying to get my needs met from people, possessions, and achievements.

Set me free, Lord, to be the woman, the wife, and the mother You have designed me to be.

Take away all my methods of self-protection that have covered up these sinful areas in my life.

I now expose my heart to You, Lord. I trust You to reveal what You are ready to heal.

I pray this in the name of Jesus. Amen.

DAY 3

The Anatomy of Flesh

BEGIN WITH PRAYER

Give God permission to shine His holy light into every "room" in your heart.
Be still and allow His Spirit to bring things to mind that you need to confess and
for which you need to ask His forgiveness.

FLESH STINKS!

What would happen if you peeled the fleshy skin off of a chicken breast, threw it in the kitchen trash, and left it for three or four days? It would stink! There is nothing quite like the smell of rotting flesh.

That's what our flesh is like. It causes a stink. It is what keeps us from receiving the flow of Christ's life. And keeps us from mothering the way we want to mother our children.

Scripture uses the term *flesh*, or *sarx* in the Greek,[3] in several different ways. Sometimes the Bible uses it to describe the earthly body—not good or bad, just human. (Genesis 2:21; Romans 1:3) Sometimes it is used to describe all of mankind. (Romans 3:19–20)

Then often it is used especially by Paul, but also by Peter and John, to describe carnality within Christians. That means people who have Christ within, but are acting as if He is not there. Today we're going to look at this third use of the word *flesh*. We're going to ask God to expose the "fleshiness" He finds in us so He will be able to get to the root of the problem.

I'm ready to get rid of my old wineskins, aren't you?

Read Romans 7:15–23.

Copy Romans 7:15 here:

_____

_____

What is the problem Paul is describing?

_____

_____

Does that sound familiar? As a Christian mother, have you behaved in a way you don't understand and done things you hate? Have you ever been inconsistent with your discipline? Conditional with your love? Been lax in teaching your kids the Word of God? Spoken when you should have been silent and been silent when you should have spoken up?

This battle between the flesh and the Spirit in the life of a Christian is the problem. Even the apostle Paul struggled with it. But he shares with us the secret to victory, so don't get discouraged. Read on.

But if I do the very thing I do not wish to do, I agree with the Law, confessing that it is good. (Romans 7:16)

In other words, I know when I'm doing wrong. I know right from wrong. It is clear from God's law written in His Word and written on my heart. The problem is not in God's Word—the law—the problem is in me.

So now, no longer am I the one doing it, but sin which indwells me. (Romans 7:17)

If I have chosen to accept Jesus' sacrifice on the cross for myself personally, I am a new creation in Christ Jesus. I share His life. But since I am still here on earth in a body that is still capable of sin, sin is in me.

The best way for me to think of this is imagining that sin is like a tumor. If I have a cancerous tumor in me, it's bad and it affects me, but does not define me. That tumor is not my identity. I am not a cancerous tumor. I have a cancerous tumor in me that needs to come out before it destroys me. I have a healthy body that functions with the exception of this tumor in part of my body.

Don't stretch the analogy too far, but perhaps it will help you see that your identity and your behavior are two different things. You are God's child, a chosen one beloved by Him. You have His life in you. He gives you your identity. But sometimes you behave in a sinful way, by your choice. That doesn't make you a dirty rotten sinner. You have fleshy, sinful areas that need cleansing and pruning, but that doesn't change who you are.

For I know that nothing good dwells in me, that is, in my flesh; for the wishing is present in me, but the doing of the good is not. (Romans 7:18)

Where is the problem located?

_____

The problem is in my flesh or self-nature. There is nothing good about my flesh. My self-strength cannot bring about fruit in God's kingdom. My self-effort may get things accomplished, but the end result will have no eternal reward. I can wish to do better as a mom all day long, but I do not have the power and strength in my own flesh to pull it off. That power and strength will have to come from somewhere outside myself.

For the good that I wish, I do not do; but I practice the very evil that I do not wish. (Romans 7:19)

This is a snapshot of a Christian walking in the flesh. Caught between what I know to do and what I end up doing, there is turmoil! It is a war! But hang on, there is a way out!

But if I am doing the very thing I do not wish, I am no longer the one doing it, but sin which dwells in me. (Romans 7:20)

Paul isolates the problem and discovers that it is _____.
The problem is sin that dwells in me. It is sin working through my flesh.

I find then the principle that evil is present in me, the one who wishes to do good. (Romans 7:21)

I have a new heart and a new mind since I am a believer in Jesus Christ. I want to do good, but I have a flesh problem that resides in me. Let me give you another word picture.

Imagine a hole in your side. The hole represents your flesh. Satan, seeing the hole in your side (your flesh) can enter your now weak defenses and flip the switch on the sin machine inside you. He has no power over you except what you give him entrance to in the fleshy areas of your life. Again, don't try to read too much into my word picture, but maybe it will help you untangle your flesh from sin, from Satan. It's hard to win a battle when you're not sure who the enemy is!

For I joyfully concur with the law of God in the inner man. (Romans 7:22)

My new nature in Christ Jesus loves His Word and His law. My "inner man," my spirit, wants His will. I want to be a godly mother whose life flows full of the life of Christ.

Please don't stop now. Keep studying just a few minutes more. I don't want you to miss this. It can change your mothering for the rest of your life. It seems a bit technical, but hold on. It will get piercingly practical. Remember, you want to be the kind of mom they write songs about!

But I see a different law in the members of my body, waging war against the law of my mind, and making me a prisoner of the law of sin which is in my members. (Romans 7:23)

Let me explain a little bit about "laws" in the Bible. Often it means a law like the law of gravity. The law of gravity is a principle that governs falling objects. If you drop something, it falls to the ground, it doesn't go flying off. The two laws described in this verse are like that.

Paul refers to two different laws in this verse. One law has two names. Name the two laws:

1._____

2._____

The two laws are the law of sin (or the law of the members of my body—since that's where sin occurs), and the law of my mind (or my inner man, my inner person).

In Romans 8:2, Paul defines these two laws even more.

What are the names of these two laws in this verse?

_____

Which law is more powerful?

_____

What does the law of the Spirit of life in Christ Jesus do for you?

_____

Eureka! Here it is! Here is the answer we've been looking for! Here is the victory for Christian moms!
What sets you *free* from the law of sin and death?

_____

Yes, it is the new law. It is the law of the Spirit of life in Christ Jesus. Your life is *in* His life. His life is *in* your life. The law of the Spirit of life in Christ Jesus sets you free from being trapped in a never-ending flesh war inside yourself. You do not have to live in bondage to your old habits and old ways of thinking. You have the very life of the Lord Jesus Christ living in you.

Can He mother your children through you without going off on a flesh trip? Yes, of course, He can. This is your victory and your freedom, Mom. I am praying that God will open the eyes of your heart so you can begin to understand and comprehend this great truth. If you do, it will truly set you free!

Prayer

Lord, I want to be free as a mom from the law of sin and death.

I don't want to bring about destruction in my children's lives by my wrong attitudes,

wrong patterns of thinking, and wrong behaviors.

Lord, set me free to live according to the law of the Spirit of life in Christ Jesus.

I offer this prayer to You in the name of Jesus Christ. Amen.

Mothering Tip

Plan a healthy dinner for tonight. Try adding more protein, whole grains, fresh fruits and vegetables, and less white flour and sugar. Set the table with plates, napkins, forks, knives, spoons, glasses, and put some candles on the table. If there are flowers in your garden, cut a few and put them in a simple vase. If possible, don't start the meal until the whole family is ready to sit down together. Then hold hands around the table and pray.

DAY 4

The Nature of Flesh

BEGIN WITH PRAYER

Ask God to peel away the layers of flesh that cover your mind and keep you from knowing the truth about yourself and the truth about Him.

CHARACTERISTICS OF FLESH

Flesh has several characteristics. Flesh is controlling, rejecting, and sometimes like an octopus. I want you to see some illustrations of the flesh that are found in Scripture. I hate to take you through this because you may get uncomfortable when you begin to see yourself, but if we are going to be free, we have to be honest with God's Word and with ourselves.

CONTROLLING FLESH

One of the main characteristics of flesh is that it is "controlling." Remember that I told you flesh reaches out to control and pulls in to satisfy.

"FIXER UPPER" OR CONTROLLING FLESH

Read Genesis 16, 17 and 21:1–21.

Who are the characters in the story?

_____

_____

What did Sarai do to take matters into her own hands instead of waiting on God?

_____

_____

Read Galatians 4:21–23. What word does Scripture use to describe Sarai's action?

_____

What was the result of Sarai's fleshy response to her problem?

_____

Sarai had "controlling" flesh. She decided God wasn't going to do anything about her infertility problem so she would take matters into her own hands. God had promised over and over that He would provide a son to her and Abram, but He was taking just a little too long. Sarai wanted action.

Sarai's choice to "walk after the flesh" instead of walking after the Spirit has had global consequences. The current war in the Middle East started with that one woman choosing to be in control instead of submitting to God's control.

In what area are you tempted to exhibit controlling flesh?

_____

_____

"CONTROLLING" VERSUS DISCIPLINING OUR CHILDREN

As mothers, we employ many methods to be controlling.

Sometimes we use hostile behavior. We yell and scream to frighten our kids into doing what we want. Sometimes we use blackmail. "If you don't do what I say, I'll…" Sometimes we have a critical attitude and attack them personally. We might be tempted to use guilt to control our children. "It makes Mom so sad and hurts my feelings when you do that." Or, "If you don't come home for Christmas Day, Dad and I will be all alone."

Often we misuse body language to get in control. We pout or stamp our feet or slam our hands on the table. We might even resort to the silent treatment, especially with our husbands or our teenagers. We choose not to speak to them so we can remain in control. We might even stoop to being sick all the time so we can control our families. If we are sick, they have to tiptoe around us and we don't have to deal with difficult parenting issues at all.

This is not good mothering. These are fleshy attempts at being in control. But aren't moms supposed to be in control?

Parents are to take authority over their children (Ephesians 6:1). We are to assume the position of responsibility for the training and rearing of the child. But yelling and screaming and all the other methods of controlling our children in the flesh reduce our position of authority. They say, "I'm trying to be in control here but I don't want to do what it really takes to discipline you. I want to control you because it meets my needs!"

There is a better way. We should set a standard of behavior for our children not because it meets our needs, but because it is in the best interest of the child. Our children need the standard set in a firm but calm manner. "Susan, look at my eyes. You may not jump on the bed." "David, listen to my voice. You must come to me the first time I call you." "Jennifer, your curfew is 10:30. It is not 10:40. You must be inside the house at 10:30 according to the digital clock in the kitchen. Are we absolutely clear on that?" Then if they do not obey, don't yell at them. Don't use manipulation and guilt to make them obey. Take action.

If your child deliberately disobeyed in rebellion against your authority, it is time for discipline. If your child is between the ages of 2 and 12, it may be time for a spanking. The Bible instructs us in the book of Proverbs to discipline with a rod.

Read the following verses from Proverbs and write out the form of discipline in each verse.

Proverbs 10:13:_____

Proverbs 13:24:_____

Proverbs 20:30:_____

Proverbs 22:15:_____

Proverbs 23:14:_____

Proverbs 26:3: _____

Proverbs 29:15:_____

Yelling is unnecessary. The reason we scream is because we are unwilling to take the appropriate action. I am convinced that those who oppose spanking and other forms of discipline see it as just a means of adults exerting fleshly "control" over defenseless children. And in some cases, they would be correct.

But biblical "chastisement" or spanking with a rod done "in the Spirit" is a means of teaching our children to submit to authority. A proper spanking is done on the buttocks with 2 or 3 firm swats with a rod or paddle that sting but do not bruise. We don't spank on the legs and we never degrade our children by hitting, slapping, or popping them on the face.

Spanking needs to be reserved for direct disobedience. Other means of discipline—such as withholding privileges—should be used for childish irresponsibility. Preschoolers are in an intense training phase. They are not little adults. Teaching an expected behavior will take months of consistent training. Monitor and adjust your discipline according to your child. It is possible to "over-spank" and to "under-spank." This is why you need to stay on your knees praying for God's guidance and listen to godly wisdom from your husband and mentors.

If you have a teenager who rebels against your authority, remove the privileges that come with responsible behavior. Most teens want to drive a car (that you bought), go out with friends, listen to the jam box (that you bought), and/or talk on the phone (that you pay for). Calmly remove the privileges that come with living in your house under your house rules. Don't respond to their emotional outbursts with your own. It is possible to take authority over your teen without resorting to walking in the flesh (but it will require a great deal of prayer!).

Sit down in the living room or at the dining room table with your preteen or teenager and outline your standards for their behavior. Set curfews, dress codes, homework rules, church attendance requirements, work and chore expectations, and whatever else is important to you. Then if they choose to disobey, resist the urge to control them in the flesh. You're going to be tempted to yell at them. However, you can calmly, but with absolute unwavering authority, take action.

The ultimate authority to which we are leading them to submit their lives to is the authority of God. If they will not submit to your authority, they will not submit to God's. If you discipline selfishly—too hard or too soft—to meet your desire to get what you want, when you want it, the way you want it, your child will suffer.

Our kids have radar about that sort of thing. They know when we are operating in the flesh. But if you discipline your children with a pure heart, desiring to lead them to submit to the authority of God, it will bear fruit in the lives of your children.

MARY AND MARTHA

Read Luke 10:38–42.

Who was the sister who exhibited controlling flesh?

_____

How did she try to exert control over her sister?

_____

What did Jesus say to her?

_____

_____

Martha had a case of "fixer" controlling flesh. Martha wanted not only to "fix" or prepare a meal for Jesus, she wanted to "fix" or control her sister! Jesus' gentle rebuke was for Martha to get her priorities straight.

With what mothering issue are you currently struggling concerning control issues?

_____

_____

Don't despair, Mom. Walking in the Spirit instead of walking in the flesh is a process. You and I are not going to "get it" all on the first day…or week…or year. But you will be amazed one day to realize that you are becoming more and more free from flesh patterns and freer to walk with Jesus through this mothering journey.

Copy Romans 7:24–25a and pray it as a prayer back to God.

_____

_____

_____

Lord Jesus, here I am. You have known about my flesh all along and You still love me. Lord,
I am amazed at that great love. Now, in Your love, guide me into all truth, especially about myself.
Thank you, Lord. In Jesus' precious name I pray this. Amen.

Mothering Tip

Those of us with controlling flesh have a tendency to make mountains out of molehills with our families. Putting things in perspective as you go through your day will help with this. Whether it's cranky children or a spat with your husband or a dirty kitchen, mud on the carpet or being ten minutes late to your child's baseball game—in reality, it's not life threatening. See these occurrences as part of normal daily life.

If your children are fussing, you can lose your cool or remember that sibling rivalry is a part of raising a family. If you get caught in traffic, you can let your blood pressure get out of hand, or spend the extra time praying for those things you never find time to pray for.

If your house is a mess, you can feel depressed and inadequate, or thank God for a place to live. Concentrate on your blessings and let God control your day.

I Gotta Have It: Beauty, Brains, and Cash

BEGIN WITH PRAYER

Ask the Father to peel away the self-protective layers of your heart and reveal its true condition.

Ask God to destroy your wrong and prideful thought patterns,

and to take every thought pattern captive to the obedience of Christ.

Years ago, when I was teaching junior high school students, I wrote a song about the flesh.

Beauty, brains, and cash that's what I really want,

Beauty, brains, and cash—I want more!

Beauty, brains, and cash that's what I really want,

Beauty, brains, and cash so I'll be complete!

I want to look just right so my friends won't laugh,

I gotta have the stuff to make 'em see I'm neat,

My looks are all I've got to give my life some class,

I really gotta shop or I can't compete for…

Beauty, brains, and cash that's what I really want,

Beauty, brains, and cash—I want more!

Beauty, brains, and cash that's what I really want,

Beauty, brains, and cash so I'll be complete!

I gotta make the grades or my folks get sore,

My Dad's got plans to send me to the top,

Everyone around's lookin' at my scores,

I gotta make the grades or I can't compete for…

Beauty, brains, and cash that's what I really want,

Beauty, brains, and cash—I want more!

Beauty, brains, and cash that's what I really want,

Beauty, brains, and cash so I'll be complete!

Beauty, brains, and cash even they can't really fill me,

'Cause when I get a little I want more, more, more…

Beauty, brains, and cash that's what I really want,

Beauty, brains, and cash—I want more!

Beauty, brains, and cash that's what I really want,

Beauty, brains, and cash so I'll be complete!

It's ugly, but it's true. We are all caught up in some fashion or another with "keeping up with the Joneses." Why do we do it? Because somehow we feel it will meet the needs of our hearts. We so desperately want to get our buckets of love and security filled that we will turn to anything we think will solve the problem. And modern advertising agencies are banking on that fact. They appeal to our "flesh."

We live in a society that rewards beautiful, smart, rich people. It penalizes ugly, dumb, poor people. That is just the way the world works. Christian mothers are not immune to this disease. We can become trapped in it so easily. We want our kids to be accepted by their peers. We want them to be on top of the heap. We don't want average kids, we want kids who are above average! And unfortunately we will do almost anything to make that happen.

We coach them and train them in the ways of the world. They must be dressed in the latest designer fashions and schooled in the best institutions—starting in preschool.

We want to parent the starting quarterback or the homecoming queen. We want superstars!

Does the Bible have anything to say on this subject? Can we really live this way and still walk in the Spirit? Is it really wrong to give your children "good gifts"?

God's Word is designed to teach us principles. I cannot tell you which purse to buy your daughter or which tennis shoes to buy your son—which one represents walking in the flesh and which one represents walking in the Spirit. The Holy Spirit will guide you as you apply His Word. My purpose is to lead you to His Word and to let Him speak. Listen carefully to God as He speaks to you from His Word as we study more examples of flesh.

LUSTFUL FLESH

Read 1 Peter 2:11.

What is at war against your soul?

_____

Read Romans 13:14.

What are we to do about fleshly lusts?

_____

I always thought that lust referred to men who are sex-crazed. Then the Lord began to convict me of my own lustful thoughts. They centered more on the mall. I lusted after new clothes and makeup and home furnishings. My thoughts were something like, "I know this stuff isn't in the budget, but I need a lift!" Buying new clothes is not a sin. But heaping up possessions to make yourself feel loved or accepted or secure is walking in the flesh. It will result in deadness in your heart. "Things" may make us feel good for a time, but the answer to our heart-needs is Jesus alone.

As a mother, perhaps you are not tempted to pamper yourself, but buying for your children might really be a problem. It is so easy to get caught up in indulging their every whim or in buying things for our children so we can feel more accepted among our own peer parents. When your daughter wears a darling outfit, you also get compliments, right? When your son drives a sporty new car, his parents also get kudos, correct? Walking in the flesh in this area is a super duper, multilane highway in America today. It is the "broad road that leads to destruction."

Read James 1:13–15.

What is the picture taken from hunting and fishing that is presented in verse 14?

_____

What is the picture taken from childbirth that describes lust in verse 15?

_____

These are graphic snapshots of lust. It baits us and reels us in like a fisherman with his catch. If we entertain lust and allow a lustful thought to be conceived in us, what will be born out in us is sin and destruction.

Read James 4:1–8.

What is the source of the problems described in verse 1?

_____

According to verse 2, why was murder committed? Why were they fighting and quarreling?

_____

Why did God not provide the things they desired?

_____

Copy verse 4:

_____

_____

What is the cure James gives in verses 7–8 for lustful flesh?

_____

The word *lust* used in James 4:2 is the word *epithumeo*. It means "to set the heart upon, i.e., long for; covet, desire, lust after."[4]

Is God shining His light on any area of lustful flesh in you? Have you set your heart on something to make you feel loved and accepted and secure other than His life and His kingdom? Journal your thoughts.

Read Galatians 5:13–15.

What "flesh trip" is described in this verse?

_____

Have you ever been tempted to walk in the flesh in this area?

_____

_____

The Women's Liberation movement of the '70s sucked me in for a while when I was a young bride. I was "woman," and I was proud of it. The women around me did not want only equality with men, they wanted dominance. The Lord had to show me a better way.

Jesus, more than any other teacher before or since, came to set women free. In His day, they were seen as the property of men. He elevated women to a position of equal worth with men but with different functions within the church and the home.

Have you shaken your fist in defiance and dominance? Are you trying desperately to demand "rights" for yourself that Jesus will give you freely if you will come to Him?

I know it's getting sticky. Sorry, Mom, but we need to look at ourselves honestly if we are ever going to be free. I've been convicted by every page of this book, so don't feel like you are alone. But I've discovered that the more open and honest I am with God, the more I am seeing Him do miracles in my life to transform my thinking and retool my mothering. The pain is worth the price!

Prayer

Lord, I am seeing myself in a new light.

I am uncomfortable facing the condition of my heart.

But Lord, even though this is a painful process, I don't want You to stop.

I want You to continue to reveal the flesh in me. I trust You to cleanse and renew me day by day.

In Jesus' name I pray this. Amen.

Mothering Tip

Lustful flesh is a problem not just for moms, but for kids too. I have had several mothers write to me that they are devastated about a twelve- to thirteen-year-old son who has been trapped in pornography. The Internet has made pornography available to almost every child on his own or on his best friend's home computer. The fall-out has been tremendous.

Pornography is an addiction. If your child is addicted to porn he or she is going to need professional help. Find a good Christian counselor, who uses biblical counseling, and make an appointment for you and your child.

There are no easy solutions, but I will pass along something my father told me. When he was thirteen, his father caught him in an abandoned building kissing a girl. His father didn't say anything, he just took him by the arm and marched him home. When they got home he told my dad, "Son, from now on, you are going to be so busy you aren't going to have time to think about that much anymore." The next morning, he got him up at 5:00 A.M. and started him working. He met him after school and took him to a job.

My dad said for several years, he worked day and night before and after school. He says that hard physical labor solved a lot of his hormonal problems! He recommends that every young man have lots of hard, physical labor—either through sports and/or a job—to keep him so exhausted he won't feel like getting into trouble! This is not to demean the very serious emotional and spiritual problems associated with pornography, but good hard work has never hurt any healthy young person!

UNIT 4

THE PRINCIPLE OF THE BRANCH:
THE "FUNGUS AMONG US!"

MOTHERING SKILL: MUSIC, MOVIES, MEDIA, AND YOUR CHILD

DAY 1
PRIDEFUL, "BUTTON-POPPING" FLESH

DAY 2
PASSIVE, "MILQUETOAST" FLESH

DAY 3
PIOUS, "GOODY TWO-SHOES" FLESH

DAY 4
PITIFUL, "BABYISH" FLESH

DAY 5
PERSISTENTLY SELF-CENTERED, "I, ME, MINE" FLESH

Now, I know what the root of the problem is, but how does this relate to me? Which mothering trap do I fall into most often?

UNIT4

Bible Study Listening Guide

1. The principle we are studying today is:

    _____

2. The key Bible verse is:

    _____

3. The illustrations used to help me remember the lesson were:

    _____

4. What I personally need to remember from this lesson is:

    _____

MotherWise Group Prayer Requests

1._____

2._____

3._____

4._____

5._____

6._____

7._____

8._____

9._____

UNIT 4
MOTHERING SKILLS DISCUSSION:
Music, Movies, Media, and Your Child

Challenge: To use discernment in what we allow our children in the consumption of media, movie, and music products and to teach them to use discernment themselves.

Do you know what your kids are watching? Are you concerned about the impact the media is having on your child? Do you have a sneaking suspicion that your eight-year-old is acting like an eighteen-year-old because of what he/she is listening to and watching on a regular basis? Are you confused about how to decide when a child is too young for certain programs? When should you allow your child to make choices on his own? This is the topic for this week's discussion.

What are your main concerns as a mom about the media and the music consumption habits of your children?

_____

_____

_____

What has your family found to be the best way to make responsible decisions about media and music?

_____

_____

_____

_____

Tools to Meet the Challenge:

Ted Baehr's ministry and *MOVIEGUIDE* subscription: The Christian Film and Television Commission. (See appendix for address and phone numbers.)

CCM Magazine. (See appendix.)

The Media-Wise Family, Ted Baehr (Colorado Springs, Colo.: ChariotVictor Publishing, 1998).

Classic "oldie" movies

Feature Films for Families, (800)347-2833, P.O. Box 572410, Murray, Utah 84157-2410.

Provide low cost family-oriented films. Suggested films: *Buttercream Gang, Rigoletto.*

Streetwise Parents, Foolproof Kids, Dan Korem (Colorado Springs, Colo.: Navpress, 1992).

Caedmon's Call web site for college kids and young adults: www.caedmons-call.com

Web site: www.crosswalk.com

DISCERNMENT

The skill we want to learn as mothers is how to have discernment concerning media choices for the family and how to teach our growing children to have discernment regarding their own media choices.

The first step in discernment is to know the "good" very well. When bank tellers are taught to catch counterfeiters, they are taught to know what a "good" bill looks like. They know every intricate detail, so when a "bad" bill comes across their desk, they can spot it immediately. It is the same with media. If you know God's Word very well, your discernment about what you see and hear will become razor sharp.

But does that mean we all should throw out our entertainment centers, never go to a movie, and make our children read the Bible all day? If we do, does that mean our kids will never see anything "bad"?

Moms, let's face it. Most of us cannot be with our children every minute of the day, everywhere they go. I believe the best insurance for our children's minds is to teach them discernment.

Help is available for Christian mothers and fathers who are seeking to teach such discernment and to walk the narrow path of spiritual and moral responsibility when it comes to decisions about movies, TV, and multimedia. Go to your Christian bookstore and check out the resources available. In doing the research for this topic, I found several books, a web site, and some magazines that were especially helpful. They are listed under "Tools to Meet the Challenge."

The Media-Wise Family, by Ted Baehr teaches practical ways for parents to protect their children from inappropriate entertainment. He also provides a guide to a child's cognitive development and at what ages and stages he should be allowed certain forms of entertainment and why. I highly recommend his book. His ministry, the Christian Film and Television Commission, produces *MOVIEGUIDE,* a monthly published guide for evaluating current movies. You may subscribe by calling 1-800-899-6684.

In *The Media-Wise Family,* Baehr gives such practical advice as this quote from a ten-year study by Dr. Sally Ward who "cautions that infants under one year should be exposed to no television while preschoolers should be limited to one hour a day."[1]

Baehr urges parents to teach their children discernment by watching and listening to media and music with them and asking questions. Here is a sample of some of the discussion we should have with our children before they watch or listen:

1. Talk about the title, images, and ideas about the plot.
2. Predict the character types and action in the film.
3. Ask what your children know that they can bring to the film.
4. Use *MOVIEGUIDE*'s "In Brief" as an introduction to the film.

QUESTIONS

First, ask questions that analyze the media product according to its separate parts: the message that the writer, director, and producer were trying to get across, the point of view and worldview portrayed, how the setting, lighting, and music helped to communicate the message.

For younger children, the questions might be, "Who was the good person in the story?" "Who was the bad person?" "How did you know which one was good and which one was bad?" "Did this story have any part about worshiping God or Jesus?" "Did the people in the story worship anything else?"

For older kids ask, "Who was the hero?" "What kind of person was the hero?" "Were they morally right?"[2] "Who was the villain?" "Why did you know that?" "What kind of a message does the character of the villain communicate?"[3] "Is religion, the church, people of faith, and/or Christians in the mass media product?" "How are they portrayed?"[4] "How is the family portrayed in this story?"[5]

Second, ask your children (and teach them to ask themselves), questions that hold up the media product to the light of God's Word.

For younger children, ask, "Did the people in the story do anything that God says is wrong?" "What did they do?" "Where does it say that's wrong in the Bible?"

For older kids ask those same questions, plus, "Does the premise of the media product agree or disagree with the Christian worldview?" For example, "Does good triumph over evil?" "Why did the story end the way it did?"[6]

If you will begin by watching and listening with your child and asking these questions, you will be on the road to teaching them discernment about their choices of movies and TV.

What about music? Some of the same questions listed above can be applied to music. There is a web site you and your teens might want to check out. It is titled the "ultimate Christian music experience on the web." There are artists profiles, samplings of current CDs, album reviews, concert schedules, and the opportunity to buy online. *CCM Magazine* is a monthly publication that reviews new albums and artists in Christian music. You can subscribe by calling 1-800-333-9643 or go to their web site, or write to CCM, P.O. Box 706, Mt. Morris, Illinois 61054-8418.

Of course, I have to put in a plug for my kids. Danielle, our oldest daughter and her husband, Cliff, head up the Christian folk band, Caedmon's Call. Their sound is very contemporary and their lyrics are thought-provoking. I think your teens and college kids would like their music. You can find their CDs at most places where music is sold and find their concert schedule on the Internet at www.caedmons-call.com.

Streetwise Parents, Foolproof Kids, by Dan Korem is another excellent resource. It was written to help parents "build up their children's immune systems for warding off deception with the following basic skills and knowledge":

- Discerning what is and isn't deception.
- The ability to distinguish between illusion and reality—with what is real and what isn't.
- The core concepts that can reveal if deception is at work.
- Awareness of current trends that can harm them.
- The importance of the family factor when defending against deceptive activities.
- How to find and cling to the good.[7]

DAY 1

Prideful, "Button-Popping" Flesh

BEGIN WITH PRAYER

Ask the Father to sweep clean every corner of your heart. Tell Him you desire a pure heart.

Tell Him you want Him to purge and purify you according to His will.

PRIDEFUL, INFLATED FLESH

Read Colossians 2:18–19 and label the type of flesh discussed.

_____

Copy 1 John 2:16.

_____

_____

_____

Read Proverbs 16:18–19.

Pride goes before _____ and a _____ goes before stumbling.

What is the result of pride?

_____

Prideful flesh can be expressed in numerous ways. For mothers it can be particularly debilitating. This variety of flesh can keep you from seeking the mentoring and teaching you need to become a good mother.

When Danielle was a baby, I thought I knew it all. I had always wanted a child, so I guess I thought that meant I knew how to do it! Wrong! My pride kept me from asking mothering questions of my mother and mother-in-law and other godly women who surrounded me. I finally gave in and began to realize that I had a lot to learn and God had provided those who could teach me.

The Hebrew word used for *pride* in Proverbs 16:18 is *ga'own*. It means "arrogancy, excellency, majesty, pomp, pride, proud, swelling."[8] When I approach mothering with pride, or *ga'own* (doesn't that *sound* bad?), I am bound to stumble.

Have your children ever embarrassed you? Does your little "pride and joy" have egg on his face sometimes? When you are embarrassed over your children, stop a moment and ask the Lord, "Am I prideful about my children? Is this flesh?"

What is God bringing to your mind concerning prideful flesh?

_____

_____

_____

_____

_____

I know you are probably ready to move on to a new subject, but we must continue with our study of the flesh, asking God to keep on working in our hearts. No one ever called heart surgery a picnic. This is the way to freedom, so roll up your sleeves and let's continue.

Prayer

Lord, don't stop working in my heart even when I scream and cry.
Cleanse me and purge me from destructive patterns in my life that affect me and everyone around me,
especially my children. I am turning my face toward You and I will not flinch as You prune my life.
I pray this in the name of the Lord Jesus who loves me. Amen.

Mothering Tip

Call your Mentoring Mom and ask your "burning mothering question" of this week. When you call, ask if this is a good time to talk. Keep the conversation to fifteen to twenty minutes unless she prolongs it. Ask her to pray for you on the phone.

DAY 2

Passive, "Milquetoast" Flesh

BEGIN WITH PRAYER

Be very still in God's presence today.

Ask Him to shine His holy light into every corner of your heart.

Remember, this is not a time of morbid introspection. Let the Lord search and try your heart

and see if there is any wicked way in you and lead you in the way everlasting. (Psalm 139:23–24)

PASSIVE, "MILQUETOAST" FLESH

Read Judges 6:11–27. (If you are not familiar with the story of Gideon, read all of Judges 6.)

According to verse 11, where was Gideon beating out wheat and why?

_____

In verse 12, what did the angel of the Lord call Gideon?

_____

What did God tell Gideon to do and what was his response?

_____

Read the passage from verse 13 to verse 27. Why did Gideon obey God under cover of night?

_____

The story of Gideon is a prime example of passive flesh. Gideon just didn't want to rock the boat. He was paralyzed by fear. It was easy for anyone to bully Gideon.

When God found him he was beating out wheat in a winepress instead of out in the open so he could hide from his enemies. At the end of our passage, he was obeying God under cover of night because he was afraid of his own relatives and the men of his hometown!

Let's look at a biblical account of two parents who exhibited passive flesh.

Read 2 Samuel 13.

Who was the parent in question?

_____

How did he exhibit a fleshly attitude of passivity with his sons instead of taking authority over them?

In verses 21–23? _____

In verses 24–27? _____

In verses 37–39? _____

In each case, what do you think he should have done instead?

_____

Read 2 Samuel 15–18 to see the end result of David's fleshly parenting. Summarize what happened.

_____

_____

_____

David, the man after God's own heart, often operated in the flesh when it came to his children. David was a passive father, getting angry but doing nothing about the gross sins of his children. David simply refused to deal with the problems, but the problems in his family didn't go away. They escalated. And destruction came to his children.

Perhaps you have a really sweet personality. Everyone likes you because you are easy to be around. You don't rock the boat. You are gentle and kind and probably have the spiritual gift of mercy. Mom, that's great when dealing with adults, but it could ruin the lives of your children if you don't know how to set appropriate boundaries with them and make those boundaries stick.

Most mothers I encounter who have this type of personality have a child of the opposite personality. They

usually have a bull-headed little tyrant who orders them around from the delivery room! Why does God assign these mothers and children to one another? Can't you guess? They become the "iron that sharpens iron." They bring balance into each other's lives. They need each other to reveal and chisel away at the flesh.

Let's examine the parenting of another such parent. His name is Eli, the priest.

Read 1 Samuel 2:12–25.

Knowing that Eli was a priest, do you see something unusual about Eli's sons described in verse 12?

_____

UNIT 4

Don't you think it's odd that Eli was a priest and yet his sons did not know the Lord? That is our first "red flag" that something is wrong with Eli's parenting!

How did Eli's sons disobey the Lord? (See verses 13–17, 22.)

_____

_____

What did Eli do about it?

_____

Eli's sons were hoodlums! They were in the direct line of the priesthood, but they were a disaster. Why? Read verses 27–29 and look for the answer to that question in verse 29. List it here.

_____

Eli was held accountable for his sons because he honored his sons above the Lord. Eli "worshiped" his boys. He would not cross them. He would not set boundaries for their behavior and make them stick. He had passive parenting flesh.

Read verses 30–36. What consequences would Eli suffer for his sin?

_____

_____

_____

Read 1 Samuel 3:10–13.

Copy verse 13.

_____

_____

_____

Read verse 14. How strongly did God feel about Eli's sin?

_____

Read 1 Samuel 4:1–18. Summarize the events in these verses.

_____

_____

_____

_____

This story has a strong message. It strikes at the heart of every mother and father. Ask the Lord to show you if you are honoring your children above Him. Be still and allow God to do business in your life. Record your insights.

_____

_____

_____

_____

I want to share a story with you. A precious mother who has passive flesh shared this story with me. She has allowed me to share her story and its effects on her daughter so that you might be spared some of the heartache she has experienced. See if some of her experiences match your own.

When my daughter was born, I had no idea that she was stronger in personality than I was. The older she got, the more controlling she became. However, I didn't see that because she had two younger siblings to boss around and my hands were more than full with three children under the age of five. It was not until she was in junior high school that I began to realize that she controlled me more than I controlled her.

I did not see this as sin in my life to be handed over to Jesus. I attempted to control her in my own strength, which made me seem very dictatorial and made her rebellious. I was tightening controls, just when I should have been able to loosen them.

As a passive parent, I realize now that I struggled with not taking care of problems when they were small ones. I let wrong attitudes and behaviors slide by. I didn't want to deal with them. I would just make things work for the moment. This promoted a false sense of peace and would catch me off guard then when things began to go very wrong. Of course, the problem would escalate until it became a major battle.

We argued and fought over nearly everything while she was in high school and since she nearly always won, she lost most of her respect for me. I had not done the hard thing many times in setting limits on her, especially in the area of her talking back to me.

When she finally left home for college, our household became much more calm and even, and I began to realize how much I had given in to her. I felt relief, but I was heartbroken when she left. We had so many unresolved issues, and after all, she was my first-born leaving for the first time. I cried for months from a mixture of emotions. A passive mother does not necessarily have passive feelings.

I have just recently begun to see how my passivity is sin for me. It even makes me look like a very good person and easy to be with. Actually it is just as deadly, if not more so, than the controlling person, because what you see is *not what you get!* It's a deception of great magnitude because it is a very subtle form of control. You see, I attempt to control others (keep them from rocking my boat), by being "sweet" and easy to be with.

The Lord gave me many opportunities at learning the lessons He wanted to teach me in taking authority over the things I was supposed to manage. Besides having a chance to learn it with my own children, I became a music teacher in an elementary school and had dozens of children to discipline.

The first year I taught school, I could not control the fifth grade boys in my class. In my effort to make music "fun," I lost control of the class and the boys were running it. One morning in my quiet time, the Spirit-inspired thought came to me that I needed to ask for the gift of godly authority. I fell to my knees and simply, desperately, earnestly, asked my heavenly Father for this gift. I felt as assured that He had answered my request as I did when I first asked for forgiveness of my sins as a child.

Over a short period of time, I began to make choices and decisions about discipline in my classroom that I had never thought of before. Teaching school became a joy as I saw my students respond to my godly discipline. I was amazed.

I also realized how I had let my own children do whatever seemed easiest for *me*. Many times I had justified my behavior with my own children by thinking I was physically weak and totally overwhelmed with my life. That was an excuse to cover my flesh. That was a big revelation to me.

The realization of this sin of passivity has opened my eyes to other areas it has infected. My marriage, for example, has been affected. By not taking godly authority over the small things in my household, fellowship with my husband has suffered. My passiveness has resulted in a break of the oneness my marriage was meant to be. One cannot be a team player all by himself. That's how my husband has felt for much of our marriage. When one partner doesn't pull all his weight, the other becomes so burdened down that love and respect are lost.

Passive parents and marriage partners are greatly deceived. We look so good! How could it be wrong to be so "nice"? But what I am learning is that being "good" and passive and being "bad" and controlling are two sides of one coin.

It is still a daily struggle to give my passive nature to God. Every time I try to discipline my children or my students in my own power, two things generally happen. I am demanding, and the children rebel. It all gets out of balance. But as I allow Jesus to discipline through me, I see His fruit in the lives of the children.

Do you see yourself in this story? Record any response you need to make.

_____

_____

_____

Prayer

Lord, forgive me for honoring my child above You.
Forgive my passive patterns of behavior regarding my child.
Lord, I need complete retooling as a parent. I am going to trust You to undertake that work for me and in me.
I pray this in Jesus' name. Amen.

Mothering Tip

We don't want to push our kids in school to make straight As for the wrong reasons…like boosting our egos. But we do want to encourage our children to grow and learn at their peak capacity. Children learn best when their parents are involved in that process—both in and out of the schoolroom. Volunteering in your child's school to tutor or read or help teachers with administrative duties and guiding him with homework gives you a powerful way to stay connected with your child and it gives your child's teachers a valuable partner in their educational process. Children need to know Mom and Dad and teachers are working together. If you and your child's teacher are on the "same page," it creates a stable learning environment for your child.

In the middle school/junior high school years, your child will probably give you a "hands off" signal about school involvement. You can respect his boundaries without dropping out completely. Take advantage of parent-teacher conferences. Sit down and really listen to your child's comments about school. Join the parent booster clubs. This will give you a more complete picture of what's really happening with your child.

If something is happening at your child's school that disturbs you, take action. Gather the data, talk to other parents, make appointments with teachers and administrators. You will be amazed at what can be accomplished when you make your voice known.

Pious, "Goody Two-Shoes" Flesh

BEGIN WITH PRAYER.

Read Psalm 139 back to God as a prayer.

Are you discovering the areas of flesh in your life?

Once you start looking at flesh, you see it everywhere!

RELIGIOUS FLESH

Read Matthew 6:1.

What is Jesus' warning in this verse?

_____

Read Matthew 6:2–4.

What is the instruction in practicing kingdom living?

_____

Read Matthew 6:5–15.

What is the instruction in practicing kingdom living?

_____

Read Matthew 6:16–18.

What is the instruction in practicing kingdom living?

_____

Jesus was preaching His great sermon on the hillside beside the large lake that is called the Sea of Galilee. He began giving His disciples instruction in walking in the Spirit instead of in the flesh. He methodically exposed common flesh patterns and then taught His disciples what kingdom living should look like. In giving and praying and fasting, it should be done in secret. Why? Because it is so easy for believers to get caught up in the praise of man even in the act of praising God!

Read Philippians 1:15–17.

Why were some in Philippi preaching Christ?

_____

Some of the Philippians were preaching out of selfish ambition. While Paul was in jail, they wanted to move in and take over his "pulpit." They were caught up in "religious" flesh.

This flesh pattern really hits home to me. If you have been reared in the home of a minister, the opportunity for "religious" flesh is ample. It feels good when people compliment your singing or speaking. It is so easy to take the glory for yourself. But God will not share His glory. I found that out in a very dramatic way.

When Danielle and Stephanie were just babies, I was invited to sing for the seventy-fifth anniversary of a large downtown Houston church. I had been a soloist there and although we had moved away, they had me come back to sing for the special service. I sang my rendition of "Amazing Grace" that had been a favorite. It went really well, and afterward the church gave me a standing ovation. Does anyone see anything wrong with that picture?

They asked me to sing an encore, and I gladly did. On the way back down from the platform to my seat, I heard God speak to me with startling clarity. "Did you enjoy that?"

"Oh, Lord," I thought. "What have I done?"

"Denise, you will never do that again."

And then the voice in my heart was silent. That solo was the last one I sang in church for a long time. I didn't broadcast my story, I just didn't get asked to sing anymore. It still gives me chills to think about it.

God could have put me on the shelf and washed His hands of me. I deserved it. But He is so faithful and rich in mercy. When the singing part of my life ended, the speaking began. I didn't know I could speak in front of people until I stopped singing. And then He began to let me sing in conjunction with my speaking, and it became a tool to express the truths of God in a special way.

I have told my story to many young musicians including the ones in my family. God will not share His glory. There is no momentary thrill of applause worth the deadness that will come in your heart if you try to take that glory for yourself. If you are the ladies' retreat chairman or the choir soloist or have the lead in the church musical or are teaching a Sunday school class or are the biggest giver in the church, I want to warn you of the temptation that awaits you. When the commendations and compliments start coming, mentally give each one to Jesus.

Copy Philippians 2:3 here.

_____

_____

_____

In the New American Standard version of the Bible, it says, "Do nothing from selfishness or empty conceit…" Those words are translated *strife or vainglory* in the King James version. I researched the original word for *vainglory* in a Greek dictionary. It is the word *kenodoxia* and means "empty glorying or self-conceit."[9] What a word picture of fruitless glorying in ourselves!

It is said that Corrie ten Boom, the famous survivor of the German death camps in Nazi Germany, testified on this point. After the war, when she spoke publicly about her experiences in the war, people would respond with praise. When she was given compliments, she imagined that each one was a rose. Mentally, she gave each rose to Jesus as they were handed to her. That kept her perspective straight. That is walking in the Spirit.

Prayer

Lord, I want to be free of religious, pious flesh.
I want to worship You in Spirit and in truth.
Teach me how to worship and give and pray in secret.
I give You all glory and honor. In Jesus' name. Amen.

Mothering Tip

Include each member of the family in tonight's dinner conversation. Take turns in giving each family member a chance to talk about their day. Ban topics that only appeal to little kids or adults.

Try these discussion starters:

- What was the best part of your day?
- If you could be best friends with any grown-up, who would it be?
- What did you like best about our last family vacation? What would you like to do next time?
- What would it be like to be a septuplet?
- What do you like best in a friend?

DAY 4

Pitiful, "Babyish" Flesh

BEGIN WITH PRAYER

Sing "I Love You, Lord" *or* "Open Our Eyes, Lord"

or a hymn that you can sing from memory.

Ask the Father to prepare your heart for His Word.

QUARRELSOME/INFANTILE FLESH

Read 1 Corinthians 3:1–3.

What was Paul's accusation of the Corinthians?

_____

What was the proof of their "fleshiness"?

_____

Read Luke 22:14–24.

Who was quarreling in this passage?

_____

What were they arguing about?

_____

The disciples were sharing the Lord's Supper with Jesus. They had just heard Him say that one of them would betray Him. They began to discuss which one it would be and then all of a sudden the topic changed to who of them was the greatest! Can you see the "flesh trip" they were on?

Read Romans 13:13–14.

List the fleshly activities mentioned in these verses.

_____

_____

Are you surprised to find jealousy and strife in that list? They are included as fleshly lusts. Why?

_____

_____

Being lustful doesn't just refer to material possessions or sexual fantasies. You can lust after position and power…even if it's just on the PTA board or the church council. Jealousy, fighting, and arguing are not exclusive elements of a group of children. Unfortunately, more often than we would like to admit, their mothers have the same problems.

Read Galatians 5:19–21.

Compare these verses to Romans 13:13–14.

What similarities do you find between these two passages?

_____

_____

We are focusing on quarrelsome flesh today, but we can't ignore the glaring list of sexual flesh and sin in these verses. One of you reading this now may be caught up in an adulterous affair with a man who is not your husband. Put an end to the affair today and go home to your family, Mom. Go home emotionally, as well as physically. Your sins can be forgiven, but you must repent. Ask God and your husband to forgive you and put this thing behind you. You cannot be free until you untangle yourself from this trap.

If this last paragraph was written for you, call for help. Call a godly friend, your pastor, or your MotherWise Mentoring Mom. The Lord Jesus can cleanse and heal and forgive. Come to Him with this today.

Now let's get back to our study.

What additional descriptions of quarrelsome/infantile flesh did you find in the Galatians passage?

_____

Read James 3:13–16.

Verse 16 tells us the result of quarrelsome flesh. Describe it in your own words.

_____

Read Proverbs 21:9 and 19 and Proverbs 27:15–16

What three pictures are used to describe a contentious, brawling wife?

_____

_____

The Hebrew word for *contentious* is *madown* pronounced "ma'don."[10] It means "discord, brawling, strife, and contesting." Could these words describe you? Journal your thoughts.

_____

_____

_____

Some of you grew up in a home where fighting and arguing was a way of life. You heard your mother and father scream at each other. You may have seen them physically abuse one another. They may have abused you.

Some of your mothers used screaming and yelling as their only form of discipline. And you may find yourself using the same ineffective means to discipline your own children.

Recognizing the hurtful ways of the past is the first step to becoming free from them. Next you need to forgive those who have hurt you—physically, verbally, or emotionally. If there was abuse, you may need professional help from a godly, Christian counselor to help you process through the grief and pain and to get to freedom on the other side of it.

Then it's time to look at your present circumstance and be honest with yourself. Is the Holy Spirit convicting you right now of your own behavioral problems as a mother?

Then come to Him. Confess your sins. Reach out to Him in prayer asking for His cleansing and pruning to take place in your life so you can be set free to love and discipline your children in His Spirit. You will be absolutely amazed at what changes He can bring about!

Prayer

Lord, I am beginning to see things from Your point of view.
Enable me to look honestly at the past and the present.
Lead me as I come to You for healing and cleansing. I pray this in Jesus' name. Amen.

Mothering Tip

There is no doubt that while you have been studying this unit on the "flesh" you have not only seen yourself, but you have probably seen your children and your children's peers. When you get a bunch of kids together, it is an "occasion for the flesh" to be sure.

While you must deal directly with your child's version of the flesh, the behavior of his peers is another thing. If your child is suffering socially at the hands of his peers, there are some things you can do. If your child says, "No one wants to play with me":

1. Take it seriously and listen very carefully. Your child has just trusted you with some very personal information. Handle it with care. Don't tell him it's not true. Don't deny his feelings and perception of the problem. That will make him leery of sharing his heart with you next time.

2. Start a conversation with your child about the situation. Has anything happened recently that caused his relationship with his friends to change? Is it always this way? Ask your child what he/she thinks the problem is when he is with his peers.

3. Pray aloud with your child about his problems. Encourage him to pray with you, being honest with God about his feelings. Spend time in prayer asking God to show you how to help your child.

4. Gather data. Talk to your child's teachers—in school, church, clubs, and sports. Get their perspective on the problem. Find out how your child is behaving when you are not around. Try to isolate the problem.

5. Teach your child how to be a friend. Friendships require being giving, caring, and friendly while maintaining a sense of one's own value. Help your child acquire friendship skills.

DAY 5

Persistently Self-Centered "I, Me, Mine" Flesh

BEGIN WITH PRAYER

Offer your heart to God as a living sacrifice.

Ask Him to take it and melt it and mold it according to His perfect will.

Concentrate for a few moments and let God do all that He wants to do in your life today.

This is our last day to study the flesh. Aren't you glad? I don't think we could have stood it for one more day!

SELF-CENTERED, SELF-SERVING FLESH

Reread Philippians 2:3–4.

Copy verse 4 here.

_____

_____

In reality, all flesh is self-centered. And being self-centered and self-absorbed has become a national pastime in America. We are told to "take time for ourselves" and "look out for number one" because no one else will. No one else will because they are so self-absorbed in themselves! Is this the way we are to live?

There is no way to be an effective mother and be centered on yourself at the same time. The name of the game in mothering is self-sacrifice. I will be the first to concede that moms need a break and there is a place for "time out" from our children. But the principle here is giving up the right to be priority number one—getting our needs met ahead of our husbands' and children's needs.

What destruction we have caused in our homes from self-centeredness! What devastation reigns in our country because we are a nation of people who are self-absorbed!

The antidote for self-serving flesh, in fact, for all flesh, is found in the rest of the passage in Philippians. Read Philippians 2:5–11.

What did Jesus do to avoid self-serving flesh according to verse 7?

_____

What price did He pay to completely humble Himself? (See verse 8.)

_____

Jesus emptied Himself and humbled Himself to the point of death—death on the cross. Is that what it takes to get rid of self-centered flesh? How can I have "this attitude that was also in Christ Jesus"?

I want you to think about those questions in preparation for the lesson next week. Don't miss Unit 5! In it we will find the way to freedom from all this flesh!

Mothering Tip

Take time today to write a note to your mom and to your mother-in-law. Tell them how much you love and appreciate them. (For some of you, this may take "emptying yourself" and becoming very humble!) Send your mother-in-law flowers on your husband's birthday. Thank her for the sacrifices and the love she poured into his life. Send your mom flowers on your birthday. Write a thank-you note for the way she expressed love to you.

UNIT 5

THE PRINCIPLE OF THE SHEARS: PRUNING THE BRANCH

MOTHERING SKILL: SETTING APPROPRIATE BOUNDARIES

DAY 1
THE PRINCIPLE OF THE CROSS

DAY 2
THE PREEMINENCE OF THE CROSS

DAY 3
THE PLACE OF THE CROSS

DAY 4
THE PRAYER OF THE CROSS

DAY 5
THE PRACTICE OF THE CROSS

Now we've discovered the problem in our love buckets. We are full of ourselves and don't have room to be filled with God! So how do we get rid of the problem? Take a few more self-help seminars? Pull ourselves up by our boot straps? The answer is found at the foot of the Cross…

UNIT 5
Bible Study Listening Guide

1. How do we put an end to our fleshly behavior as a mom?

_____

2. The principle we are studying today is:

_____

3. The key Bible verse is:

_____

_____

_____

4. The object used to help me remember the lesson was:

_____

_____

5. The story Denise tells to help me understand the principle is:

_____

6. The drawing used to help me understand the principle is:

_____

7. What I personally need to remember from this lesson is:

_____

_____

_____

MotherWise Group Prayer Requests

1._____

2._____

3._____

UNIT 5
MOTHERING SKILLS DISCUSSION:
Setting Appropriate Boundaries

Challenge: To clearly set and enforce age-appropriate boundaries for our children in the areas of attitude, behavior, speech, and work.

We have a big job. The work of mothering is vast in its scope. But one of the most critical arenas of mothering is that of establishing boundaries for our children and enforcing those boundaries. Wise mothers discipline their children according to God's standards. But how do we practice it? This is the topic for today's discussion.

What area of discipline and boundary-setting is the most challenging to you? Getting your child to obey? Getting your child's respect? Establishing bedtimes? Curfews? Food and clothing choices? Manners? School and housework? Choice of friends? Attitudes? Entertainment?

_____

_____

_____

_____

Why do you think you struggle with that area?

_____

_____

_____

List some age-appropriate boundaries for each of your children.

Child 1:

_____

_____

_____

Child 2:

_____

_____

_____

Child 3:

_____

_____

_____

Child 4:

_____

_____

_____

Tools to Meet the Challenge:

Author's Note: In every book, you will find parts you agree with and disagree with. These books are no exception. However, I found some helpful words in each one. Read them with discernment.

What the Bible Says about Child Training, J. Richard Fugate (Elkton, Md.: Full Quart Press, an imprint of Holly Hall Publications, 1998).

Making Children Mind without Losing Yours, Dr. Kevin Leman (Old Tappan, N.J.: Fleming H. Revell Company, 1987).

How to Really Love Your Teenager, Ross Compbell, M.D. (Wheaton, Ill.: Victor Books, 1993).

Helping Teens in Crisis, Miriam Neff (Wheaton, Ill.: Tyndale House Publishers, 1993).

Boundaries with Kids, Dr. Henry Cloud and Dr. John Townsend (Grand Rapids, Mich.: Zondervan Publishing House, 1998).

- Boundary 1: Take authority over your child while he still depends on you. He or she must obey you. It is your job to set that boundary and to enforce it. This boundary is based on Ephesians 6:1.
- Boundary 2: Children must respect their parents. Honoring parents starts with an attitude and proceeds to action. This boundary is based on Exodus 20:12.
- Boundary 3: Children must relate to others in an acceptable manner. These boundaries have their foundations in the last five of the Ten Commandments in Exodus 20:3–17 and the further explanations of them by Jesus in Matthew 5–7.
- Boundary 4: Children must follow the boundaries set that are unique to your family. These include decisions about bedtimes, curfews, eating and dressing habits, cleanliness, entertainment, friends, church attendance, and acceptable attitudes.[1]

Your child will learn his boundaries when he receives consequences for operating outside the boundaries, when he takes ownership or responsibility for his own actions, and when he deals with the boundaries of others.[2]

Part of training a child to understand his boundaries is establishing and enforcing clear, fair, appropriate boundaries for your child and part of his understanding of boundaries comes as you become a boundary for your child.[3]

AGE-APPROPRIATE BOUNDARIES

Many moms ask me, "What can I expect of my child? How do I set standards and boundaries that are age appropriate?" Whereas no two children are alike in their growth and maturity rate, some very basic and general guidelines are helpful as long as you don't get legalistic about them! Remember, God made your little Suzy or Johnny unique! These are some boundaries for young children to school-aged kids based on an excellent resource for parents, *Baby and Child Care for Christian Parents*, by Grace Ketterman and Herbert Ketterman.[4]

Sometime in the first year to year and a half, most children can learn to accept limits and obey your simple, clear instructions. They can learn to avoid dangerous situations. However, Mom, children under two need *constant* adult supervision. It is inconvenient and tiresome, but it is what is right for your child. This is the time for some serious bonding with your little one. Relax and enjoy it because before you know it you'll have to make an appointment to spend time with him.

Between two and three, children can learn to pick up their toys with some help. He can obey your instructions if you make them simple. He/she will more often stay within the boundaries you set for him if he faces immediate, consistent consequences. During this stage a child learns to use the toilet, dress himself, play within safe limits, and he starts to be considerate of others. He/she can be a big "helper" for mom and dad.

By the time he is four to five, most children can button, zip, and tie on their clothing and shoes. They can eat with fewer messes. Most of them have the ability to be cooperative in a group as they can submit their personal wishes to a larger group's agenda. Since children at this stage are very trusting, they need help in knowing who they can trust and who they cannot.

To preschool or not to preschool is a major concern for many parents. Take it to the Lord in prayer first! Ask the Lord for wisdom and discernment. Get counsel from godly parents in your church.

Then take an honest look at the maturity level of your child. Do they obey your simple instructions? Could they take instructions from a teacher? Can they focus their attention and sit still for short periods of time or are they "all over the place"? Are they still needing long afternoon or morning naps? Do you have an eager beaver who talked early and whose mind is a little sponge? Do you have a quiet little one who loves to be home with Mom and hates crowds and noise?

Look at your financial picture. Can you afford tuition and uniforms for a private school? Would it be best to homeschool up to a certain point?

We went through all those scenarios with each of our children. We did different things with each one because each situation was unique. It is a big decision, but Mom, it's not life and death. Whether or not they go to preschool usually will not decisively alter the course of their lives!

When children enter school, they enter a new world. They have a new adult authority figure every year, they are in a competitive peer environment and want to please their parents with school success. If you have a school-age child that does not know basic obedience and responsibility start now. Set clear boundaries and enforce them.

Many school-aged children respond to charts that help them develop responsible habits. Often the chart is placed on the refrigerator and stars or stickers are used to reward success for each task accomplished. Some duties that might be on the chart are listed here.

CHORE CHART

Wake self with an alarm clock

Make the bed

Brush teeth

Take a bath

Get dressed on time

Do homework on time

Feed pets

Help with garden and yard work

Help with sweeping

Help with dusting

Take out the trash

Put groceries away

Set the table

Clean up messes after eating

Take dishes to the sink

Help fill the dishwasher

Put dirty clothes in hamper

Answer the telephone appropriately

Tell parents whereabouts when playing

Go to bed on time the first time you are told

ATTITUDE CHART

An attitude chart to be filled out at the end of the day could have some of the following categories:

If in your culture it is polite, said "yes ma'am," "no ma'am" (or "sir" to father)

Used polite table manners

Did not whine

First time obedience to instructions

Did not interrupt conversations

Thoughtful of others

Kind to others

Honest and truthful

Generous

Not lazy; worked hard

Not bragging or boastful

The teen years bring on new challenges in setting boundaries. These years become a balancing act for you as you begin the process of letting your child have more and more responsibility and less and less directives from you. The goal is to send your eighteen-year-old out into the world equipped to take over his life with maturity and responsibility.

I suggest that you set up a form on your home computer (or copy mine). I've put it on a separate page so you can copy it if you desire. Adjust the categories to fit your family. If you have a compliant teen, you may want to whittle the list to only a few important points. If you have a very belligerent teen, trim the list to only the battles that you are willing to fight and win.

OUR FAMILY BOUNDARY AGREEMENT

Curfew

What time to be in the house on school nights?_____

 What time to be in the house on weekend nights?_____

What time for friends to be gone from house on weekend nights?_____

What time for friends to be gone from house on week nights?_____

Consequences for noncompliance: _____

Cleaning room

What jobs need to be done?

1. _____

2. _____

3. _____

4. _____

5. _____

How often? _____

Consequences for noncompliance:_____

Cleaning bathroom

What jobs need to be done?

1. _____

2. _____

3. _____

4. _____

5. _____

6. _____

How often? _____

Consequences for noncompliance: _____

Car care

What jobs need to be done?

1. _____

2. _____

3. _____

4. _____

5. _____

How often? _____

Consequences for noncompliance:_____

Kitchen help

What jobs need to be done?

1. _____

2. _____

3. _____

4. _____

5. _____

How often? _____

Consequences for noncompliance:_____

School work

Acceptable grade range: _____

Homework expectations: _____

Attitude toward teachers, administrators, and schoolwork: _____

Consequences for noncompliance: _____

Church attendance

Minimum attendance standard: _____

Church activities attendance: _____

Consequences for noncompliance: _____

Allowance

Weekly amount: _____

Expectations on work outside the home for pay: _____

Expectations for what teen is responsible to pay for:

1. _____

2. _____

3. _____

4. _____

5. _____

Consequences for noncompliance:_____

Attitude toward parents

Requirements to show honor and respect:

1. _____

2. _____

3. _____

Consequences for noncompliance:_____

Attitude toward siblings

Requirements to show respect and kindness:

1. _____

2. _____

3. _____

Consequences for noncompliance:_____

Ask your teen to fill out the form by a set time. Review the form with your husband and be prepared to compare your own completed form with your teen.

Set a time for an appointment with your teen and your husband when everyone can be relaxed, comfortable, focused, and not rushed. Listen without comment as your teen describes what he/she thinks his boundaries should be regarding each item.

Clarify his comments without judgment on whether you agree. For now you are just listening. Thank him for his time and input and tell him you will get back to him when final decisions are made.

Spend time in private with your husband talking carefully through each boundary you will set. When you have the final list, put it in writing, and call another meeting to discuss it with your teen. You may be surprised at the wisdom your teenager might display if you give him an opportunity to have input in setting his own boundaries. Remember your ultimate goal for him is that he will set internal boundaries for himself and abide by them by the grace of God.

There are many great resources for parents today. If you haven't taken the MotherWise course, "Wisdom for Mothers," I encourage you to do that at the completion of this course. Also, look on the shelves of your local Christian bookstore for resources to help you learn to set boundaries for and discipline your child.

DAY 1

The Principle of the Cross

BEGIN WITH PRAYER

Ask the Father to remove any barrier that keeps you from Him.
Ask Him to work in your life this week in a powerful way to accomplish His purpose.

We want Jesus' life to flow unhindered through us to our kids. We know that what blocks His life flow through us is our flesh. For the past two weeks we have done an autopsy on our "flesh" or self-nature. And it hasn't been pretty. I'm ready for the cure, aren't you? This week we will uncover the remedy that Jesus has provided for our self-nature. It is so awesome it will "blow your hair back"!

Read John 15:1–6.

Who are the branches?

_____

What does God do to branches that do not bear fruit according to verses 2 and 6?

_____

PRUNING DEAD BRANCHES

Jesus' words to those who do not bear fruit at all is very strong. He says that those who are not receiving their life from the vine and bearing fruit will be taken away, cast into the fire, and burned. What is Jesus saying?

Those who do not know Him as Savior of their lives, who have not asked forgiveness for their sins and have not asked Him into their hearts, will die and go to hell. Hell is a very real place. God did not create it for human beings, He created it for Satan and his demonic angels. But Jesus' words are chillingly clear. If a man or woman refuses His way of salvation, they will die in their sins. And the penalty for dying a sinner is eternal hell.

We learned in Unit 2 that Jesus paid the price for our sins. Read 2 Corinthians 5:21.

Who actually became sin for us?

_____

Since He took the penalty for sin, what did that allow us to become?

_____

Jesus exchanged His sinless life for your sinful life. He took on your sin, so you could take on His righteousness. But you must receive it as a conscious choice. It does not happen to you because you were raised in a Christian home. You do not escape hell because you go to church. You must recognize that you are a sinner and ask forgiveness for your sins. If you have not turned your life over to Jesus at some time in your life or as suggested previously in this study (see Unit 2, Day 1) and you want to do so, consider praying a prayer something like this right now:

Lord, I am a sinner. I need a Savior. Please forgive me of my sins.
I ask You now to come into my heart to be my master and Lord and Savior.
I want to become Your child. Thank You for dying on the cross for me.
Please count Your death as the payment for my sins.
I ask this in the name of Jesus Christ the Messiah, the risen Lord. Amen.

If you have taken this step in trusting Jesus just now, you need to tell someone about it. Call on your pastor or MotherWise group leader or a Christian friend and share this important decision.

PRUNING LIVE BRANCHES

Many of you have already made that one-time commitment to Him. You are His branch. So what are His words to you?

Reread John 15:2.

What does God do to branches that bear fruit?

_____

God prunes branches that bear fruit. You may say, "Wait a minute. You mean if I am a believer, and I am bearing the fruit of love, joy, peace, patience, etc., He will come into my life with the pruning shears and start cutting? Why would He do that?"

What does the verse say? So that you will bear *more* fruit. If we truly want to bear more fruit, to live lives that are pouring forth love and joy and peace, then we will need to submit to the heavenly pruning shears. We will need to allow Him to cut away that which keeps us from bearing more fruit.

We discovered in the last two units what needs to be cut away. It has a name and the name of it is "flesh." Let's review what "flesh" looks like by using another illustration.

PICTURE OF THE FLESH

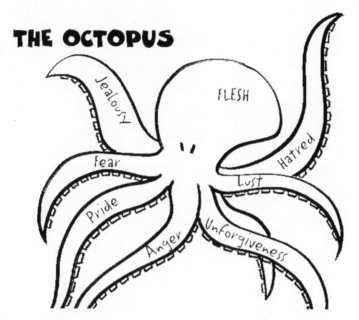

Flesh or our self-nature is much like an octopus.

We could label the arms "jealousy," "hate," "anger," "fear," "pride," "lust," "envy," and "unforgiveness." The arms of your own personal "flesh" octopus might have different titles. Titles like "gluttony," "greed," and others might be on a "flesh" octopus. What would be on yours?

1. _____   5. _____

2. _____   6. _____

3. _____   7. _____

4. _____   8. _____

Most third-graders know what happens when you cut off the arms of an octopus. They grow back! If you want to permanently get rid of an arm of an octopus, there is only one thing to do. You must kill the octopus. There must be a mortal wound to the head.

Read Galatians 5:16–21.

List the "deeds of the flesh" given in these verses.

_____

_____

_____

Here is a detailed list of some patterns of the "flesh" or self-nature. Do any of these look familiar?

Anger	Opinionated
Anxiety	Overly sensitive to criticism
Argumentative	Overly submissive
Bigotry	Passivity
Bitterness	Pride
Boastful	Profane
Bossy	Rebellion at authority
Causing dissension	Resentment
Conceited	Self-centered
Controlling	Self-confidence
Critical tongue	Self-depreciation
Depression	Self-hatred
Envy	Self-indulgence
Fear	Self-justification
Feelings of rejection	Self-pity
Feelings of worthlessness	Self-reliance
Gluttony	Self-righteousness
Hatred	Self-sufficiency
Idolatry	Sensuality
Impatience	Sexual lust
Impulsiveness	Slow to forgive
Impure thoughts	Stubbornness
Inadequacy	Temper
Indifference to other's problems	Too quick to speak
Insecurity	Undue sadness
Lazy	Vanity
Loner	Withdrawal
Materialistic	Workaholic
Negativism	Worrier[5]

Okay, we know that flesh or the self-nature often rears its ugly head even in devout believers. But there is a cure and we find it documented in the book of Romans.

Read Romans 8:1–2.

What two items of good news are proclaimed in these verses?

1._____

2._____

Read Romans 8:3–4.

How did our rescue from "living in the flesh" occur, according to Romans 8:3–4?

_____

LAW OF SIN AND DEATH VERSUS THE LAW OF THE SPIRIT OF LIFE IN CHRIST

The Old Testament or Old Covenant stated that if you walked in the way of sin, you would reap death (Deuteronomy 30:15–20). That is called the law of sin and death. When you live out the attitudes and actions of your fleshy self-nature, you are living according to the law of sin and death.

If you indulge yourself in gluttonous behavior, your body will be put on a path of destruction. If you are unforgiving of some offense against you, your mind and spirit are cut off from the life flow of Jesus and you will experience deadness. (This doesn't mean you are no longer a Christian, but that your fellowship with Him is disrupted.) When Jesus died on the cross, He set us free from that law of sin and death.

Here's how He did it. He became sin, and so He died. That was the legal payment for becoming a sinner. So He fulfilled the law of sin.

But then, because He is God of the universe who is all powerful, He victoriously rose from the dead in full resurrection power and came to life again. That's how He set us free from the law of death. His death paid the penalty of sin and His resurrection life set us free to live. We are no longer trapped into a sin and death cycle.

Do you hear that, Mom? You are free! If you have accepted His death in place of yours as payment for your sins, you are truly free! You are free to live according to the law of the Spirit of life in Christ Jesus instead of according to the law of sin and death.

What does all that mean for a mother with a bunch of whiny kids, dirty dishes in the sink, teenagers who talk back, or adult children who never come home for a visit, or even worse, young adults who have moved back home? It means that if we are in Christ, we do not have to be trapped by our self-nature or "flesh" into destructive patterns of thinking and responding to those trying, mothering situations.

We don't have to lash out at whiny children, or condemn ourselves for dirty dishes in the sink, or fall into rejection when teens talk back, or pout when adult children never come home, or despair over young adults who are drifting. We don't have to be constantly defeated by our own behavior. We aren't bound to the law of sin and death.

Let me give you another example. Let's say you come from a long line of women who scream at their children to get them under control. Your grandma may have screamed at your mom and your mom screamed at you. So when you had children, it was "natural" to scream at them whenever you wanted to get them to obey you.

So can that cycle be broken? Can you stop screaming and start giving firm, but kind commands to children who will obey the first time they hear your calm voice? Is that a dream? Would you like to be free?

UNIT 5

FREEDOM FOR MOTHERS

Jesus died on the cross and rose again just so we could be free in situations like that. Sometimes we think He died and rose again just so we could go to heaven. Of course that is true, but there is so much more to it than that! He died and rose again so you could live in freedom here on this earth in very earthy situations like screaming or not screaming at kids. The cross of Jesus is very, very practical. If you understand it, it will change your daily routine. It will affect every moment of your life. You will never be the same.

Yes, Mom. You can be free from screaming or any other fleshy response you have with your children and your husband. There is a way out of that defeating cycle of sin and death in your relationships. But it is the way of the cross.

The cross is the pruning shear in God's hand. But how do we make the cross work to get rid of the problem of our self-nature or "flesh"? How can we truly be free?

Let's reread Galatians 5:16–21, then read verses 22–24.

How do we keep from carrying out the desire of our flesh?

_____

_____

Why do I experience a battle inside myself between doing good and doing bad?

_____

Contrast the "deeds of the flesh" with the "deeds of the Spirit."

For example:

1. Immorality-Impurity-Sensuality	versus	Love
2. Outbursts of Anger	versus	Patience
3. _____	versus	_____
4. _____	versus	_____
5. _____	versus	_____

What radical action needs to be taken on our "flesh" according to verse 24?

_____

We all want to be moms who exhibit love and joy and peace on a daily basis in every relationship. We want our kids to see us living in peace and harmony with them, with our husbands, and our coworkers. We want the fruit of the Spirit to flow from us. According to verse 24, there is only one way to accomplish that.

If we want the heavenly vinedresser to enable us to bear more fruit, we will have to let Him get to the root of the problem and cut away with His heavenly pruning shears.

Flesh doesn't need mending. Flesh must die! We don't need to just clean up our flesh; it needs to be crucified. Copy Galatians 2:20 in the space below.

_____

_____

_____

How has the ruling power of the old sinful, fleshy life been broken?

_____

Who is now living in the life of a believer?

_____

Could Jesus Christ mother your children effectively?

_____

Could He handle your marriage?

_____

How can we now live our lives?

_____

_____

THE PRINCIPLE OF THE SHEARS: THE CRUCIFIXION PRINCIPLE

Here it is! Here is the answer to how we can be free! "I am crucified with Christ." Nothing short of death of my fleshy self-nature will set me free. I can't mend it and hope it will get better. I can't use self-help to get stronger. I don't need to learn to cope with it; I need to take it to the cross.

The apostle Paul said, "My strength is made perfect in weakness" (2 Corinthians 12:9).

It is not in becoming stronger that I will win the battle over my flesh, *it is by coming to the cross and dying that I gain victory.*

Mom, you do not have to live according to the pull of your flesh. You do not have to be bossy and controlling just because women in your family have "always been that way." You do not have to be weak and passive and let your husband and children run all over you because you've "always been that way." Jesus came to set you free. He died on the cross so that you could live according to His Spirit—His power source—and not your own.

Come to Him today. Come to the cross! Choose this day to "put to death" the deeds of the self-nature. Deal a mortal wound to the flesh. I urge you to get on your knees and lay yourself on His altar.

Prayer

Lord Jesus Christ, I thank You for Your sacrifice on the cross for me.
Now, Lord, I choose to die to my flesh, my self-centered nature. I don't want my will,
Lord, I want Yours and Yours alone. I want to know the truth that will set me free.
I pray this now in the matchless name of Jesus. Amen.

Mothering Tip

Make time for little things. When you greet your husband in the evening, take time for a smile and a hug. Try to spend at least ten to fifteen minutes giving each other eye-to-eye contact and your full attention. Tell your husband how much you love him.

DAY 2

The Preeminence of the Cross

BEGIN WITH PRAYER

Be still and know that He is God.

It is He who has made us and not we ourselves.

Submit yourself to God. Humbly bow yourself before Him.

If we want the heavenly vinedresser to enable us to bear more fruit, we will have to let Him get to the root of the problem and cut it away.

NO LONGER SLAVES

Read Romans 6:4–7

How many references to death are there in these verses?

_____

According to verse 6 what happened to our old self?

_____

We are no longer slaves to_____

There are seven references to death in verse 4, so we need to pay attention to what has died. The Lord Jesus died and our old self-nature died. We have been crucified with Him. This was so we could be freed from our old self or old fleshy self-nature. We are no longer slaves to it.

Read Romans 6:11–14.

According to verse 11, what is my relationship to sin?

_____

What is my relationship to God?

_____

What does not have "lordship" or dominance over us according to verses 12–14?

_____

I don't have to obey my fleshy inclination to lash out or scream or pout to manipulate and control the people around me. I can choose to present my mind and my body and my heart to Jesus so that He can live His life through me. That is freedom! I am to "consider myself" dead to sin. That means I choose with my "chooser" to die to sin. I take myself to the cross.

Act Like Who You Are

A story is told about Queen Elizabeth. When she was a young teenager, she talked back to her nanny. The nanny grasped her by the shoulders and said, "Do you know who you are? You are the future Queen of England. Now start acting like it!"

It is time we began acting like who we are. We have been freed from the law of sin and death. Jesus has paid the price for our freedom. We are no longer in bondage to the flesh patterns of our parents and the fleshy habits of our personalities. We are children of the King! We are mothers who have the very life source of the Lord Jesus Christ Himself living in us! He is our life!

Read Romans 8:12–13

What is the result of living in the "flesh"?

_____

What is the result of living in the "Spirit"?

_____

According to verse 13, what action do you have to take to live according to the Spirit?

_____

The flesh brings death and the Spirit brings life. If I am a mother who manipulates and controls my children to get my needs met, it will bring about a spiritual deadness in all of us. The Spirit will be quenched. It will cut off the flow of Jesus' life through me.

If I submit myself to the indwelling life of the Lord Jesus and allow Him to guide and direct my children through me, springs of life flow from me to my children. That spells *freedom.*

I want you to see that the cross was not just a place in time and history, although it certainly was that. It is also a principle that operates in the life of a believer on a continual basis. This crucifixion principle is dying to "self-nature" or dying to "flesh." It is absolutely necessary to obtain the freedom in Christ Jesus that we are promised.

When the Cross "Crosses" You

If you continue in your journey with God, longing to move forward in knowing Him, He will inevitably lead you to the cross. His cross will somehow, someday cross your path. At the place where He crosses you, you will have a decision to make. Will I live in the flesh, getting what I want, when I want it, the way I want it, or will I choose to go to the cross with what I want and get in on what God wants? Will I give up and give in, or will I go my own way?

Copy Philippians 1:21.

_____

_____

Journal your thoughts.

_____

_____

_____

Prayer

UNIT 5

Lord, I admit that I don't even begin to understand all that You did for me

on the cross and all that You are doing in me with the cross now.

Keep working even when I don't understand what You are doing.

Don't allow me to be satisfied with where I am spiritually.

Keep me hungering and thirsting for more and more of You.

All I want is You. I pray this in Your name. Amen.

Mothering Tip

The beginning step in setting the standards for your child is to carefully explain them to him.

Stop your child and tell him in a calm but authoritative voice what you expect him to do. Get down on his level and look him squarely in the eye. Make sure he is focused. Only then will you be able to hold him accountable for first-time obedience.

For example, "John, you must come to me when I call you. When you hear your name, stop what you are doing and come quickly. Do not continue playing. Do not continue talking to someone else. Drop what you are doing and come to me. Do not argue. Do not fuss. Listen to my voice and obey. Do you understand?"

Then let John repeat the rule: "I must come to you the first time you call me. I must not keep playing. I must come right when you call me." Then say, "John, are we really clear about the rule? I don't want you to get in trouble for breaking the rule if you don't understand it." Let him respond. "Yes, Mom. I understand the rule."

The Place of the Cross

BEGIN WITH PRAYER

Ask the Lord to open your understanding of the cross today.
Thank the Lord for all that He did there for you to make you free.

There is an illustration in Dr. Larry Crabb's book, *The Marriage Builder,* that may help you understand the crucifixion principle more clearly. We have permission to use it here.

Imagine yourself standing at the edge of a cliff.[6]

The Cliff of Surrender

The cliff represents your self-strength and being in control. It is familiar and there you feel safe. You look down into the chasm below the cliff and it is frightening.

If you were to jump off the cliff, you would lose control. You might be rejected. You would have to face your fears. You might lose the very thing you are holding onto.

But now imagine that there is a rope around your waist. That rope is the rope of God's love. His love is a love that will never fail. It will sustain you. It is a rope tied securely at the top around Jesus.

He is urging you to jump off the cliff of self-strength and hang only by His strength and love. But you may look over the edge of the cliff and think, "Wait just a minute! If I jump off, the rope might be too long and I might crash at the bottom. Or the rope might break. What if God can't be trusted to really be there if I trust Him?"

Most of us experience the panic of the "hang time" that comes even after we commit to fully surrender and trust in God. It may not seem like He's there. It may not look like He is able to hold you securely when you're dangling over the cliff.

But if you will surrender fully to Him in complete abandon, He will always be there for you.

Read Hebrews 13:5.

Copy the words that the Lord Himself has said to you:

_____

_____

THE PLACE OF SURRENDER

UNIT 5

The cliff represents the "place" of the cross. It is the place of total surrender. To surrender yourself, you will have to jump. You will have to take the leap of faith, letting go of relying on yourself and your own way of controlling your life and allow Him complete control.

For some of you, that may mean that you have to let go of your fears. You may be afraid of having enough money or afraid that your children will be safe from harm. You may be afraid of losing your health or you may be afraid of being dependent on someone else. Your fears may be wrapped up in your child's future and what it will bring.

Your jump from the cliff may represent letting go of being in control. You may have been controlling your children and your husband so you could have your own way. You may have controlled those at work or manipulated those on a committee at church.

Or jumping off the cliff of safety for you may represent letting go of bitterness and anger and unforgiveness. Perhaps you have been badly hurt. You may have been nursing that hurt for a long time. It has become the cliff of safety for you. You feel you have a right to keep the hurt. You want to punish those who have hurt you.

You see, when you commit yourself to living the principle of the cross, there will be a time and a place where you will have to make a decision. It will be a crucifixion moment for you much like standing on the edge of a cliff.

You will have a choice. The choice is to jump into the arms of God or to stay on the cliff of your own will. You are facing the decision of your life. What will you do? Will you let go of everything in your life that keeps you from total and complete dependence on Him? Are you ready to surrender to Him?

Read Matthew 10:37–39.

Who may it affect if we choose the way of the cross?

_____

What will happen if we hold onto our lives?

_____

How do we find "life"?

_____

Mom, you will never discover life as it was meant to be lived if you don't give in to the cross. You will never be free to bear the fruit of the Spirit in your children's lives if you resist its call. If you hold on to your self-life, you will lose your whole life.

But if you surrender to the cross, you will find your life. The process begins with the "death" of your will, but soon His life will come springing forth.

Did you experience a crucifixion moment today?

Are you struggling to let go of someone or something that you've been holding onto? Is it a child or a job or a parent or a house? Let it go. Take it to the cross. There you will find restoration and healing and wholeness and forgiveness.

Journal your decision.

_____

_____

_____

_____

_____

_____

_____

_____

_____

_____

_____

_____

Prayer

Lord, I have been crucified with Christ. It is no longer I who live, but You who lives inside me.
Help me to grasp the message of the cross, Lord. I am holding tightly to You as I let go of everything else.
Give me the grace I need for this day. I pray this in Your precious name. Amen.

MOTHERING TIP

Write age-appropriate love notes to your children. Leave them on their beds. Leave them on the bathroom mirror. Tuck them into their lunches. Leave them on the seat of the car where they most often ride. Tell them what you appreciate about them.

If your children are grown, write letters, e-mail, or faxes to them at home or work. Make it short, but include what you love about them and their spouse. Pour on the encouragement.

DAY 4

The Prayer of the Cross

BEGIN WITH PRAYER

Pray for your husband today. Ask God to anoint his day with blessings.
Ask God to put a hedge of protection around him and keep him safe.
Ask the Lord to remove all barriers in your husband's heart to hearing the Word of truth.

God applied the Principle of the Shears, the Crucifixion Principle, to the life of His beloved Son for the same reason He applies it to your life. For Jesus to exhibit the full love of the Father's heart for the world, He had to offer His life to the Father. He had to submit to crucifixion so that resurrection life could occur for Himself and all who would believe in Him.

So today, we will look at the precious Son of God and His trip to the cross. When was Jesus "standing on the cliff" making a decision to fully surrender to the heavenly shears?

PLACE OF DECISION

Read Matthew 26:36–39.

Where did Jesus face the decision of going or not going to the cross?

_____

Was this an easy decision for Jesus? Copy the verses that prove your answer.

_____

_____

_____

_____

Where do you see documentation that Jesus made the decision to die to His own will and to submit to the will of the Father? Write out the phrase.

_____

If you decide to follow Jesus to the cross, it will not be easy. It will probably be the most challenging thing you've ever done. It will require that you endure pain. It will have a great price tag. It will cost you your life.

Read Luke 9:23–25.

What were Jesus' three requirements for those who want to come after Him?

1._____

2._____

3._____

What is the paradox of verse 24?

_____

_____

What is the exchange Jesus illustrated in verse 25?

_____

Now reread Matthew 10:37–39.

What is it that Jesus is calling you to bring to the cross?

_____

_____

Copy verse 39 here:

_____

_____

_____

Read Galatians 6:14.

What gives Paul cause to boast?

_____

Why? What has happened to his relationship with the world?

_____

JOURNEY TO THE CROSS

Going to the cross with your fleshy self-nature is not a one-time occurrence. It is the lifestyle of the believer who wants to fully know God.

My cross journeys have for the most part been in the area of mothering. The first time I was consciously aware of the cross in my life was when the Lord crossed my life with infertility. When I went down on my face before Him, gave up my "right" to have children and committed myself to His Lordship, it was a crucifixion moment in my life. The cross crossed my path again when it was time to let go of my firstborn, Danielle. I had to give up my "right" to my child and commit her into His hands. It was another crucifixion moment for me. There have been many others.

Each of my personal trips to the cross has been painful. I have wanted to writhe my way out of it with a little more prayer, or penance, or giving, or confession. I have even tried to "fix" myself so God wouldn't have to do it.

But there is no cure for the flesh. There is nothing to do but go to the cross. Nothing but complete surrender to Jesus will bring complete healing in you.

It reminds me of going to surgery. When the doctor announces that surgery is necessary, it doesn't seem so bad, but the closer it gets to the day of the operation, it starts getting more and more scary. The day of surgery, you may want to cling to the walls as they roll you down the hall toward the operating room. But once you submit to the process, you know that this is where healing begins. You have to allow the doctor to cut away the bad so the body can heal.

We can follow Jesus to the cross, or walk in the deadness of the flesh. If we choose to keep company with the flesh for a while, it will make us "heart-sick." It will always begin to rot and stink. Rotten flesh stinks. My "flesh" stinks. It is never worth hanging onto.

I am learning to submit to the way of the cross more readily. Day by day, I am learning that when something crosses me, and I begin to fret that I am not getting my way, that something is the cross of Christ. And I have a decision to make. I can take the leap off the cliff into the arms of God or I can hold onto my feeble, self-produced security.

Has the light begun to dawn on your understanding of the cross? Do you see it as a principle that applies to every facet of your mothering and your life?

Do you have a child who is giving you trouble and embarrassing you? What flesh patterns is Jesus exposing in you? Prideful flesh? Controlling flesh? Fearful flesh?

Do you have a child who refuses to obey when you call? What flesh patterns is Jesus revealing in you? Passive, fearful flesh? People-pleasing flesh? Lazy flesh?

Do you have a child who is begging for attention by being sick or whining or irritating others or failing in school? What flesh patterns is Jesus revealing in you? Self-centered, self-absorbed flesh? Or the opposite, which is over-protective flesh?

Your child's sinful, fleshy behavior is not your fault. He has his own will, but you are responsible before God for your response to your child's behavior. When your child embarrasses you by acting out in front of your friends, do you act out of your pride and try to cover it up with an excuse? "He's just tired," or "She's been sick." Do you yell and scream at your child to try to control him? Or use guilt and fear to control him just to make yourself look better? Do you collapse in fear at what he might do if you really discipline him?

Or are you ready to take those issues to the cross for crucifixion, so that Jesus' life can be borne out through you to deal with your child in the Spirit? Remember, you can discipline a child with a rod "in the flesh" or discipline him with a rod "in the Spirit." You can set boundaries for a teenager "in the flesh" or set boundaries for him "in the Spirit." Do you see the difference?

I am praying for you. I know by experience how challenging mothering can be. You and I are on a very important lesson plan written just for us by our heavenly Father. He knew exactly which mother to place with which child to expose and reveal flesh and in whom He desires to pour out His life. Come to Jesus. Jump off the cliff and jump into the arms of Jesus where true freedom and real life begins.

Selfer's Prayer

Father, I confess that I have been holding on to my self-strength and I have been
trying to live the Christian life by self-effort. I have been trying to get my love bucket
filled by seeking intimate relationships, by increasing my possessions, and trying to impress people.
I now give up on my self-strength and self-effort and commit my life completely into Your hands.
I give up all my rights and expectations and give You complete control
over my life to do with it whatever pleases You.
I trust Your Word that I have been crucified with Christ,
and it is no longer I who live, but Christ who lives in me.
I choose as an act of my will to affirm that Christ is my life.
I yield myself totally to the indwelling work of the Cross in my life.
Bring glory to Yourself through me, Lord. In Jesus' holy name I pray this. Amen.

MOTHERING TIP

List five things about your husband for which you are grateful. Write them on a card and mail it to him at work.

If you are a single mom, list five things about your ex-husband for which you are grateful. Tell your children the things you appreciated about their dad.

DAY 5

The Practice of the Cross

BEGIN WITH PRAYER

Express to the Lord praise and worship for His holiness.
Pray something like, Lord, You are holy.
You are the holy Lord over all the earth. Glorious is Your matchless name.
You are Lord of lords and King of kings and I worship You.
I love you, Lord, with all my heart.

Jesus lived a life of total and complete surrender to the Father. He lived the principle of the cross every day of His life on earth before He went to the place of the cross.

Read John 8:28–29.

What did Jesus do on His own initiative?

_____

To what did He fully surrender?

_____

The principle of the cross is so practical. When you begin to understand it, you will see that it guides every aspect of your life. You will recognize the work of the cross in every relationship of a woman's life.

First Priority: Relationship with God

In your relationship with God, there is an overriding principle. It is found in Exodus 20:3, *"You shall have no other gods before Me."*

In this one commandment, God establishes His place in our lives. He is priority number one. No other thing in our lives should compete with His place. No relationship, no possession, and no agenda in our lives should become a god to us. He alone is worthy of taking the position of God.

Can you see where the cross crosses you at this point? It is so easy to let the "thorns and thistles" of this world creep into the place of god. We can have a relationship with a spouse or child that turns from pure love to codependence. We can get wrapped up in an organization that is very "good" but consumes all our energy and time. We can be so in love with a house or car or place that our lives begin to revolve around the keeping of it.

And then the cross is presented to us. Will we die to that which we hold so dear to become alive to where the Spirit is leading? Will we loosen our grip on that which has become god to take hold of the one true living God of the universe?

Is there any relationship or activity or possession God has brought to mind? What is it that has become a god to you? Journal your thoughts.

_____

_____

_____

_____

Second Priority: Relationship with Husband

The second priority of a mother's life is her relationship to her husband. If you are a single mom, please keep reading. These principles are important information for dealing with the past as well as leading to the future.

Read Ephesians 5:22, Colossians 3:18, 1 Peter 3:1.

What is the commandment stated in these verses?

_____

Describe how the cross is presented to a wife in these verses.

_____

_____

_____

We are commanded in Scripture to submit to our husbands. It is not vague or ambiguous. It is very clear. But do you feel the hair rising up on the back of your neck? Submit to him? What?

The cross looms before us. Will I go to the cross with my rebellious attitudes and defiant tongue? Will I choose to put off pride and stubbornness? Will I put on humility and meekness? Do you see the cross before you as it crosses the path of your marriage?

Take a few moments to pray right now. Close your eyes and enter into His sanctuary. Ask Him to speak to you about your marriage in a way you can hear Him and understand Him. Listen to His voice and obey.

Record your thoughts.

_____

_____

_____

_____

THIRD PRIORITY: RELATIONSHIP WITH CHILDREN

The third priority of a mother's life is her relationship to her children. There are three gifts that I believe every mother should give her children. These gifts are to be given in order. The first gift a mother needs to give her children is the gift of unconditional love.

The First Gift

Read 1 Corinthians 13:1–8. Insert the words "unconditional love for _____" and insert your child's name into each place where you see the word "love."

List the attributes of unconditional love given in 1 Corinthians 13:4–8.

1. _____   9. _____

2. _____   10. _____

3. _____   11. _____

4. _____   12. _____

5. _____   13. _____

6. _____   14. _____

7. _____   15. _____

8. _____   16. _____

Did the Cross cross your path? Did you see where God's unconditional love for your child and your love for your child are out of alignment? Write down the thoughts that come to mind.

_____

_____

The Second Gift

The second gift a mother can give her child is the gift of firm and fair discipline.

Copy Proverbs 19:18 here:

_____

_____

What is the strong inference of this verse?

_____

If we don't discipline our children, we could be a willing party to their death! That is strong language!

Conduct a "Proverbs read through." To do that, read through the list of Scripture references in Proverbs in the order given, without stopping. It would be very helpful if you would read them aloud.

Proverbs

10:13	13:18	15:5	19:18	23:13	29:17
10:17	13:24	15:10	20:30	23:14	30:17
12:1	14:1	15:31–32	22:6	26:3	
13:1	15:2	16:18	22:15	29:15	

Go back over each verse carefully and write down any questions that these verses raise in your mind.

_____

_____

_____

Now stop and use those questions to form a prayer. Ask the Lord to be your teacher and instruct you in the discipline of your children. Discuss your questions with your husband. Your Mentoring Mom can help you further.

Did any of the Proverb verses bring conviction to your heart? Did the cross cross your path in the area of discipline? Journal your impressions.

_____

_____

_____

The Third Gift

The third gift a mother should give her child is the "Bread of Life"—the Word of God. I have heard some parents say that they are not going to decide for their children what "religion" they will embrace so they don't take them to church or teach them anything that might influence that decision. Satan must lick his chops when he hears parents say that. He is not so neutral in his approach to influencing the innocents.

We cannot make the decision to accept or reject Christ for our children, nor should we. But we can create an atmosphere where they can choose for themselves whether or not to follow Christ. Why would we not share the greatest news on earth with our own children?

To share Christ with our kids, we must first live our own life transparently and honestly, seeking God with total abandon. Have you ever been around someone who lives like that? The power of the life of Jesus operates through them in such fullness that it is contagious. You just want what they have. Our children are looking into our faces to see if they can see the face of Jesus. What will they see in your face?

Secondly, we expose our children to the Word of God. It is important to take them to Bible classes at church on a regular basis, but nothing replaces what they learn at home. At home, the Bible is in the laboratory. When your child is afraid in the middle of the night, he can most readily learn, "When I am afraid, I will put my trust in You" (Psalm 56:3).

When your teenager is overwhelmed with research paper deadlines and play-off games and "love" interests and college applications, "Cast your burden upon the Lord and He will sustain you" (Psalm 55:22) will mean more to him.

Finally, pray with and pray for your children. From the time they are toddlers in high chairs, begin teaching your children to pray. Say a simple prayer and let them pray it phrase by phrase after you. Pray over them at bedtime. Let your words in prayer be the last thing they hear before they go to sleep.

When your children are older, you will be blessed at the joy of having a family prayer time. Each week set aside a time where you pray with your children over the issues they are facing.

Read Deuteronomy 6:1–8.

What is the generational blessing of verses 1–3?

_____

_____

How are parents to transfer the baton of faith according to verses 7 and 8?

_____

_____

Did the cross come into view when you thought of how your children are being trained in matters of faith? Is Jesus speaking to your heart concerning your diligence in this vital responsibility?

_____

_____

_____

FOURTH PRIORITY: YOUR WORK INSIDE AND OUTSIDE THE HOME

The fourth priority of a mother's life is her work, which either builds or tears down her home. This includes housework, volunteer work, full- or part-time employment, recreation, and hobbies.

Put each of your activities to a biblical test and see if they pass.

For test number one, read Proverbs 14:1.

Does your work build your home or tear it down? Examine each activity in your life by this test. What did you discover?

_____

_____

For test number two, read Colossians 3:17.

Can you do your work—your activities—in the name of Jesus? Would Jesus be doing what you are doing?

_____

_____

For test number three, read Colossians 3:18.

Does your husband want you to do this work? Does he want you to stop?

_____

_____

For test number four, read Colossians 3:22.

Do you work with a servant heart under the authority of the person in charge?

_____

_____

Reflect on the cross. Does anything about your work or play habits need to go to the cross? Do any of your activities fail the tests?

Record your thoughts.

_____

_____

_____

FIFTH PRIORITY: YOUR MINISTRY

The fifth priority of a mother's life is her relationship with the world through her ministry.

Read Jeremiah 18:1–6.

Which form of art does God use in these verses to describe his relationship with us?

_____

What does the clay have to do in the potter's hand?

_____

The key word to the fifth priority is to *yield*. The clay must yield to the potter's hand as he shapes and molds the clay to be used as a vessel. The beginning of ministry is yieldedness to God. It is answering yes to Him before you know the question.

PUTTING OFF THE OLD—PUTTING ON THE NEW

Read Colossians 3:5–10.

Compare these verses with the act of putting on and taking off clothing.

_____

_____

UNIT 5

Why don't you spend a few moments in prayer right now. As if you are taking off layers of clothing, consciously take off and "lay aside" the five filthy, fleshy garments listed in Colossians 3:8 that do not belong on a daughter of God. Specifically pray this prayer in regard to your relationship with your children.

Your prayer may go something like this: *Lord, I am taking off the garment of anger right now. As an act of my will, I die to any anger that is in my heart toward my child or anyone else. I choose to forgive them of wrong-doing. I choose today with my "chooser" to "put on" Your unconditional love whether or not my "feeler" feels like being loving.* Go through each fleshy attitude listed in verse 8 and pray a similar prayer making it personal to your situation.

Read 1 John 3:14–16

What is the ultimate ministry for others?

_____

Besides physically laying down your life for others, what are other ways to demonstrate this principle?

_____

_____

Where does the cross fit in this picture? Do you see it? Where are you being asked to lay down your "life" in ministry?

_____

_____

_____

Only when the cross becomes the power base of your relationship with your children will you experience mothering as it is intended in the heart of God. A mother who willingly goes to the cross with her flesh is one whose children can experience the life of Jesus in tangible form. They see His eyes looking out through her eyes. They hear His voice in the firm but gentle tones of her voice. They feel the touch of His hands and the caress of His arms through her touch. "She speaks with wisdom and in her tongue is the law of kindness." It is all accomplished when a mother goes to the cross.

Prayer

Lord, I see the cross more clearly now. It has crossed my life many times.

Jesus, make me aware when Your cross crosses my will.

I surrender my will to Your will to be Yours alone. I love You, Jesus.

I pray this prayer in Your name. Amen.

Mothering Tip

Finish these statements:

"The most wonderful thing my husband ever did for me was…"

"What I've learned from my husband over the years is…"

"My dreams for our future include…"

Share these over a romantic dinner with your husband. Set the table with your best dishes and linens, put on romantic music, light the candles, and voila!

UNIT 6

THE PRINCIPLE OF THE SHEARS: CUTTING AWAY

MOTHERING SKILL: COMMUNICATING WITH YOUR CHILD

DAY 1
THE PICTURE OF THE CROSS

DAY 2
THE PERSONAL CALL OF THE CROSS

DAY 3
THE PROOF OF THE CROSS

DAY 4
THE POWER OF THE CROSS

DAY 5
THE PRODUCE OF THE CROSS

Letting go and letting God control our circumstances is often hard for moms. I'll begin this unit with a personal story that may help.

UNIT 6
Bible Study Listening Guide

1. The main object used to help me remember the lesson was:_____

2. The parts of the "Picnic Table" illustration and their meanings are:

   A. _____

   B. _____

   C. _____

   D. _____

   E. _____

   F. _____

   G. _____

   H. _____

   I. _____

3. What I personally need to remember from this lesson is:

   _____

   _____

   _____

   _____

   _____

   _____

   _____

   _____

   _____

   _____

   _____

   _____

UNIT 6

MotherWise Group Prayer Requests

1. _____

2. _____

3. _____

4. _____

5. _____

6. _____

UNIT 6

MOTHERING SKILLS DISCUSSION:

Communicating with Your Child

Challenge: To keep the lines of communication open through connecting with your child in timely, sensitive interaction.

At every age and stage of mothering, we communicate with our children. From the day we give birth to the day we take our last breath, we want to have great communication with our kids. But how can we talk in a way they will listen? How can we listen and really hear their hearts? When are we sure that the important messages we are sending are getting through?

How would you describe the quality of communication in your family? Hot? Cold? Lukewarm?

_____

When is the best time to communicate with your child?

_____

Where is the best place to communicate with your child?

_____

When do you have difficulty with communication?

_____

Do you have more trouble talking or listening?

_____

Does your child have more trouble talking or listening?

_____

If you could dream up a perfect world, what would present and future communication with your child look like?

_____

Tools to Meet the Challenge:

How to Really Love Your Teenager, Ross Campbell, M.D. (Wheaton, Ill.: Victor Books, 1993).

What Every Child Needs, Elisa Morgan (founder of MOPS) and Carol Kuykendall (Grand Rapids, Mich.: Zondervan Publishing, 1997).

Grandparenting: It's Not What It Used to Be, Irene Endicott (Nashville, Tenn.: Broadman and Holman Publishers, 1997).

Mom's Guide to Raising a Good Student, Vicki Poretta and Marian Edeman Borden (Aurora, Colo.: Alpha Books, 1997).

21 Days to Helping Your Child Learn, Cheri Fuller (Grand Rapids, Mich.: Zondervan, 1998).

The Way They Learn, Cynthia Ulrich Tobias (Colorado Springs, Colo.: Focus on the Family Publishing, 1994).

The development of language through the listening and talking that goes on in family conversation is one of the most important building blocks of learning. In fact, the better that kids are at using spoken language, the more successful they are in learning to read and write and the better they will function in school and at work. With that kind of motivation for communication, we want to make our family conversations meaningful. But how?

- Dinner Table Talk—Use the time at the evening meal to look each child in the eye and ask about their day. Ask specific questions about classes they are taking or activities in which they are involved. Turn off distractions like the television and loud music and focus the conversation with each family member. Avoid unpleasant subjects like nagging about unfinished tasks, dealing out punishment for misbehaviors, and hashing out problems.

    Encourage your children to swap stories, talk about what they are reading, or share the best part of their day. Brainstorm answers to questions like, "What do you think the world will be like in twenty years?" Talk about current events in the news. Include even the youngest members of the family in conversations by allowing them to share an event from their day and teaching them to listen quietly to others without interrupting.

- Bed Time—Sit down on the bed beside your child and chat before bedtime. This is especially effective with kids between the "little child stage" and the teen years. Most middle school girls and some guys respond to this invitation.

- While your teenage daughter is taking off her make-up at night, go stand in the bathroom. Even if it's very late, take the time. You will have to sacrifice your sleep to have good communication with most teens. The most meaningful conversations I've had with my teens and young adults are after midnight.

- With young children, even babies, speak with gentleness and love, but don't always use baby talk. Baby talk is fine when expressing love and affection. But when you are teaching them the names of objects and giving simple directions, use the correct names of objects and events.

- Be specific when giving directions to your children. Instead of "clean your room" say, "Please pick up the toys and clothes off the floor and put them in the drawers where they belong."

- Play board games or work puzzles as a family to stimulate times of conversation.

- In the car, play games like "I Spy" with license plates and road signs to get the family talking.

- With teenage daughters, make an appointment to fix tea in the afternoon and find a quiet place to sip and talk. You might take your teen son to a good steak house or fishing hole for casual conversation.

These ideas are just starters. Brainstorm with your group about ways to get your family talking! Take notes here on what you learn.

_____

_____

_____

_____

_____

_____

_____

_____

_____

_____

_____

_____

_____

Day 1
The Picture of the Cross

BEGIN WITH PRAYER

Pray today for your children.
Ask God to give each of them a hunger and a thirst
for His Word and to fill them with His presence.
Ask Him to protect them and keep them safe today.

Last week we ended our study applying the cross to our priorities. Today, I will share one of my "crucifixion moments" with you. Sometimes God speaks to us through the testimony of others.

NEW YEAR'S PRAYERS

Every New Year's Day, David spends all morning in our small study. He reads his Bible and prays until God gives him the prayer he is to pray for our family for the coming year. Then he prays that prayer every day all year. We don't disturb Dad when he is in the study on New Year's Day. Serious business is going on in there!

On January 1, 1993, David came out of the study and told me he was going to pray that God would deliver him and our entire family from fear, the love of money, and a critical spirit. I said, "David, are you sure you want to pray all three of those in one year?"

True to His Word, God began answering David's prayers. On February 8, David lost his job. The heavenly Vinedresser took the pruning shears and began to snip. That one event made us face fear. Losing financial security was the thing David had feared most; it made us deal with the love of money—now there wasn't any money to love. It also exposed a critical spirit—"How are you going to respond to the people who did this to you?"

Then, four weeks later while we were still reeling from David's job loss, the heavenly Vinedresser picked up the shears and began working on me. Before I describe the events of that time, let me give you a little background.

When our oldest daughter, Danielle, was growing up she was the sweetest, gentlest, easiest child to live with that you can imagine. (That is, after she outgrew colic, asthma, and allergies.) So when she began to push against us at age seventeen, we were in shock.

Danielle had started singing with an acoustic Christian band, which seemed very nice at first. They were singing in Sunday school classes and at local youth functions, and we were very proud of her. But then in her last year of high school, the band began to travel further and further from home to sing. She began making life-changing decisions based on what the band wanted to do instead of what we wanted her to do. And we didn't like it.

Friction began to show up in our relationship with Danielle. She was almost a 4.0 student and had been considering some very prestigious universities. Now she was talking about singing with the band and not attending college at all. As David tells our friends, "Every dad is afraid his daughter will run off with a rock band!" We were anxious to say the least.

Because I was upset with the decisions she was contemplating, I began picking on her for cleaning her room and helping more around the house. I fussed over her choice of clothing and the way she wore (and didn't wear) her make-up. The more I nagged, the more belligerent she became.

It seemed that we couldn't be in the same room for five minutes without an argument erupting between us. We limped through the rest of her senior year in high school and in the fall, we moved her into a university dorm in town. The day she left, I felt like someone had sawed off my right arm. It would have been hard enough if she had left peacefully, but as it was, the wound had not healed. I cried and prayed myself to sleep almost every night.

THE PICNIC TABLE

On a September night that fall, I woke at 3:00 A.M. and saw something very strange on my bedspread. I do not usually see visions, but what I saw that night was unmistakably from God.

I saw a picnic table setting lying out before me. The tablecloth was blue-and-white checked and the plate, cup, and place setting was white plastic dinnerware. There was a red bandana for a napkin, a salt and pepper shaker, and a little glass vase in the shape of a cowboy boot with silk bluebonnets in it.

I recognized the setting as items in my kitchen cabinets stored away for picnics. I knew God was trying to communicate with me, but I couldn't see any spiritual symbolism in the display.

I shook David and said, "David, I think God's trying to talk to me!" He didn't even open his eyes. He just said, "Well, go in the kitchen and write it down and tell me about it in the morning." So I grabbed my robe and headed for the kitchen.

I pulled out all the items I'd "seen" and set the table with them. Then I sat down and said, "Lord, I don't know what you're trying to say. This doesn't look very spiritual."

Within moments I sensed God saying, "Unset the table."

UNSETTING THE TABLE

I took up the dialogue. "Lord, I don't know how to unset a table. I know how to set a table, but I don't know how to unset a table."

"Yes, you do, Denise. Pick up the spoon. You've been spoon-feeding Danielle. You've been telling her how much mascara to wear and how to wear her hair and clothes. Stop spoon-feeding her and give her the spoon."

That struck home. I knew I was guilty. This was God speaking and I knew it was true. I slowly picked up the spoon and laid it across the table at Danielle's place.

Next I "heard" (not with my ears, but I distinctly understood these words inside my mind), "Pick up the knife. You've been knifing Danielle in the back. Stop knifing that child and give her the knife."

I had to stop and admit that I had been angry and frustrated with Danielle and had taken it out on her with criticism. I didn't want to be nice to her. She wasn't being nice to me. But I asked the Lord to forgive me for antagonizing her and with conviction placed the knife at her place.

Then I heard, "Now pick up the fork. Danielle is at a fork in the road. It's not your fork, it's hers. Give her the fork." At this I began to argue.

"But Lord, what if she makes the wrong choice?"

I felt like her life was hanging in the balance. It scared me to death to think about turning the controls of her life over to her while she was in that state. What a mess she would make!

"Give her the fork." The words were unmistakable. I put my head down on my arms and sobbed.

"Lord, look at the decisions she's making. What if she throws away her life?"

He said, "If she chooses the right or the left, the light or the darkness, that is not your affair. She is my child and I will deal with her. Give her the fork." It took me a long time to get up the courage, but with trembling hands, I picked up the fork and placed it at Danielle's place.

Next I sensed that I was to put the bandana napkin under my chin tucked into my collar, like you would put one on a child. "You have had the napkin of overprotection on Danielle all her life. You have protected those little white collars from every gravy stain, every mustard blop, and every ketchup drip. Now it's time to take off the napkin of overprotection. Let the gravy fall. Let the ketchup drip. I'm a master at spot removal."

I was convicted with the truth I was hearing. I took off the napkin and folded it next to the fork.

Then I understood that I was to get a square sticky note and place it on the plate. I was to write on it these three words: major, mate, and mission. Those were the three big decisions facing her and all three were life-changing, pivotal choices.

I could not imagine that God would have called Danielle—my quiet, sweet, beautiful, smart, straight-laced child—to go off on a bus with a bunch of boys traipsing around the country and not getting a traditional college education. I didn't care that it was in the name of ministry. She told us this was her mission, and I said, "Danielle, God wouldn't have said that!

Then, there was the issue of her mate. She and the leader of the band had begun dating when she was sixteen and he was nineteen, the year they started the band. After they had had three dates, she told us she was going to marry him. We went nuts. We loved the boy, but had told her, "You are too young and could not possibly know if he is *the one*." You can imagine the chaos that created.

The decision over her college choice and her major sent me into orbit. When she did decide to go to college, she chose to stay in town so she would be available for the band. She had given up the opportunity to go to a well-respected Ivy League institution.

The icing on the cake was when she decided to be a French Literature major. "Oh great, you can get a lot of jobs with that degree!" David and I were beside ourselves.

"Give her the whole plate—the whole enchilada. [When God speaks to me it is always in Texan language that I can understand.] Her major, her mate, and her mission are between Danielle and Me. This is not your life, it is hers. Give her the plate."

I held onto that plate for a long time knowing that if I "gave" it to Danielle I could never take it back. God was challenging me to give up my right to tell Danielle what to do with her life, and I didn't want to let go. Finally, with tears, I submitted and carefully, reverently laid down the plate.

"Pick up the salt and pepper."

"Oh, I know what this means, God. It has something to do with the salt of the earth from Matthew 5."

"No, Denise. It has nothing to do with that. Imagine that you went to lunch with your friend, Jan, and when you got your food, she picked up your plate. What if she salted and peppered your food to her taste and then gave the plate of food to you to eat? What would you say?"

"I'd say, 'Rude, Jan! You don't salt and pepper *my* food to *your* taste!'"

He said, "That's how Danielle feels about the way you are trying to tell her what to do with her life. You wouldn't get on a bus with a bunch of guys and sing in a band, but she would. You wouldn't wear overalls and go without make-up, but she would. Let her season life to her own taste. It's not your taste, it's hers that counts. Give her the salt and pepper."

We came to the cup. "You have been pouring out the cup of wrath on Danielle. Now give her the cup of kindness."

"Okay, Lord, but how?"

"Go get her loafers out of the closet." I knew exactly which ones. Danielle had been asking me to resole the loafers, and I had refused. The loafers were very inexpensive and a new sole would have cost almost as much as a new pair. Anyway, I just hadn't wanted to be nice to her and get the shoes repaired. In those days, I stayed half-angry at Danielle most of the time.

But, the next day, I did have the loafers repaired and felt impressed to place them where Danielle came once a week to get her mail. I didn't say anything about them, but when she saw the loafers with the new soles, I got the first warm hug I'd received in months. She got the message, "Mom still loves me." It broke the ice between us and began the healing process.

"Pick up the flowers." I took the little boot-shaped glass vase full of silk bluebonnets, the Texas state flower, in my hands. "Flowers are a sign of intimacy. If some man gave you three red roses with a card that said, 'I love you,' David would be, to say the least, very upset with him. Go read Ecclesiastes 3:5."

I had no idea what it said in that verse, only that the third chapter of Ecclesiastes was about "a time for this and a time for that."

I read these words in the second part of the verse, "A time to embrace and a time to shun embracing."

"Lord, you mean there is a time when I can't embrace my child?"

I had been so hurt that Danielle was creating space between us. She was so distant and unavailable. Until that big seventeen-year-old turn-around, we had been almost inseparable. We were best friends who shared everything. And I loved it. Now she was cold and evasive. It had broken my heart.

The Lord said, "Denise, give Danielle her space. This is the time to refrain from embracing. Give her the flowers and let her go." With tears running down my face, I placed the flowers on her side of the table.

THE FINAL PIECE

All that was left was the tablecloth. I said, "Okay, Lord, just wrap me up in it and throw me in the river." He must have been laughing.

"No, the tablecloth stays on. She is always welcome to come home. The light is always on and the table is always ready. She can come for a visit any time and then she can leave again."

And then it was over. I sat for a long time absorbing all that God had just communicated with me. It was a powerful word picture and it hit home. I wish I could tell you that I instantly processed the whole message and that Danielle and I were perfectly fine the next day, but that's not what happened.

It took me over a year of steps forward and a few steps back to make progress in letting Danielle go. It was a dramatic trip to the cross for me that had many crucifixion moments. A few days after the "picnic table" revelation, I was still tearful about letting her go. I was crying as I was driving to one of Stephanie's volleyball games when I distinctly felt the presence of the Lord with me in the car.

"Denise, aren't you the mother who told me before Danielle was born that it was okay if you never had a child, what you wanted was Me? Now you don't 'have' this child. So what is that to you? You told Me that was all right with you."

I numbly nodded in agreement. "I did give her to you, Lord. She is yours."

Each day and month that passed became easier and less painful for both of us. When I knew it was time, I got out all the picnic paraphernalia and went through the whole story with her. It was therapeutic for both of us.

THE HAPPY ENDING

Let me tell you "the rest of the story" as I see it today. Danielle is happily married to Cliff Young, the leader of her band. I could not choose a more perfect husband for Danielle, a man who loves the Lord and loves Danielle so completely. After all we put him through, he even loves David and me. Amazing grace! They are so in love and so happy and we love them both dearly. We have a wonderful time together as a family. Watching them grow and mature together is the delight of our lives.

As for her mission, many of you reading this will recognize the name of their very popular band, Caedmon's Call. What I thought was a little garage band has now ministered to thousands and thousands of college students and young single adults all over America and England. Had we demanded that Danielle go off to college and drop out of the band, she would have missed God's great call on her life.

Yes, she was young. Yes, she was inexperienced. And yes, she was hearing from God and I was not. God gave His plan for Danielle's life to her, not to me. And to make it possible for her to follow Him, He had to use the pruning shears on me and lead me to the cross.

Our family will never be the same again after the events of 1993, the year David prayed those bold prayers. Did we know what was coming? No! Would we do it again? Yes, yes, a thousand times, yes! By the way, David did get a wonderful job with a Christian businessman eight weeks after he lost his job. That eight weeks seemed like eight years, but it was one of the most fruitful times in our lives.

Mom, is there someone or something—a child, a husband, a parent, a friend, a job—of which you need to let go in order to take hold of the life of Jesus? Journal your response here:

_____

_____

_____

_____

_____

_____

_____

_____

_____

_____

_____

_____

Lord, I lay down my life. I let go of every person and everything that I am grasping and I take hold only of You.

I want the cross to have its full effect in my life. Here is my life.

Take it and use it as You will. Lord, keep working even if I whine and cry.

Don't stop using Your pruning shears until I am clean. I make this prayer in the name of Jesus Christ. Amen.

DAY 2

The Personal Call of the Cross

BEGIN WITH PRAYER

Sing the hymn "Holy, Holy, Holy" to the Lord.
Make it a personal praise to Him.

Once a little peach seed lived in a drawer in the master gardener's shed. He waited and waited to be chosen by the master. Finally one day, the master opened the drawer and chose him. Placing the little seed in his hand, the gardener started walking out into the sunshine.

The little seed was so proud. "He's chosen me!" and he looked smugly about the garden to make sure all the other plants saw him. The gardener knelt down on one knee and began to dig a small hole. The hole got deeper and deeper as the gardener continued to dig. When he was finished digging the gardener took the little seed and placed it in the bottom of the hole.

The seed looked up and said, "It's dark in here. And it is a little damp. But if this is where the gardener wants to put me, I trust him. He knows what he's doing." Then the gardener took a hand full of dirt and threw it in on top of the seed. The seed wiped his eyes and said, "You just threw dirt in my face!" About that time the gardener threw a little more dirt in. The seed called out, "Hey, this is me. The one you chose. Stop throwing that dirt down here!" But the gardener continued to pile more and more dirt into the hole. As the hole completely filled up, the gardener took his boot and tamped down the dirt to compress it onto the little seed.[1]

Have you ever felt like that little seed in the heavenly Gardener's hand?

Read John 12:24–26.

What illustration from farming did Jesus use to describe the cross?

_____

Describe the paradox in verse 25.

_____

Skim John 12:27 through John 13:1–3.

What is the context of these verses? What was happening in Jesus' life?

_____

In John 12:26 He says, "If anyone serves Me, he must follow Me...." Where was He going? Where are we to follow?

_____

Jesus was on His way to the cross. He called to His disciples to follow Him there.

Now He is calling your name. He is asking you to follow Him to the cross. It is there that flesh and sin must die.

Reread Matthew 16:24. Copy it here.

_____

_____

We must take a hard look at the cross of Jesus. What is Jesus asking of us? Where will this cross experience take us?

The cross is not an event that only existed in time and space, it is an eternal principle. The indwelling cross in me is an internal altar where I sacrifice my will to His will, my wants for His wants.

Lord, I want to follow You.
I give up all that has kept me from total surrender to Your will.
Hear my heart's cry, Lord. I pray this in Your name. Amen.

DAY 3

The Proof of the Cross

BEGIN WITH PRAYER

Pray for your church, your pastor, and the people who are the staff members of your church.

Ask the Lord to shield and protect your church from attacks from Satan.

Ask Him to empty your pastor of his flesh and fill him with the life of Jesus.

Ask God to bring about revival and repentance in your local church body.

THE FIRST MARTYR

When the cross is present in the life of a believer, his life takes on a decided difference. No one is able to be in his company without being affected by it. The life of one of the disciples of Jesus was such a life. He stands tall above the rest.

Read Acts 6:8 and describe this disciple.

_____

_____

See Acts 6:9–10.

Record the response of unbelievers to Stephen.

_____

_____

According to verses 11–14, what did their frustration with Stephen prompt them to do?

_____

_____

The presence of the cross was so apparent in Stephen's life it changed his appearance. Read Acts 6:15 and describe it.

_____

_____

The principle of the cross led Stephen to witness to the Jews knowing what he would endure because of his preaching. The place of the cross came for Stephen in a showdown with the Jewish council. The presence of the cross made Stephen's face shine on the outside because of the glory within.

But did the cross keep Stephen from experiencing difficulties? Hardly! Read Acts 7:54–60.

According to Acts 7:54, what was the first response of the Jewish Council to Stephen's sermon (recorded in verses 2–53)?

_____

_____

How did Stephen respond to their anger and rejection?

_____

_____

How did Stephen carry out the message of the cross as stated in John 15:13?

_____

_____

Stephen entered into the fellowship of Jesus' suffering by giving up his life. The cross cost him dearly. But do you know what happened as a result of Stephen's martyrdom? Christianity spread from Jerusalem into the entire world. The disciples of Jesus, running for their lives took the gospel message into every part of the earth. Kingdom fruit was born out of Stephen's ultimate sacrifice.

The fact that you are reading this Christian book written by a female, Gentile author two thousand years after the event is a result of the indwelling cross of Christ in the life of Stephen. One disciple took seriously the message of the cross and the world will never be the same. That is the power of the cross.

Will you allow the presence of the cross into your life? Will you commit to laying down your life "for your friends"? Will you follow the cross at any cost to yourself? Will you be the kernel of wheat that falls to the ground and dies that it may bear much fruit? Write out your prayer to the Father.

_____

_____

Prayer

Lord, give me the grace to follow the cross.

I open my heart and ask You now to plant the cross there.

Have mercy on me and give me the courage to follow You at any cost.

I ask all of this in the name that is above every name. And that name is Jesus. Amen.

UNIT 6

Mothering Tip

If you have young children, encourage them to dress up and create a "show" for you and your husband. Provide them with costumes and props and get them started on a story to act out. Take videos or still pictures and share them with the grandparents.

This was a favorite Friday night activity of our girls when they were young. We have some of the most adorable videos of our little actresses dressed in either old ballet costumes or my clothing and high heels and lots of jewelry. The girls still like to watch those old tapes. I can't wait to show them to my grandchildren someday!

Of course, I still have many of the old costumes and plan on having "shows" with my grandchildren in the future. My mom and dad used to shop garage sales and buy any little ballet/dance costumes they could find. My mom kept them in a special closet at her house and pulled them out when we went for the holidays.

All the little cousins put on shows for the whole extended family. (If you can believe this, she had six granddaughters born in five years and three more granddaughters to follow! Then we finally had a "little prince" to join the family much later. Of course we adore him!) The video and still pictures of those precious performances are among our larger families' sweetest memories of time spent together.

Day 4

The Power of the Cross

BEGIN WITH PRAYER

Come before the Lord on behalf of your children today.
Pray for your children that they will know the power of the cross.

Fruit trees produce fruit after their kind. Apple trees produce apples and orange trees produce oranges. Fruit is an outward sign of the life within the tree. Believers also produce fruit in keeping with the life within.

We have studied the principle of the cross, the place of the cross, the practice of the cross, and the presence of the cross. Today, we will see that the power of the cross is the evidence that the work of the cross is complete.

The power of the cross is the way God works through believers. When you or I take the cross to heart, God can work through us to reach another heart that is ready for the cross.

Read 2 Corinthians 4:7–18.

What is the power source described in verse 7?

_____

Compare Stephen's experience with verses 8–10.

_____

_____

Copy verse 10 here, then begin working on memorizing it.

_____

_____

In verses 11 and 12, Paul summarizes the exchanged life. What is the exchange?

_____

_____

According to verse 15, why is it worth going to the cross?

_____

Verses 17 and 18 tell us the reward for living life with the cross. What is that reward?

_____

Our power source is in Christ, it is not in ourselves. It enables someone like Stephen to "carry about in his body the dying of Jesus so that the life of Jesus might be manifested in his body."

The definition of the exchanged life is that I die to my self-life so that Christ's life can be lived out in me. I exchange the old nature for the new one.

One of the benefits of paying the cost of the cross is that through our dying to our self-life, others can share in the grace of Jesus Christ. The ultimate reward for exchanging my life for His life is that I can know Christ and the power of His resurrection. I can see Him in a way I cannot if I hold onto my self-strength and self-sufficiency.

Imagine that you and your children are the only people in the world. Now reread 2 Corinthians 4:7–18 and insert your name every time Paul uses the words *we* or *our* or *us*. Insert your children's names when he is speaking to the Corinthians using the words *you* or *yours*.

Do you and I really want to produce godly offspring? Do we want to see our children producing fruit in the kingdom? Then it will cost us something. It will require a trip to the cross.

Lord, I am willing to carry about in my body the dying of Jesus so that the life of Jesus may be manifested in my body.

Lord, use me as Your instrument in my children's lives to accomplish Your purpose.

Enable me to love and discipline and disciple them according to Your plan for each of them.

Let me see them through Your eyes. I pray this in Jesus' name. Amen.

ℳothering 𝒯ip

Gather the family at the table and get a pack of Post-It Notes. Let family members suggest alternatives to watching TV. Stick the notes on the television. When someone in the family is tempted to veg in front of the TV, have them close their eyes and pick a note.

Some suggestions are:

Read

Draw/color

Phone grandparents or other family members

Put on a puppet show

Make cookies

Take a walk or bike ride

Play jacks

Draw on the sidewalk with sidewalk chalk

Listen to music

Take a nap

DAY 5

The Produce of the Cross

BEGIN WITH PRAYER

Ask the Father to carry out the work of the cross in your life.
Ask Him to take the cross and cross your life with it.

I want to pick up Stephen's story from day 3 where we left after his death. We will see the power of the cross in his life as it was demonstrated in the life of another young man.

Read Acts 7:58–60; 8:1–3; 9:1–18.

Who enjoyed witnessing Stephen's stoning?

_____

_____

What changed his life?

_____

FROM SAUL TO PAUL

Stephen had been full of grace and power and was performing great wonders and signs among the people. He was at the height of his ministry. Before his death, he argued with men from Cilicia and Asia. Tarsus was the key city in Cilicia. Is it possible that Saul had argued with Stephen and had lost because he was unable to cope with the wisdom and Spirit with which Stephen was speaking? Saul, the lawyer, lost an argument? It is no wonder he stood by triumphantly as Stephen's murderers laid their garments at his feet.

But don't you imagine that the lovely face of Stephen would not leave the mind of Saul? The pure sacrifice of that life must have haunted Saul's dreams. And then when Jesus addressed Saul, He said, "Why are you persecuting Me?" Was Saul persecuting Jesus? Jesus had already ascended to the Father. Jesus was referring to His life being lived out in the life of Stephen and the other disciples. When Stephen laid down his life, it allowed the power of the cross to reach Saul. And then Saul took the gospel outside the walls of Judaism to the Gentiles.

Now read Saul's words (whose name was changed to Paul) in Colossians 1:24–29.

Copy verse 27 here:

_____

_____

Can you believe this is the same man who watched Stephen's stoning? These words sound like they could have been Stephen's. Do you see that Stephen's sacrifice was one of the things that resulted in the power of the cross moving in Paul's life?

To fully realize the power of the cross, you must adopt the principle of the cross as a way of life. Dying to self and living to Jesus must be as constant as breathing out and breathing in. The place of the cross will one day cross your path. To fully realize the power of the cross, you must align your will with the Father's in that critical time and place where there will be a crucifixion moment of decision.

You have an opportunity to practice the full power of the cross each day as you walk in brokenness with God, with those in your family, and with the world. The presence of the cross's power in your life will be revealed in the window of your eyes and the glow on your face. The awesome, dynamic power of the cross will reach beyond you into the hearts and lives of those who will see it in your life and be forever changed.

Read the following list. It will show you if you've made your trip to the cross.

Signs of Brokenness

All rights surrendered.

Willing to be out of control.

Not believing in or living by feelings or old patterns but by Christ within.

Willing to fail.

Willing to be weak.

A sense of total inadequacy in self-strength.

Recognizing God's power in my weakness.

Trusting God in whatever circumstance. Resting even with external turmoil.

Seeking Christ Himself more than His benefits.

Forgiving of all.

Willing to be rejected.

Transparent—willing to share weakness.

Vulnerable—willing to share failures.

Readiness to let others receive credit.

Genuine humility.

Placing value upon those who have little or no value to myself.

A readiness to affirm others.

Teachable.

Willing to be misunderstood.

Willing to be broken again....[2]

Prayer

Lord, I offer my heart as a living sacrifice. Place the cross upon my heart.

I die to self and flesh and sin and I live to You alone. Pour out Your life into mine.

Do all that is in Your heart and mind to do in my life. I make this prayer in the holy name of Jesus. Amen.

Mothering Tip

Mothers of girls, please do not allow your daughter to call boys. Even in the fourth and fifth grades, some girls will be tempted to call boys to get a boyfriend or to be popular. Among junior-high age girls, it is an epidemic. I know too many moms who not only allow it, they encourage the practice. Why? Because when daughters are popular—particularly with the opposite sex—their mothers also get their "love buckets" filled. Why not let our girls call guys? Because it starts off male-female relationships on the wrong foot. We want to teach our daughters to follow the scriptural admonition to submit to their husband's authority someday. When they start off as nine- and ten-year-old girls initiating and directing relationships with boys, why would we expect them to suddenly do an about-face fifteen years later as a wife?

Most girls mature faster than boys, and driven by their need to "belong," they often want to aggressively "get" a boyfriend. Their mothers, driven by their need for acceptance, encourage them!

Most boys in the preteen and early teen years are still "little boys." They may look at girls and talk about girls, but most aren't quite ready to start relationships with girls. This is as it should be, because they aren't ready to take on the responsibility that goes with relationship.

So Moms of girls, be tough and don't allow your daughter to call boys for the purpose of flirting and "chatting." (I would also extend this to chatting on the computer.) Moms of boys, don't allow your sons to receive calls from girls. Teach him to say, "My parents don't let me take calls from girls." Mom, if you answer the phone and it is a girl calling for your son, take the message and explain your rule. Monitoring this is relatively easy when you have only one phone line and it is not in your kid's bedroom!

UNIT

THE PRINCIPLE OF THE BUD: GRAFTED TO THE VINE

MOTHERING SKILL: NOURISHING THE FAMILY

DAY 1
A NEW LIFE

DAY 2
A NEW HEART

DAY 3
A NEW POWER

DAY 4
A NEW PLACE

DAY 5
A NEW MIND

———✇———

How a mother views herself—who she is and why she is on the earth—
makes all the difference in her mothering. Mothering from a poor self-image
makes for poor mothering. Mothering from an overly
positive self-image may be even worse.
We mothers need to know who we are. We need to know why we are here.

———✇———

Bible Study Listening Guide

1. The principle we are studying today is:

_____

2. The four-part illustration used to help me remember the lesson was:

   A. _____

   B. _____

   C. _____

   D. _____

3. The key Bible verse is:

_____

_____

_____

_____

4. What I personally need to remember from this lesson is:

_____

_____

_____

_____

_____

_____

_____

_____

MotherWise Group Prayer Requests

1._____

2._____

3._____

4._____

5._____

6._____

7._____

8._____

9._____

10._____

UNIT 7

MOTHERING SKILLS DISCUSSION:

Nourishing the Family

Challenge: To take responsibility to provide wholesome, nourishing food for the family.

One mother recently told me that she has a real problem with establishing a family dinnertime. Her husband works late and didn't grow up in a home where the family ate together. They have two preschoolers who eat and go to bed early, and the mom hates to cook and eat alone.

Another mom admitted that she's gotten out of the habit of even thinking about cooking dinner. When the family comes in tired and hungry at the end of the day, they look at each other and try to decide where they can stand to eat out again. These scenarios are common in our current American lifestyle. It has become increasingly hard for families to sit down together at home to share meals.

Do you think it is important for families to sit down at a table at the beginning or end of the day to eat and talk? Why or why not?

_____

_____

What is your family's greatest problem in eating together?

_____

_____

What is your biggest difficulty in providing nourishing food for your family?

_____

_____

Tools to Meet the Challenge:

Eating for Excellence Cookbook, Sheri Rose Shepherd (Sisters, Ore.: Multnomah Publishers, 1998).

Fit for Excellence, Sheri Rose Shepherd (Dallas, Tex: Creation House, 1998).

There is a famous "homemaker" on television who cooks everything from "scratch," whose house is decorator perfect, whose yard is wonderfully manicured, and who has plenty of time for handmade baskets full of homemade goodies for her friends. Every meal is a delight and every dish exquisite. She also has a full staff of secretaries, chefs, yardmen, designers, and housekeepers. I could do all that too with that kind of help.

So what can real moms with real families do to get good, wholesome food on the table at a reasonable hour and get the family to come eat it? Share your best mothering hints for getting the family together to eat at least one meal each day.

_____

_____

Share your best recipe for a dinner entrée that is nutritious (low fat, low sugar, low salt) and tasty.

_____

_____

_____

_____

_____

When do you grocery shop? How do you keep grocery bills low, food quality high, and keep food preparation simple? Share your best secrets.

_____

_____

_____

_____

Here are some hints we've gathered over the years:

- Grocery shop just before the weekend to have ingredients on hand for cooking larger quantities of main entrées. Serve leftovers on busy week nights.

- If you are a stay-at-home mom, start dinner right after breakfast. That way you won't get to the 5:00 P.M. crazies and end up eating out.

- Cook one of your husband's favorite dinners at least once a week. Call him at the office in the morning and tell him what you are cooking.

- Shop around the edges of the grocery store. The refrigerated units and the produce units are around the edges so they can be plugged into electricity and water sprayers. The freshest, most nutritious foods are around the edges of the store. Foods that are canned or boxed with lots of preservatives are sitting on shelves in the middle of the store. If it can be stored for four years in a can, how healthy can it be?

- Cook simple dinners. Cook a meat, a green vegetable (don't count corn, which is a grain), a bread or other whole grain (like wheat pasta or brown rice). Serve fruit for dessert. Voila! You have a simple, nutritious meal.

- Buy a new cookbook for healthful eating. Sheri Rose Shepherd's *Eating for Excellence* is wonderful!

- Buy a wok and experiment with stir-frying chicken and vegetables that your family likes (or at least will try). We like stir-frying chunks of skinless, boneless chicken breasts, thin slices of onion, fresh broccoli and carrots. We serve it with brown rice and sprinkle on a little soy sauce. Yum!

- Experiment with Mexican spices like cumin and chili pepper and tomatoes and green chilies. Try them in chicken and rice soups and ground meat and corn tortilla casseroles.

- Try out some Italian spices like oregano on sauteed chicken pieces, mushrooms, carrots, and zucchini served over whole grain pasta with bottled pasta sauce. Make a salad and warm some French bread to complete the meal.

DAY 1

A New Life

BEGIN WITH PRAYER

Worship the Lord as the giver of all life.
Praise Him for burying your old life and for giving you new, resurrected life in Him.
Tell Him you long to walk in newness of life.

We hear a lot about women's self-esteem. I've talked to many moms who say that when they quit work to stay home with their kids, they lost it. Others say their self-esteem plunged when they had to leave their kids to go to work. Still others say they've had low self-esteem all their lives. Then there are a few who think people with self-esteem problems should just get a grip.

How a mother views herself—who she is and why she is on the earth—makes all the difference in her mothering. Mothering from a poor self-image makes for poor mothering. Mothering from an overly positive self-image may be even worse.

We mothers need to know who we are. We need to know why we are here. It is the only solution in having an accurate perception from which to mother our children.

I have incredibly good news for you. I can't wait to share this week's lesson with you because there are some liberating truths in God's Word that can change the esteem you have for yourself forever. In fact, the Bible has some pretty radical things to say about who you are and why you are here.

To get started, I want to review the crucifixion principle with you, and give you an overview of the resurrection principle. Mom, you are getting ready to find out something amazing about yourself. Ready?

THE TRUTH ABOUT YOU AND ME

Let me put it as simply as I can. You were born with a desperately sinful nature (Romans 1:18). It was not responsive to God at all. When you came to Christ, that old sinful nature died (Romans 6:6). It no longer exists. In its place is your newly created nature that responds to God and His love (2 Corinthians 5:17). Your new inner being, sometimes called *"spirit man,"* is a container inside you for God's life. So now you—the real you deep inside—is a new creation who is deeply loved by God.

If you have not yet been born again and asked God for this rebirth, you have a reason to feel bad about yourself. I hate to tell you this, but you are bad. You need a complete overhaul before you can become the loving, giving, healthy mom you want to be. Come to Christ for His salvation today!

If you are a believer, you may get confused about that "you" inside that is supposed to be good. Let's face it, sometimes we don't look like a saint. That's because we live on earth in a fleshy body that can still sin. It can go on a real "flesh trip" (Romans 7). That's the part that makes us feel bad about ourselves as a mom. We mean to do good to our children but sometimes we really mess up. It's enough to make you really depressed.

Although your spirit—that person deep inside—is completely righteous and good (2 Corinthians 5:21), your mind, your emotions, and your will are still under construction (Romans 12:2). They are in a process of being changed gradually.

When your new inner self was created, it was left to live in a body with a mind, will, and emotions that needed reprogramming. That process of reprogramming happens when we choose as an act of our will to "die" to our fleshy attitudes and actions and to allow Jesus to live in us and through us. It doesn't happen one time. Each wrong attitude and each wrong habit and behavior have to go to the cross. Layer by layer we are transformed by the renewing of our minds.

As we progress and have more areas in our lives where Jesus' life is expressed through us, we walk in freedom and love and joy. We exhibit the fruit of the Spirit (Galatians 5:22–23) more completely. Do you see how that affects your mothering? Moms who have Jesus' life flowing through them without hindrance are free to love their children unconditionally; discipline fearlessly, firmly, and fairly; and their lives beam with the radiance of Christ. When the children see Mom, they see Jesus shining through her. It is a powerful witness.

That's how mothering is supposed to work!

UNIT 7

So now let's take time to explore the resurrection principle. I will take you to God's Word. I will give you illustrations and examples. I will share my own testimony with you. But these truths will have to be revealed to you by God alone. I cannot teach them to you. I will lead you to the truth, and then you will need to take Jesus' hand and let Him walk you through it.

We will start by looking at the historical resurrection of Jesus. This time as you study, focus not only on the events, which are probably very familiar to you, but look also at the power you see evidenced. Ask yourself, what changes occurred in Jesus after His resurrection? What changes occurred in His disciples? Does the resurrection of Jesus really make a difference? Could that kind of power make a difference in my mothering?

That old hymn, A Risen Savior, captures the message of the resurrection. He lives! I know this may sound elementary to some of you, but did you know that Jesus really is alive? Do you know what impact that has on your mothering? "He walks with you and He talks with you." If you are a believer, a living Jesus is on the inside of you every minute of every day with His full and powerful life always available.

Do you need wisdom for that big child-rearing issue? He is a living source of all wisdom. Do you need to get rid of the crushing burdens you are carrying about a difficulty with your child? He has offered for you to "cast all your cares on Him, because He cares for you." Are you worn out and exhausted and frazzled? He is a constant source of power and strength. He is not an idea, a belief, a story, a pattern of thinking, or a picture. He is a person. And He is alive.

Read Matthew 28:1–10.

In verses 5 and 6, what explanation did the angel give to the women who came to Jesus' tomb?

_____

What two emotions did the women express?

_____

What did Jesus do for Mary Magdalene and the other Mary?

_____

_____

Read Matthew 28:11–20.

After commissioning His disciples, what were Jesus' last words recorded by Matthew?

_____

_____

_____

We have gotten very blasé about Jesus' resurrection. It is such a familiar story that we are in danger of forgetting the basic fact. Jesus died but came back to life and is still alive. Just as He appeared personally to several of His disciples after the resurrection, He still appears and talks with His disciples now. He said He would be with us to the end of the age, and He meant it literally.

Read Mark 16:1–20.

What was the first response of the disciples, according to verse 11, when Mary Magdalene and the two disciples who were walking to the country told them about Jesus' resurrection?

_____

_____

_____

What was the nature of Jesus' rebuke of the disciples?

_____

_____

I want to ask you a question. Please take a moment to seriously consider it. Do you really believe that Jesus literally, actually resurrected from the dead? In your heart of hearts, what do you know beyond all shadow of doubt about that fact?

_____

_____

Jesus is nearer than your heartbeat. He is nearer than your breath. He is alive and He is here. You are not alone. Take some time right now to stop and meditate on His present nearness in your life.

Prayer

Lord, I proclaim that You are truly alive. You are here with me now. I am not alone.
I bless You and I praise You. I draw near to You now in Jesus' name. Amen.

Mothering Tip

Take your children or grandchildren to the library this week. Check out books on a variety of subjects. You might even check out CDs and tapes.

If you have teens, make sure they have their own library cards and know how to go to the central library in your area to do research. Help them learn to use the computer catalogue and how to ask for assistance at the information desk. Librarians are always available to provide assistance.

UNIT 7

DAY 2

A New Heart

BEGIN WITH PRAYER

Ask the Father to teach you how to walk and talk with Jesus all throughout your day.
Ask Him to make the living Lord more real to you each day this week.

I have a lot of Scripture for you to read today. Please don't skip it. It is so important for you to see what is in God's Word for yourself. E-mail me after today and let me know how you are doing. Are you learning and growing? Do you have questions? Let me hear from you by e-mail at deniseglenn@motherwise.org or regular "snail mail" at:

MotherWise

P.O. Box 1271

Houston, Texas 77251

Now, read Luke 24:1–35.

How long do you think the disciples on the road to Emmaus walked with Jesus without recognizing Him?

_____

How long have you walked with Jesus without recognizing Him?

_____

What was the first thing the disciples in Jerusalem told the two from Emmaus?

_____

So far we have seen that Jesus appeared personally to Mary Magdalene and to Simon Peter and in 1 Corinthians 15:7 it is recorded that He appeared to James. We know from 1 Corinthians 15:8 and from Acts 9 that He appeared personally to Paul.

Why do you think He appeared individually to these four? What do you know about them that would justify a private meeting with the risen Lord?

_____

_____

_____

Mary Magdalene had been demon-possessed and Jesus had cast out seven demons from her. She loved much because she had been forgiven much. She needed reassurance that He would never leave or forsake her. Peter needed a different kind of meeting with the Lord. Just days before the resurrection, Peter had blatantly denied even knowing Jesus. He needed a time for reconciliation. James, His half-brother, had lived with Him in unbelief. He needed some family time to express his newfound belief. Paul had persecuted Jesus' followers. He had to have a face-to-face confrontation with Jesus or he probably would never have believed.

Each one had a "history"—a seedy past—and needed personal time with the Lord. Can you relate to any or all of them? Jesus made it a point to seek them out. In love, He pursued each one. And He is pursuing you.

Read Luke 24:36–48.

What did Jesus do to help His disciples perceive that He had really come back to life?

_____

Compare verses 27 and 45. What did Jesus do for His disciples after His resurrection in a way that He couldn't do before the resurrection?

_____

Make verse 45 into a prayer. Rewrite it here:

_____

_____

Jesus was so practical. He ate a meal in front of His shocked disciples to prove to them that He truly had risen and was with them again. He was able to open their minds and to explain the Scriptures like He had never done before. He now had proof that the Scriptures were literally true and accurate. Now that they had been through His death and burial and resurrection it all came together and made sense. They got it!

Do you get it? The whole point of the good news about Jesus is that He is a living God. He's not dead like Buddha or Mohammed. We have a personal mentor who doesn't just leave us a written holy book to follow. We have the author of the book inside our hearts, personally instructing and guiding us toward the light! That is radically different. Are you seeing the impact of the resurrection on your daily life? Some of you might be thinking, "Oh great. God is with me all the time. He's watching over me to see when I mess up, and He's going to zap me. I don't want to think about the resurrection because it interferes with my lifestyle."

If you think that, you just don't know Him well enough yet. Just like you hover over your child to guide and lead and protect and train him in his best interest because you love him, Jesus is hovering over you. You are His baby. His precious one, dearly loved. And He has not left you alone. He is ever-present, ever-watching, ever-knowing because He loves you.

Read John 20:1–18.

What changed Mary's perception of the "gardener"?

_____

What was Mary's announcement?

_____

Jesus is calling your name. You personally. He sees, He cares, and He knows. Can you say with Mary, "I have seen the Lord"? Ask Jesus to open your eyes so that you too can see Him. Focus your attention this whole day on the risen Lord Jesus Christ. Record your thoughts here.

_____

_____

_____

Read John 20:19–31.

What was Thomas' real problem?

_____

What was Jesus' solution?

_____

What was Jesus' gentle rebuke to Thomas?

_____

According to verse 31, what is the reason John gave for writing his book?

_____

_____

What benefit comes from belief in Jesus' resurrection?

_____

John wrote his record of the events in Jesus' life culminating in His resurrection so that we too would believe and that believing we also would have *life* in His name. Will you believe? Can you take it in? Christ is risen! He is risen indeed!

Prayer

Lord, open my blind eyes to see the power of Your resurrection life. I have heard this story so often,
it doesn't mean anything to me anymore. I want to know You and the power of Your resurrection in my life.
Scrape away the calluses on my heart and let the truth sink in. I pray this in Jesus' name. Amen.

Mothering Tip

Keep your promises and insist that your children keep theirs. Broken promises break down the trust level in a relationship. Even strong family bonds can be seriously injured by not keeping your word.

We had a rule in our house when the children were growing up: "A word is a promise!"

Day 3

A New Power

BEGIN WITH PRAYER

Worship the Lord as the giver of all life.
Praise Him for burying your old life, and for giving you new, resurrected life in Him.
Tell Him you long to walk in newness of life.

CATERPILLARS AND BUTTERFLIES

God gave an illustration in nature to help us learn about the principle of resurrection life, the life of the butterfly. It goes through four life-cycle stages to come to full maturity. Look with me at how the stages of butterfly life coincide with our kingdom walk.

First, there is a tiny butterfly egg.[1] Can you see the little dots on the leaf?

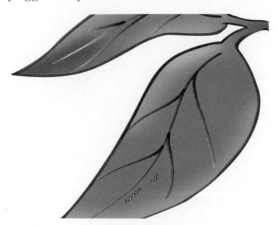

Before we know Christ, we are locked away from a relationship with God. We are in our "shells" until the time of rebirth. Our old sinful natures—our deep innermost selves—are separated from God. They cannot have a relationship with Him.

UNIT 7

The next phase of the butterfly life cycle is the larvae or caterpillar stage.

The caterpillar comes out of the shell ready to begin life. He eats constantly. He eats so much and grows so fast that he literally splits his sides. His exoskeleton does not grow, so when he grows too big for it, it splits and he sheds it. The caterpillar goes through this process many times.[2]

When we accept Christ Jesus as our Lord and Savior, we come out of "death" into a new life. We emerge from the "eggshell" as brand new creations capable of relationship with God. We are hungry to know Him. We devour everything that can feed us spiritually.

We grow and then have to shed those "skins" because they can't contain our new knowledge. Then we eat more and grow some more until again, our "skin" has to be shed. We get pretty excited about being big, fat "caterpillars." We are fairly amazed at our own growth. We grow and grow until we come to the place of total commitment and we think we cannot grow any more. Then God is ready to take us to the next phase.

The third phase of butterfly life is the pupa.[3]

When the caterpillar is ready for full maturity, he spits out a sticky substance forming a pad on a branch or twig. While suspended only by a silken thread, he flips up and thrusts the clawed structure at the end of his abdomen into the pad, leaving him hanging head down.

Soon the soft structures of the pupa begin to harden and a hard shell is formed. The pupa stays motionless while dramatic changes are taking place on his internal structures. He is being changed from caterpillar to butterfly. It happens in the dark. It happens on the inside. It takes time. But the change is worth it. It prepares him to fly.

If we are serious about going on with God, growing beyond our comfort zone into His will for our lives, there will come a time when we enter the "cocoon" phase so God can transform us. It will be a crucifixion time where we die to the former ways we have thought and believed and acted and where we are being retooled for a new dimension in living. It often feels lonely, and we may be in the dark. It may seem that God has forsaken and forgotten us. Life may not make sense. But if we will be still and patiently wait for God's work in the process, one day we will experience life on a level we never thought possible. We will be set free.

The final stage of butterfly life is the mature, adult phase.[4]

When the metamorphosis is complete, the butterfly emerges from the shell. At first, his wings are flat and damp. His body is soft and wet. Then he uses his muscles to begin pumping air into his body and wings, inflating and drying them to prepare for flight. After an hour or so, the butterfly is ready to fly off to find his mate and to begin reproducing butterfly life.

In a very real sense, the old caterpillar has died and has been replaced with a completely new life. The old has gone, the new has come. When we decide to make Jesus Christ not only our master and Lord, but our *life*, we are ready to live life on a higher plane. Mature, flight-ready Christians emerge from the "crucifixion cocoon" with new internal equipment.

We are changed and we are free. Old thought patterns and behaviors have been replaced by new ones. Anger and frustration have changed to peace and love. Jealousy and envy have changed to sincere praise and appreciation. Depression has become joy. Intolerance and impatience have become patience. Harshness has changed to gentleness. It is more than trying to do better. It is more intrinsic than a step-by-step self-help program. Real internal change has occurred. We are ready to fly. We are ready to bear fruit.

WHO ARE YOU, MOM?

Mother, if you are in Christ, let me tell you who you are. You are a new creation. You are a different species from any other on the face of the earth. Jesus recreated you in such a way that now you can contain His life. Before, when you were in Adam, you were hostile to Him. You were warped and deformed and could not contain Him. But now, you have been made brand new and you are perfectly suited to be a living temple that is filled with Jesus' life.

He made you and He loves you. In fact, He died that you might be pulled from His bleeding side to be His bride just as the first Adam's bride was pulled from his bloody side. Right now you are in a period of "engagement" to Him. He has sealed you with His promise. You have the engagement ring of His Holy Spirit. And some day in the fullness of time, He will take you to the home He's been getting ready for you. You will celebrate a wedding unlike any other, with a magnificent feast. And there you will finally be joined to your Bridegroom.

You are righteous. That new created you—that innermost you—was created by Christ Jesus to be holy and righteous. You are no longer a dirty, rotten sinner. You are a saint created for good works. Mother, do you see who you are?

The resurrection has implications for your past, your present, and your future. In your past, Jesus brought you from the death of life in Adam doomed to hell, to life in Him destined for heaven. In your present, Jesus is transforming you by the renewing of your mind through the process of death to your fleshy nature. In the future, at your physical death, He will bring you into eternal life in Him to join Him as His bride.

The resurrection tells me who I am. It establishes my identity. I am not a helpless sinner (Romans 6:6). I am a new creation wearing His robe of righteousness (2 Corinthians 5:17–21). I am not Jesus' slave. I am His friend (John 15:15). I am a son (daughter) of God (Galatians 4:7). If I don't understand the resurrection, I miss out on the great purpose for which I was born. I was born, and then reborn, to be an "earthen vessel" carrying around the life of the Lord Jesus here on earth. Now I know whose "letter jacket of identity" I'm wearing!

Now, reread Romans 6:3–14.

Describe your newness of life according to verse 14. What have you just learned?

_____

_____

According to verse 6, what happened in the past to your old "body of sin"—your old Adam life?

_____

Now that it has died, what has happened?

_____

Starting in verse 11, Paul's discussion turns to your present "crucifixion" and "resurrection." Now what has died and what is alive?

_____

Paul describes in a practical way how we should go about crucifying flesh and living the resurrected life in verses 12–13. Give his instructions in your own words.

_____

_____

Read Romans 8:9–11.

According to Paul, what is the condition of your body if you are a Christian? What is the condition of your spirit?

_____

_____

Mother, you are alive. You have to live in an earthy body that still has flesh, but the real authentic "you" is vibrantly, thrillingly alive. This is why you can "esteem" yourself, love yourself. You are a beautiful, new creation in Christ Jesus. He dispensed with the old self that was displeasing to God, and recreated you brand new with the capacity to be full of His life.

We don't need to pull ourselves up by our boot straps and try to work on our "self-esteem." That would be just building up our flesh, making stronger what actually needs to die. What we need is to know who we are. We are His workmanship, created in Him for good works.

Yes, we are going to go through some struggles that resemble Romans 7. Our flesh is going to war against our spirit. Old fleshy patterns of thinking will result in fleshy behaviors. But as we cooperate with God, change will occur.

Let me illustrate it. Suppose a family who owns a home decides to sell. The new owners love the floor plan and the overall structure of the home, but the decor is not to their taste. Over time, they take out the old and put in the new. They replace the carpet and paint the walls. They change the drapes and put in new furniture. The home begins to reflect the character of the new owners. Don't stretch the illustration too far, but you get the general idea.

You are a new creation in Christ. You've been bought by a new owner. He now resides in you. He has given you a completely new inner man. That "inner man" or spirit can contain the life of Jesus and can respond in faith to Him. He is in the process of transforming your mind, will, and emotions. He is remaking you on the inside to match who you really are.

Will you receive the truth about yourself? Will you believe who you really are? Journal the thoughts and questions that come to your mind.

_____

_____

_____

Lord, thank You for the wonderful truth that I am a new creation, a lovable person.
Lord, help me to know this truth that can truly set me free.
I pray this prayer in Your holy name. Amen.

If you are a working mom, you will probably want to limit your social obligations. Your relationship with God and bonding with your family should be the top priorities when you are not at work.

Your kids and husband need your focused attention and with all the other things that press in on you just to survive, there isn't time for many "extras." Someday, when the children are gone, you'll have lots of time to pursue other things.

DAY 4

A New Place

BEGIN WITH PRAYER

Ask the Father to transform you by the renewing of your mind.
Ask Him to bind your mind to His mind and your heart to His heart.

I want to clarify the difference between who you are and who you are becoming. They are two radically different things and will affect your mothering in very basic ways.

A NEW CREATION

Who you *are* is a new creation, loved by God. You are a completely different species of man than a non-Christian. They have dead spirits that cannot contain the life of Jesus. Your spirit has come alive and can contain the life of Jesus. You have no excuse to feel defeated and inferior and inadequate. You simply aren't! You are a magnificent, new creation of God.

Copy 2 Corinthians 5:17 here.

_____

_____

_____

_____

Read Galatians 6:15.

How did Paul describe your new life?

_____

Read Romans 8:10–11.

Even though your body is "dead" because it still has the ability to sin, your spirit is_____.

Read Romans 8:15–17.

According to verse 15, what have you not received?

_____

What have you received as a result of your new creation birth?

_____

Verse 16 makes an amazing statement about our true identity. Who are we?

_____

As children of God, to what does that entitle us according to verse 17?

_____

Read John 3:3.

How did Jesus describe the new life we have?

_____

Our new life is "born again." He starts over and completely recreates us!

The best way I know to illustrate this is when my daughters were teenagers. I knew if one of them was in love. It showed all over her. All of a sudden, she started working on her hair and taking lots of time on her make-up. Every outfit worn to school was a major decision. She walked with a lilt in her step and the little everyday annoyances of life just didn't seem to matter. She knew who she was. She was a loved woman. That knowledge was enough to enable her to see herself as worthy and valuable. When she saw herself that way, it changed her whole perspective.

If we know who we are, Mom, we don't have to try to feel good about ourselves by accumulating possessions. We don't have to spend the national budget on our faces and figures to find meaning in life. We won't need to achieve career success at the expense of our families so we will know who we are. We do know who we are, and it has nothing to do with any of that.

We can settle down and get to the real issues of life. We can focus on being God's woman—a lovely, feminine container of His holy life. We can accept our role which is to pour out that life into the lives of those He places around us. Our husbands and our children and our world will know Him because they know us.

I want to encourage you to take the time to finish the following exercise. Get your Bible and trace what it says about your true identity. I believe you may be amazed at what you will find.

Find the Scripture reference and fill in the blank.

Matthew 5:13	I am _the salt of the earth_ _____
Matthew 5:14	I am _____
John 1:12	I am _____
John 15:5	I am _____
John 15:15	I am _____
John 15:16	I am _____
Acts 1:8	I am _____
Romans 6:18	I am _____
Romans 6:22	I am _____
Romans 8:14–15	I am _____
Romans 8:17	I am _____

1 Corinthians 3:16; 6:19   I am _____

1 Corinthians 6:17   I am _____

1 Corinthians 12:27   I am _____

2 Corinthians 5:17   I am _____

Galatians 3:26, 28–29   I am _____

Galatians 4:6–7   I am _____

Ephesians 2:10   I am _____

Ephesians 2:19   I am _____

Ephesians 4:24   I am _____

Philippians 3:20   I am _____

Colossians 3:3   I am _____

Colossians 3:4   I am _____

Colossians 3:12   I am _____

1 Thessalonians 1:4   I am _____

1 Thessalonians 5:5   I am _____

Hebrews 3:1   I am _____

1 Peter 2:5   I am _____

1 Peter 2:9–10   I am _____

1 Peter 2:11   I am _____

1 Peter 5:8   I am _____

1 John 3:1–2   I am _____

Psalm 23 and 100   I am _____

I am:

the salt of the earth

the light of the world

a child of God (a part of His family—not just created like the angels)

part of the true vine, a branch through which His life can flow

Christ's friend

chosen and appointed by Christ to bear His fruit

a personal witness of Christ for Christ

a slave of righteousness

enslaved to God

a "son" (daughter) of God

a joint-heir with Christ sharing all of His inheritance with Him

a temple where God's Spirit dwells

joined to the Lord and my spirit is one with His spirit

a part of Christ's body—we are organically related

a new person, a new species of man able to house God's Spirit

a son (daughter) of God and one in Christ Jesus

an heir of God since I am a begotten child

God's workmanship, newly created in Christ to do His work, that He planned before the foundation of
     the world

a fellow citizen with the rest of God's people that are in His family

righteous and holy

a citizen of heaven and seated in heaven right now

hidden with Christ in God

an expression of the life of Christ because He is my life

chosen of God, holy, and dearly loved

a son (daughter) of light and not of darkness

a part of the holy brethren and a partaker of a heavenly calling

a living stone that is being built into a spiritual house and a part of a holy priesthood to offer up spiritual
     sacrifices with my prayers

a part of a chosen race of people, I am royalty, I am part of a priesthood, holy and God's own personal
     possession for the purpose of proclaiming how excellent God really is. I have come from darkness into
     light

an alien and stranger in this world because I am different as a result of my new creation by God at my
     new birth in Christ

an enemy of Satan

a child of God who will be like Jesus when He comes back to earth

a sheep in His pasture and I have everything I need[5]

When your children are fighting in the backseat of the car, or your teenage daughter gets jilted by her boyfriend, or you have a wreck on the freeway, or your husband gets laid off, it is hard to remember who you are in Christ. It is so easy to focus on the event of the moment. We might think, *what difference does it make if I know who I am, I've got to deal with what's right here under my nose!*

Knowing who you are in Christ won't change your circumstances, but it can change how you look at them. It won't change the problem, it will change you.

If you are fundamentally an earthling who is trying to get the best you can out of this earth experience, then all of the above situations are going to frustrate your goal. You will get angry and depressed, and if the situation isn't settled quickly, you might even despair.

If you are fundamentally a child of God—a citizen of heaven—who is living on the earth for a short time for the purpose of bringing Him glory, then each of the situations mentioned are opportunities to express His life and His grace. We don't sit around trying to decide what Jesus would do in the situation, we ask Him to do whatever He wants using our hands and feet.

My fighting children don't threaten who I am as a mother. I know who I am and I simply have a job to do to bring my children into submission and peace. The rejection my teenage daughter is experiencing doesn't mean she is unworthy and unloved. I don't have to put up shields of self-protection. I know it is a part of God's plan to lead her to the understanding that Jesus alone can meet the needs of her heart. No human being will be totally faithful in meeting that need.

The wreck on the freeway doesn't mean I am a stupid and incompetent person who is a failure. I know I am a daughter and friend of the Living God. Even when my behavior doesn't line up with who I am, it doesn't change my fundamental personhood. (No matter what the other driver or my husband says about me, I know who I am! That makes all the difference!)

When my husband gets laid off from his job, it doesn't mean God has abandoned and discarded us. I know I am a sheep in His pasture and He will take care of my every need. As we listen to His voice and obey, He will lead us and guide us to His provision.

We often confuse our behavior with our identity. If I mess up, I think that's who I really am. When I know who I am and to Whom I belong, then I can see my behavior as being consistent or inconsistent with who I am. This is very critical to your role as a wife and mother.

When you know the truth, you won't be on an emotional roller coaster trying to use "good" behavior to please your family so they will affirm that you are an "okay" person. You are already an "okay" person because God said so. Your behavior only has to please *Him*. Now you can do the right thing for the right reason because you are an all-right person. All right?

We have dealt with who you are. Now let's talk about who you are becoming. Let's talk about the process.

A WOMAN OF FREEDOM

Who you are *becoming* is a woman of freedom. Freed from the barriers within your heart that squelch His life, you are being transformed by the renewing of your mind. With each passing season, you are becoming more transparent and able to display His glory.

Read Romans 8:12–13.

What is the principle Paul gives in verse 13 for living free in Christ?

_____

_____

Lord Jesus, thank You for my new life in You.

Continue to unfold the truth to me in a way I can receive it.

I love You with all my heart, Lord.

Now take my heart and let it be Your throne.

I pray this in Your name. Amen.

Try to spend time alone with each child at least once a week. Talk, read, walk, cook, or play to connect with that child even for a little while. Tell the siblings they will have their turn. Make an exclusive date really exclusive.

My pastor's wife, Mrs. JoBeth Young, shared these wonderful mothering tips with me and has allowed me to share them with you. Her youngest son is my oldest son-in-law so I can vouch for her great mothering!

1. When a child has a negative behavior trait, look for any indication of the positive in that area and praise his action. This will encourage a repetition of the positive. For instance, if carpool time has become hectic and chaotic, look for a quiet, cooperative interlude in which you can praise that action and encourage it to continue.

2. Be aware of the individuality of each child and guide him or her in that way. A sensitive, thoughtful child will have one set of needs and a happy-go-lucky, outgoing child will have another.

3. Stop, love, and listen! Stop your activity and pay attention; demonstrate your love to your child; and listen attentively.

DAY 5

A New Mind

BEGIN WITH PRAYER

Ask the Father to flood the eyes of your heart with light
so that you will know the hope of His calling.
Ask Him to fill your mind with His thoughts and your heart with His love.

Today, we are going to discover some of the wonderful blessings that come with our new creation status. We will examine the first five chapters of Acts to see what happened to Jesus' followers after His resurrection. In other words, when resurrection happens, what comes next? Is there a change?

As we look at the record of what happened to the disciples after the resurrection, we are going to see their flesh patterns demolished and new patterns of thinking and behavior appear. That is resurrection power working! It was not just for them, it is for you and for me. I'm ready for resurrection to work on me and work in me, aren't you? As a mother, I want to be "transformed by the renewing of my mind."

I have one caution as we enter this territory. As you read these passages of Scripture, you will come across things that the disciples experienced that you will question. The church you belong to has a particular belief and doctrine about many of these events.

The purpose of our study is to focus on the change that occurred in the people who witnessed the resurrection of Jesus. I want you to just read the Scripture honestly for what it says and document those changes. Don't get hung up on details and miss the main point. We are observing the events of resurrection living to grasp more of the principle. Agreed?

NEW POWER

Read Acts 1:1–5, 8.

When the Holy Spirit would come, what were the disciples of Jesus going to receive?

_____

Now go on a Scripture hunt. Read Acts 2:2–4, 38, 43; 3:1–8; 4:13; 5:12a; 6:8–10.

What were the evidences of the new power the disciples possessed?

_____

_____

_____

The Holy Spirit didn't creep up on the disciples in a gradual process. There was one decisive moment when the power of heaven connected with the hearts of men. It must have sounded like a tornado hit, because the sound was heard all over the city (Acts 2:6).

The brand-new creatures in Christ sat huddled together in one place. They had emerged from the dark cocoon, but they sat with soft fragile hearts and wings that were limp and useless. From somewhere up in heaven, the Father gave the signal and the wind began to stir. As it moved toward earth, it picked up speed until it exploded though earth's atmosphere. Finding its target, it engulfed the room with its presence. As it pumped itself into each empty, waiting heart, something like fireworks began to go off around each one of them. There was no way to contain this presence. They were so filled with the super-intelligence of the Spirit of God that their brains began to process information that hadn't been there moments before.

Did they need to witness to people who couldn't understand their language? The language was given them. Did they need to heal the sick? The healing power was given them.

Compare Luke 22:33–34, 54–62 with Acts 2:14–36.

What difference do you find in Peter? How was he changed?

_____

_____

Before Jesus' resurrection, Peter was a cowering, cursing liar. In the courtyard of the high priest he denied the Lord for whom he had vowed to go to prison and to death. But look at him now! He is preaching openly in the temple porches, shouting at the top of his lungs, proclaiming Jesus. He boldly accuses the Jews of putting Jesus to death, and proceeds to explain the resurrection.

Can you believe the change in this man? Did the crucifixion change him? After the crucifixion, Peter was still cowering behind closed doors. No, it was after the resurrection of Jesus, when the Holy Spirit was released onto the earth that Peter changed so suddenly and so completely. It was resurrection power that changed Peter.

Mother, are you ready for that kind of change? Are you cowering in your present circumstance, defeated and depressed? Remember who you are! Remember what you have! You are a new species of mom. You have been created with a capacity to be filled with God Himself. Furthermore, you may ask Him to fill your heart and your mind with His heart and His mind. You have direct access to Him. The same power that raised Jesus from the dead is at work in you.

Read Ephesians 1:18–20 and Ephesians 3:16.

What does Paul pray for the Ephesians concerning power?

_____

_____

I am echoing Paul's prayers for you. I want to put my arm around your shoulders and give you a hug. I want to look you in the eye and tell you, "Mom, you can do this mothering job. Not because you are going to learn how to get 'strong' in your flesh, but because He is strong. You are not limited to your own strength and knowledge. He has equipped you to house His life and as you learn to put off flesh and put on His life, you will become a powerful overcomer. Mothering will become the joy it was intended to be."

Lord, I want to be an overcomer. I want to live in freedom and victory.
Accomplish in my life Your whole plan and purpose. I pray this in Your holy name. Amen.

MOTHERING TIP

When your child is recovering from an illness at home, try some of these time-tested home remedies:

1. Make tapioca pudding. For some reason, it seems to soothe tender stomachs.
2. Keep clear carbonated sodas and saltine crackers on hand for middle of the night illnesses.
3. Hold a cool, wet washcloth on fevered brows.
4. Keep a flexible ice pack in the freezer for strains, sprains, and bruises. If you don't have one, frozen peas or corn work great!
5. Serve fresh cut-up oranges to patients with a cold.
6. Make a pot of tea and add honey and lemon for sore throats.

UNIT 7

UNIT

THE PRINCIPLE OF THE BUD: NEW GROWTH

MOTHERING SKILL: FINANCIAL FINESSE FOR FAMILIES

DAY *1*
NEW PURPOSE

DAY *2*
NEW COMMUNITY

DAY *3*
NEW POSSESSIONS

DAY *4*
A NEW BLANKET, RIBBON, AND JACKET

DAY *5*
PERSONAL TESTIMONY

❦

The book of Acts describes what it was like for the disciples to experience
the new freedom of life in Christ. Denise discovered what it was like to have a
new heart and a new mind from a miracle one Christmas.

❦

UNIT 8

Bible Study Listening Guide

1. The key Bible verse is:

_____

_____

_____

_____

2. What I personally need to remember from this lesson is:

_____

_____

_____

_____

_____

_____

MotherWise Group Prayer Requests

1._____

2._____

3._____

4._____

5._____

6._____

7._____

UNIT 8

MOTHERING SKILLS DISCUSSION:

Financial Finesse for Families

Challenge: To exercise self-control in spending and saving and teach our children to appropriately delay gratification of their desires for material things.

Our children are growing up in a very different world from the one we knew. Especially in the area of money. Even four- and five-year-olds respond to commercials and get the "gimmes." Teenagers are tempted to blackmail their parents into purchasing expensive clothing and technology. What's a mother to do?

Use the following scenarios to discuss financial finesse with your MotherWiss group.

1. Your seventeen year-old daughter wants to go to the mall and get a $50 haircut. She expects you to pay for it because she lives under your roof.

   a. You pay for her haircuts, but feel you can only afford $35 haircuts for yourself.

   b. You tell her no, she can cut her own hair.

   c. You give her a percentage of the budget amount for haircuts for the family and tell her she can either stay within that budget or supplement it with money of her own.

2. Your five-year-old wants the newest toy he has seen advertised. It is very expensive.

   a. You tell him your family doesn't waste money on junk like that.

   b. You use the opportunity to start an allowance for him and explain savings, spending, and tithing. Tell him the cost of the item and how much both you and he will need to contribute to split the cost of the toy. Ask him if he is sure he still wants that toy or would he like to choose another that's less expensive and would take less of his savings.

   c. You pull out your credit card and get the toy as soon as possible.

3. Your twelve-year-old wants to spend every Saturday at the movies and mall with friends. He asks for $25 to spend each time.

   a. You give him the money because he's been struggling with popularity and you want him to have friends. You're afraid if you don't give it to him, he's going to be an outcast.

   b. You tell him, "Absolutely not!" and remind him of how much $25 would buy in your day.

   c. You offer to pay him for Saturday chores that are to be done before socializing can take place. You establish ground rules for friends, movies, and the mall. If he earns the money and stays within the ground rules, you let him go.

4. Your young children want to know who they will go live with if you die while they're still home.

   a. You tell them to stop talking about it because nothing bad like that will happen while they are children.

   b. You ask if they would like to go live with Aunt Judy (because that's who is named in your will as their guardian in case of your death). Then you call Judy and tell her the kids are asking and that you want to verify that she will take them. You tell her about your life insurance coverage and the children's college accounts.

    c. You tell them that it's all worked out and not to worry about it.

5. Your teenage daughter has earned her own money at a part-time job at the mall and comes home with the most hideous looking clothing from her earnings. The clothing is not immodest, but is in terrible taste.

    a. You bite your tongue and use body language to communicate your displeasure.

    b. You tell her to take it all back and sit her down to explain good taste from bad taste.

    c. You tell her how proud you are of her for working. You ask to see her outfits and find *something* to compliment. You honestly say that her taste is different from yours but that she can wear anything she buys that is not immodest and doesn't break school or work dress codes.

6. You are tired of the clothing in your closet and have been feeling down. You need a lift. You go to the mall and pick out the most darling outfit that exactly matches your hair and eyes. Your husband blows up when he hears how much you paid for it.

    a. You put it back in the sack with the receipt and take it back the next day. You don't speak to your husband for a week and even then the air is icy between you.

    b. You apologize to your husband and offer to take back the outfit. You express your need for a clothing budget amount every month so you can save toward purchases.

    c. You fix your husband a great meal, offer him sex, and hope he forgets about the expenditure.

I think the best answers are:

1. c

2. b

3. c

4. b

5. c

6. b

What do you think?

_____

_____

_____

What financial issues are you working through with your family?

_____

_____

Tools to Meet the Challenge:

Miserly Moms—Living on One Income in a Two Income Economy, Jonni McCoy (Elkton, Md.: Full Quart Press, 1996).

The Complete Cheapskate: How To Get Out of Debt, Stay Out and Break Free from Money Worries Forever, Mary Hunt (Nashville, Tenn.: Broadman and Holman).

Cheapskate in the Kitchen, Mary Hunt (New York: St. Martin's Mass Market Paper, 1997).

DAY 1

New Purpose

BEGIN WITH PRAYER
Read Psalm 103 back to the Lord as a prayer.

Read Acts 1:8, 22; 2:31–32; 3:15; 4:8–10, 20, 31, 33; 5:20, 29–32.

What was the new purpose of the disciples of Jesus?

_____

What was the specific subject of their witnessing?

_____

The disciples now had a purpose. They were not just fishermen from Galilee, they were powerful witnesses to the resurrection of Jesus Christ. They had focus and direction for the rest of their lives. Life was meaningful and significant. It all made sense.

Mother, if you are in Christ, your life has meaning and purpose. Your life is extremely significant. You are one of the live witnesses to the fact that Jesus Christ is a living God and not a dead one. You are a witness to the fact that your own personal life has been and is being transformed in ways you did not think possible. You are on a mission

Who is your mission field? Start with your children. Do they know and understand the truth about the resurrection of Jesus? When you talk to them, don't focus on what Jesus did or what He would do, focus on *who He is.* He is alive and He speaks to us. That is astounding! He is a part of every minute of every day. That is almost unbelievable, but it's true!

Now do you see your love bucket? Are you grasping how Jesus fills your every heart need? Your need to be significant, to get a blue ribbon, is met in Him. He doesn't just make you "feel" significant, you really are—whether you feel like it or not! Your feelings have little to do with the facts, and, as women, we need that reminder.

The fact is that you are a significant part of the family of God. You have power and you have purpose. For some of you this may be hard to accept because of the wrong thinking patterns that have dominated your life. For now, you may have to choose to believe the truth about yourself whether your feelings line up or not. But the facts remain. Jesus has created you brand new. He has created you for a purpose.

New Prayer Life

Read Acts 1:14; 2:42; 6:4.

What characterized the prayers of the disciples after Jesus' resurrection?

_____

With one heart and one mind, the disciples prayed. They devoted themselves to prayer. Mother, pray! Prayer provides the fuel for a mom to get to her main destination with her children. One of the three most critical gifts a mother can give her children is the gift of her witness about Jesus. If she will love her children unconditionally and unselfishly, and if she will discipline them fairly and firmly, she will have an opportunity to share with them her faith in Jesus Christ. Prayer will open the pathway for that witness to occur.

Read Romans 8:26–30, 34.

Whose heart is being searched when it cannot even express its prayers?

_____

What does my heart need to be connected to in prayer?

_____

Who intercedes for us, connecting heaven to earth?

_____

Look carefully at the prayer picture drawn for you in Romans. Here you are with your requests that are so deep you can't even express them in your language. English or Spanish or Cantonese words just don't describe what is in your heart. Now we are told that the Spirit searches our minds and knows exactly what we are trying to express. He also knows the "mind of the Spirit"—He knows God's will for our circumstance.

Now He connects the two—my request and God's will—by His intercession to the Father. God's will comes down to the earth through the intercession prayers of Jesus to me as I open my heart to pray. Prayer is so much more than telling God what we want. It is hearing from God what He wants. He transforms us by the renewing of our minds as we pray!

How does that affect your prayer life as a mother? Mom, it sets you free! You don't have to pray with pain and agony over your children supposing that if you just pray harder you can make them do what you want. He knows what your heart's desire is for your children. Your response in prayer is to open your heart to Jesus asking Him what the Father's heart's desire is for your kids. Allow Him to transform your prayers and your thinking to match His. Then let your actions in your children's lives flow from that point.

Do you see the difference this kind of praying can make? If only a few mothers would take seriously the "devoting themselves to prayer" aspect of resurrection living, it would change their mothering and that would change the world.

Could you commit some time today to prayer? Would you devote yourself to prayer this day for the sake of your children? Take some quiet moments to absorb today's lesson. Ask the Holy Spirit to lead you into all truth concerning His power, your purpose, and prayer. Listen and record what He says.

_____

_____

_____

_____

Lord, I want to understand the power of the resurrection in my life.
I want to experience Your power working in me. I want to be transformed by the renewing of my mind.
Don't just change others, Lord, change me. I open my heart to hear
Your voice. Jesus, express the mind of the Spirit to me in a way I can hear You and understand You.
Hear my heart's cry. I pray this in Jesus' name. Amen.

*M*OTHERING *T*IP

Ask your older children if they feel they can talk to you freely and openly about anything. You may be surprised at their answers. Talk about the climate in your family. Is it cold or warm? Open a discussion about your family communication levels. Discuss a plan for improvement.

If your children are too young for this discussion, ask the questions of your husband. Work together on a plan to communicate clearly and more effectively.

DAY 2

A New Community

BEGIN WITH PRAYER

Bless the Lord by telling Him how wonderful and marvelous He is.
Praise His power and praise Him for His love.

We will continue looking at the first five chapters of Acts to see what changes occurred in the lives of the disciples after the resurrection. As you study, ask the Father to reveal to you more about your identity in Him and what that means for you as a mother.

NEW PLACE

Read Acts 2:1, 44, 46; 5:12.

What is the common characteristic of the believers in these verses?

_____

The disciples had a new unity and community they had never before experienced. They were all together in one place. They didn't want to be separated. The phenomenal events they had witnessed had bonded them into a unit. They ate meals together. They even sold their property and shared all they had with each other.

When resurrection power is at work, there is unity. God's people want to spend time together. There is a place to belong and it feels like home.

NEW PRIORITIES

Read Acts 2:42, 45; 4:32, 37.

List the priorities of the disciples as given in these verses.

_____

_____

All of a sudden, the disciples' lifestyles changed. They listened to teaching, had fellowship, ate, and prayed together on a continual basis. Their possessions became offerings to God for His use. "Church" happened every day, all the time.

NEW PERSECUTION

Read Acts 2:13; 4:1–3, 16–18, 21, 29–30; 5:17–18, 33, 40–41; 6:9–15; 7:54–60.

What was happening to the group of believers?

_____

The degree of commitment on the part of the believers brought about an equal amount of opposition. Persecution began slowly and picked up strength. The stoning of Stephen sent the believers scurrying to leave Jerusalem. Resurrection life is powerful, and Satan knows it. There will be opposition!

NEW PEOPLE

Read Acts 2:41, 47; 4:4; 5:14; 6:7; 9:31, 35, 42;

Also read Acts 11:21, 24; 14:1, 21; 16:5; 17:12.

Was Christianity growing in small, medium, or large numbers?

_____

_____

Look at the number of new believers! When revival is happening, people flock to join other believers.

UNIT 8

Lord, I pray for my church. I pray for the community of believers that I belong to.
I ask You to protect us, guide us, purify us, and fill us.
Wash us with the water of Your Word. I pray that Your Spirit will be so free to work through us
that many people will come to know You. I pray this in Your name. Amen.

Mothering Tip

Compliment every family member at least twice today. Encourage everyone in the family to get in on the act!

New Possessions

BEGIN WITH PRAYER

Sit very quietly in God's presence.

Acknowledge that He is Lord of lords and King of kings.

He is ruler over all and He is in control.

Read Romans 8:32.

Read Matthew 6:33 and Romans 8:32.

What possessions did the disciples have here on earth?

_____

Read Romans 8:16–17; Ephesians 1:11, 18; 3:6.

What possessions did the disciples have in heaven?

_____

On earth, the disciples had *all of the things* they would need. God would freely meet their every need. (See also Matthew 6:25–34.) They also had inherited all of the kingdom of God. Everything Jesus now has in the heavenly realm would be theirs because they were now joint heirs with Jesus able to inherit everything from the Father. While still living on earth, He gave them the Holy Spirit to live inside them and to be with them as a small portion of their inheritance to enjoy now, knowing that the full inheritance was waiting for them when they got to heaven.

These poor, uneducated fisherman had just inherited the mother lode! They now possessed everything in heaven that Jesus possessed. On earth they now had everything they would need. No wonder they started selling their possessions and sharing them with each other. That's the way the kingdom is supposed to work. No one selfishly hoarding to protect himself against want. No one grasping; everyone giving. No one living in self-indulgence. Everyone looking out for his brother. Wow!

NEW "PAPERS"

Read Romans 8:14–16 and Ephesians 1:5; 2:19.

Circle the answer that best describes the position of the believers.

Slaves   Sons

A slave serves his master in fear. A son serves his father out of love. The believers had moved from a position of slavery to sonship. They had their adoption "papers" that declared them to be sons of the Father.

Do you see the difference the resurrection makes? Look at the lives of the believers before and after the resurrection. While they lived and walked with Jesus, they were learning and growing (like "caterpillars feeding on the leaves"). They were constantly growing and needing to shed their old ideas and enlarge their capacity to understand the kingdom.

But then it was time not just for growth and for total commitment (they had done all that), now it was time to take a supersonic leap into a completely new existence. To do that, they had to experience death to all they hoped for and believed in. They watched Jesus die, and they were in utter confusion and sorrow that went far beyond their sorrow over losing Him physically.

It was the end to all they had understood and believed about God. Jesus took them through this death into a completely new life. When they emerged from that week where they had lost all and then gained more than "all," the changes in them were nothing short of coming from death to life.

They went from owning nothing to owning it all. They changed from cowards to lions. They were transformed from ignorant fishermen to eloquent orators. They changed from being a little band of scattered followers to being a mobilized army of believers who changed the world. This is the power of the resurrection!

Do you think the resurrection—if you truly understood it—could make a difference in your life?

Go back through each of the changes in the disciples that we have studied in these past two days and evaluate your mothering issues according to each one. Can you see evidence of the resurrection in any of these areas in the relationship you have with your children?

New Power: _____

New Purpose: _____

New Prayer: _____

New Place: _____

New Priorities: _____

New Persecution: _____

New People: _____

New Possessions: _____

New "Papers": _____

Lord, I want to experience resurrection power in my mothering.

I want to see dramatic changes that can only come as You bring about death to my old mindsets.

You said that You would live in and through me.

Here I am. I offer myself to You. Change me, Lord. Mold me and shape me after

Your will. I pray this in the name of my Jesus. Amen.

Mothering Tip

As a family, read aloud a biography of a famous Christian. Or encourage your children to read some on their own. Choose the life of someone who has totally committed himself or herself to Jesus Christ. Check your local Christian bookstore for some good titles. You might enjoy Elisabeth Elliot's *The Life and Legacy of Amy Carmichael: A Chance To Die*. It is wonderfully inspiring.

One of the biographies that influenced my life as a child was *Bill Wallace of China,* by Jesse Fletcher, the story of a missionary who gave his life serving Christ in Asia. It is still available from the publisher. My Grandmother Durham encouraged me to read biographies of dedicated Christians every summer when I spent time at her house.

DAY 4

A New Blanket, Ribbon, and Jacket

BEGIN WITH PRAYER

Ask the Father to open your heart to whatever new work He wants to do.
Give Him full permission to change your thought patterns, actions, and attitudes.

When we began *Freedom for Mothers*, we started with our empty love bucket. Remember? Let's take another look at it.

In the bucket that represents your deepest heart of hearts, you need love, acceptance, and security (that we illustrated with a blanket); you need to know that you are significant (that we illustrated with a blue ribbon); and you need to belong to someone you care about (that we illustrated with a letter jacket).

BLANKET OF UNCONDITIONAL LOVE, ACCEPTANCE, AND SECURITY

Let's review what Christ has done to meet your need for unconditional love.

Read Ephesians 3:17–19.

In verse 17, what gardening and building terms did we discover that describe Christ's love for you?

_____

How much does Christ love you?

_____

_____

According to verse 19, what fills up your bucket?

_____

Read Romans 8:35–39.

What cannot separate you from the love of Christ?

_____

_____

_____

Jesus fills your need for love so fully and completely that Paul says he's praying that we will be able to comprehend that love. It is so broad, so long, so high, and so deep that we are going to have trouble containing it. It surpasses our ability to take it all in!

Absolutely nothing in the spiritual realm nor on earth can separate us from Christ's love. Nothing!

Read Romans 15:7.

Who has accepted you?

_____

Read Romans 8:31–35.

What are the five questions Paul encourages you to ask yourself?

1. _____

2. _____

3. _____

4. _____

5. _____

What are the five answers?

1. _____

2. _____

3. _____

4. _____

5. _____

To what degree are you accepted by God?

_____

Who is against us if God is for us? No one that counts! Will He not freely give us all things? Yes, He will! Who will bring a charge against God's elect? No one that matters because God has justified us. Who is the one who condemns? Only Jesus has the right to do so and He died for us and intercedes for us. Who will separate us from the love of Christ? Nothing, and no one, never ever! Is that strong enough for you? Do you get the picture, Mom? YOU ARE LOVED!

You may have experienced rejection in your life. You may have been rejected in the home where you grew up. Or rejection may have come in marriage or work. All of us have experienced some type of rejection. We all have a few holes in the bottom of our buckets.

What does God's Word say about that? You—that deep personal you—were totally accepted by God when you came into His family. You did not have to earn it with good behavior. He accepts you completely because you are His.

Read Hebrews 13:5.

Christ has said to you, "I will never _____."

How secure are you in Him?

_____

You may have been left by those you loved and trusted, but He will never leave or forsake you. It's interesting that the first part of that verse refers to our insecurity about money and possessions. For many of us, that is where we demonstrate our insecurity and our lack of trust in Him. He has promised to take care of us. In Him we are safe and secure.

BLUE RIBBON OF SIGNIFICANCE

Read Ephesians 1:4.

Who chose whom?

_____

Read John 15:16.

Who chose whom?

_____

Read 1 Peter 2:9.

What are the four descriptions of a Christian?

_____

Could it be any clearer? God chose us! He specially selected us to be in Christ Jesus. You are a royal, priestly person chosen by God. You can't get more significant than that!

LETTER JACKET OF IDENTITY

Read Ephesians 1:5.

God decided before our birth to bring us into His family by _____.

Read John 15:15.

You are not a slave in God's household, you are called a _____.

Read Colossians 2:9–10.

True or false:

_____ You are not complete in Him. You have to work to be identified with Christ.

_____ You are complete in Him. He did everything necessary for your identification with His family.

Your love bucket is brimming full to overflowing! In Him you are full and complete.

Lord, I receive Your love today by faith.

I am a new creation capable of being filled all the way to the top with Your love.

I believe that You love me because the Bible tells me so. Now, Lord, I want to love You back with my whole life!

In Jesus' name I pray this. Amen.

Mothering Tip

On the Subject of Sibling Rivalry:

1. Everyone wants to be loved for who they are uniquely. Celebrate each child's individuality.

2. Try to let your children work out their differences, but set a few ground rules. (Like no hitting, name-calling, etc.)

3. Don't ask, "Who started it?" It will just escalate the war and there is no way to "prove" who is right. It takes two to tango in fights between siblings, and it's usually not the case that one child is right and the other is wrong. They most often both had something to do with the start of the argument.

4. Your children sometimes fight just to get your attention.

5. Being "fair" is treating the child according to what he needs at the time, not making everything the same for everyone all the time. For example, when your son or daughter goes off to college, he needs extra clothing and dorm room equipment. Every other child in the family left at home may need to sacrifice a little at the beginning of school to make that allowance. Or when it's one child's birthday, he gets the gifts, not the other children in the family.

*Ideas adapted from *Loving Each One Best: A Caring and Practical Approach to Raising Siblings*, Nancy Samalin (New York: Bantam Books, 1996).

DAY 5

Personal Testimony

BEGIN WITH PRAYER

Spend a few minutes in adoration of the Lord.

Then ask Him to show you anything you need to confess as sin.

Ask His forgiveness. If you need to ask forgiveness of someone else,

put down this book, and take care of that now.

Thank the Father for all His blessings to you.

Ask Him to fill you with His presence today as you listen to His voice.

To end this section, I want to share a personal testimony of resurrection that occurred in our family. I'm praying that it will enable you to see what it looks like when someone goes from "death to life" in an area of their lives. To prepare you for the story, please read the Scripture that God used to change us.

Read 2 Kings 4:1–7.

What was the woman's problem?

_____

What resource did the woman have?

_____

What were Elisha's four instructions to her?

1. _____

2. _____

3. _____

4. _____

What happened?

_____

_____

Now that you have the Scripture as the setting to our story, let's begin.

THE MIRACLE CHRISTMAS JAR

Christmas is my favorite time of year. I'm a hopeless romantic about it. I love everything about Christmas, but most of all I love buying gifts. And like most people, the gifts I love buying the most are the ones for my children.

However, something happened a few years ago that completely changed Christmas for our family. David and I began a prayer experiment. We didn't intend for the experiment to change our holiday celebration, but as we discovered, that was precisely what God had in mind.

I had just been introduced to a new way to look at Matthew 16:19. In that verse Jesus says: "I will give you the keys of the kingdom of heaven; and whatever you shall bind on earth shall be bound in heaven, and whatever you shall loose on earth shall be loosed in heaven."

It was suggested that we bind our minds, hearts, wills, and whole lives to Jesus Christ and loose ourselves—through prayer—from wrong thinking patterns, actions, and attitudes.[1]

In preparation for this study, I found Jesus, in John 15, describing Himself as the vine that gave life. In fact, He said all life was in Him and unless we were bound to Him to receive His life, no fruit would come from our lives. We could do nothing. When I put the two concepts together, it seemed clear that I should pray that God would bind me to Himself so that His own life could flow freely through me and that I should ask God to "prune" or loose me from fleshly attitudes and actions. I decided I would try praying this way for a few months to see what would happen. We didn't have to look far to find out where to start.

David and I had made a lot of progress in obeying God with our finances, but we knew God wasn't finished working in that area of our lives. So we agreed to separately and privately begin praying the "binding" and "loosing" prayers concerning our attitudes and actions concerning money.

We asked God to bind our minds to His mind, our hearts to His heart, our wills to His will, and our lives to His purpose specifically concerning finances. We asked Him to loose us and set us free from the love of money, and every wrong attitude and habitual pattern of thought concerning money. Though we prayed expectantly, we had no idea where this prayer experiment would lead.

The first thing He convicted me about was the grocery store. I wanted to say, "Lord, not the grocery store!" But I couldn't get away from His gentle, yet convicting nudge that I was being self-indulgent at the grocery store each week. You see, I'm a spender and David is a saver. As a result, we tended to try to fix each other by becoming extreme in our own prejudice. I would spend to keep him from hoarding and he would save to keep me from being self-indulgent.

Somehow our efforts to change each other had only brought disharmony in an otherwise harmonious relationship. So naturally, God started with me in the area of over-spending on food.

Because David never goes to the grocery store, he doesn't know how much food items cost. I used that to my advantage. We had to have food. He couldn't argue with me there, so I satisfied my fleshly self-indulgence at a place where he wouldn't hold me accountable…the local supermarket.

At my grocery store you can practically buy tires! You can buy make-up and drug items and get the cleaning done. You can get pictures developed, buy stationery, gift items, and T-shirts. You can rent movies and buy books and…oh yes, get food that's already cooked, along with organic veggies flown in from the islands.

I had become a "leak in the boat" of our finances as I swamped our budget with expensive trips to the grocery and discount stores. Of course, that caused my cautious husband to want to save (yes, hoard) even more.

As God dealt with me about my spending, I was pierced by overwhelming conviction about being honest with David. If I was really going to be set free from the wrong attitudes and actions about money and let Christ's thoughts flow unhindered through my mind, I had to confess my sins to my husband. I'm ashamed to say how difficult it was for me to be brutally honest about my secret spending sprees. Yet I finally mustered my courage and poured out my heart to David.

He responded with confessions of his own about over-saving and faithlessly overprotecting the family. That day, real revival began at our house. But it didn't stop there.

OUR CHRISTMAS MIRACLE

I hate math. So not surprisingly, I'm terrible at it. David, on the other hand, is a geophysicist and was a math minor in college. Nevertheless, God led me to put a budget on the computer that would enable us both to track spending and saving. That budget was like a miracle. As soon as it was all on paper, there were no arguments. Our financial picture was no longer an idea or belief, it was a fact. It was crystal clear what we could and could not spend and save. We even realized that without leaks in the boat, we had a small surplus each month.

It was with that surplus that God began to work our Christmas miracle.

As I said before, I love buying Christmas gifts for my children. For years it was my main occupation in November and December. But this year was to be different.

I clearly sensed God leading me to put the surplus from our budget into a jar. It was to be a jar like the one in 2 Kings 4:1–7. That was the jar of the widow who gathered empty vessels and poured the oil out of her own jar until it filled every vessel. It would be a jar that we were to pour out of at Christmas.

I had no idea where God was leading me with this, but I obediently cleaned out a mayonnaise jar, put a little tinsel around the top, and set it in the middle of the kitchen table. At the end of the next pay period, I took the surplus left in the checking account, got it in cash, and put it in the jar. I knew how much money was in the jar and it wasn't much. In fact it was one-tenth of what we usually spent on Christmas. I couldn't imagine having much of a Christmas with what was in that jar.

I started preparing our daughters for the likelihood that Christmas that year would be lousy. In fact, I actually think I said, "Girls, this year, Christmas is going to stink." My attitude was pitiful. But I was determined to stick with God's plan, even though I thought He was being a real killjoy.

At that time, I taught piano lessons, so I took the money I earned from the lessons and put it in the jar also. As every two weeks rolled around, the surplus was added, and the jar began to gradually fill.

With our prayer experiment still underway, I began to feel impressed by God to purchase only three gifts for each of my daughters. I had recently heard someone say, "If three gifts were enough for God's Son, three gifts are enough for our children as well." Though it stung, I knew that comment was for me. With so little to buy, I finished the whole shopping list for the girls in one short afternoon.

As I placed the nine wrapped gifts under the tree, I thought, "Okay, God, it looks a little skimpy, but if that's what You want…" and with a sigh I indulged in a brief pity party.

The next morning in my time alone with God, I had barely started praying when I sensed the Lord saying to me, "The rest of the gifts are in the house." I thought, "Oh great! Now I'm making up stuff and calling it prayer. This can't be God trying to speak to me." But the more I tried to "get serious" and pray, the stronger the impression that I was hearing correctly.

So I began a conversation with God. "Lord, I don't get it. What do You mean, 'The gifts are in the house'?"

"Go get the quilt that your grandmother made and wrap it up for Stephanie." Stephanie had been eyeing that quilt and had already asked for it.

I had refused her, saying, "When I die you'll get the quilt. I love that quilt!" So this was where I was to begin. I took down the soft, warm quilt that had been lovingly stitched by Grandmother, and wrapped it up for our Stephanie.

Next, I distinctly heard in my heart, "Give Danielle the wedding bowl." I knew the bowl immediately. It had been given as a wedding gift to David's grandmother in 1915. It was an exquisite, delicate, hand-painted china bowl. I began wrapping it gently for my Danielle. Brittany's gift was to be a quilt square from another great-grandmother to be placed in the frame that had been made from wood taken from David's grandparent's barn.

Now we had three gifts under the tree that were big and mysterious. The excitement in our house grew. So did the joy in my heart.

After that, the gift ideas began to pour in. While cleaning out some lingerie drawers (that's right, since I wasn't at the malls, I was so bored I was cleaning out sock drawers!), I came across three little boxes. Each box contained a little pearl and diamond drop necklace. I had bought them for the girls one year for Easter when David's business had boomed. The girls had been five, seven, and nine at the time. I had carefully packed them away and had promptly forgotten all about them. When I rediscovered them, I heard a still, small voice say, "There is the jewelry for the girls for Christmas!" I quickly wrapped each little box and added it to the growing collection under the tree.

Danielle had a boyfriend with whom we felt close enough to exchange gifts. I wondered out loud in prayer one morning, "Lord, what do I get him?"

Immediately I remembered my Beatle record collection. I still had some old 45 records that I instantly knew would be a hit with this young man. (Who, by the way, is now my son-in-law.)

Our God is so wonderful. He even found a way to indulge my love of Christmas shopping. I had time that year to do the Christmas shopping for a family whose child was in the hospital. It was so much fun to purchase and wrap each gift for them. And then on Christmas Eve, David and I took baskets of homemade bread and fresh coffee beans to two families—one Hindu and one Muslim—with whom we had been establishing a growing relationship.

Resurrection in a Jar

Just before going to bed the night before Christmas, I sensed that it was time to get the jar. Each gift had been purchased with money from that little glass container. We had even spent double our usual budget on our parents. But money was still in the jar. I was curious to see just how much remained.

David had only asked for one thing. David has the gift of giving. He had asked me to save out some money from Christmas so he could give it to several ministries he wanted to support. I had thought to myself, "There won't be any left, because there is hardly anything there to start with!" But I answered with a pessimistic, "We'll see."

When I started counting the money in the jar that Christmas Eve, I was shocked. There was $100 dollars more in the jar than we had started with. I didn't know how it had happened, only that we had put in the surplus and taken out what was needed to be obedient. Tearfully, I put the bills and change into a Christmas card to my faithful, servant husband and went to sleep with a full heart.

Christmas morning I was bursting with joy. I got the girls up early. I couldn't wait to open the gifts. They opened the first three gifts with the usual, "Oh, thanks, Mom and Dad" and laid each gift aside. Then Stephanie opened the package with the quilt inside. Tears sprang to her eyes as she instantly realized what that gift meant to me. We both had to cry a bit as we hugged warmly. Danielle opened the gift containing the beautiful bowl with "Oh, Mother!" and Brittany tore into her framed quilt square and flashed us her famous dimpled grin.

Christmas had just taken on new meaning. They understood the sacrifice behind each gift and somehow, our gift exchange moved up to a higher plane.

David had even gotten into the spirit of that year's gift giving. He dug out three articles of his clothing the girls had begged for. He still had a belt and a jacket from the '70s that were now collector's items! One of the girls had begged for his old—now fashionably—holey jeans. His gift wrapping was vintage David. He used about four different kinds of paper on each one, taping it all together in a hodgepodge of color. The girl's eyes glistened as they unwrapped the treasures from their father.

I'll never forget the looks of happy surprise on their faces as they opened the little pearl and diamond necklaces. They had forgotten the jewelry even existed. Stephanie recently wore that precious little drop on her wedding day.

Then when they got to one giant gift addressed to all three, I had to explain. "This is a gift for the future. It's for all three of you to share."

They unwrapped my old doll trunk containing my dolls dressed in the garments each girl had worn home from the hospital. I had had a ball washing and mending each little outfit and putting them on my Chatty Kathy doll, my Revlon doll, and my Tiny Tears. "Girls, these gifts are for your little girls. You might even want to let them wear your outfits home from the hospital themselves!" We all had a good laugh and cry as we thought about that.

We were to the end of the packages and it was time to give David the gift only I could give. I took the envelope from the tree where I had placed it and handed it to him ceremoniously. He slowly opened the heavy envelope and as the money spilled out he read the card. Tears formed in his eyes and trickled down his cheeks. And, of course, we all joined him. He thanked me with a hoarse voice choked with emotion.

When I thought I couldn't contain any more joy, my twenty-year-old Danielle gave me a special gift.

As you know, she and I had struggled through the final years of her teens with an unaccustomed gap in our relationship. It had been healed in stages, but we weren't quite yet on the same page. That Christmas morning, after all the gifts had been presented, she said, "Mom, I have a gift to give."

Without another word, she came and got in my lap. She wrapped her arms around me and snuggled into my neck whispering words of love and asking for forgiveness. I totally lost it. With sobs we embraced and forgave and loved and were restored.

I have never experienced a day quite like that one. God released His resurrection life into our family. Where there had been deadness, there was now new vitality and joy. We experienced revival as a family. By choosing to die to the old way of thinking and acting, we got to experience the resurrection life of Jesus.

And it all began with an experiment in prayer during one Christmas season.

Lord, You are an awesome God. I know You want me to experience life fully and abundantly.
Forgive me for grasping to meet my own needs.
Lord, I open my hands to let go of what I have so I can take hold of what You offer.
I pray this in Jesus' name. Amen.

UNIT 8

Talk about your holiday celebrations as a family. What traditions do you want to keep? What needs to be revamped or eliminated?

Read my Christmas story to the family and get their reactions. Would your family be willing to begin praying now about how to celebrate?

UNIT 9

THE PRINCIPLES OF THE FRUIT: RIPENING TO MATURITY

MOTHERING SKILL: FAMILY DEVOTIONS

DAY 1
SEATED

DAY 2
SEEKING AND SETTING

DAY 3
STANDING

DAY 4
SUBMIT

DAY 5
THE SWORD

You want to live a lifestyle of love, joy, peace, patience,
kindness, goodness, faithfulness, gentlenes, and self-control.
But there's a battle for your mind and now you need a strategy to win.

UNIT 9
Bible Study Listening Guide

1. The key Bible verse is:

_____

_____

_____

_____

2. The illustration used to help me remember the lesson was:

_____

_____

3. What are the two parts of the ascension principle?

   A. _____

   B. _____

4. What I personally need to remember from this lesson is:

_____

MotherWise Group Prayer Requests

1._____

2._____

3._____

4._____

5._____

UNIT 9

MOTHERING SKILLS DISCUSSION:

Family Devotions

Challenge: To commit yourself to a season of meaningful, workable family devotions.

We often want to get the family together to have meaningful devotions, but many times the reality is far from our dream.

What is your goal for family devotions?

_____

_____

What did you like/dislike about the devotions your family did or did not have as you grew up?

_____

_____

What will be the greatest challenge you face in trying to establish or maintain family devotions?

_____

_____

Tools to Meet the Challenge:

Together at Home; A Proven Plan to Nuture Your Child's Faith and Spend Family Time, Dean and Grace Merrill (Wheaton, Ill.: Tyndale House, 1996).

52 Fun Family Devotions: Exploring and Discovering God's Word, Mike Nappa and Amy Nappa (Minneapolis, Minn.: Augsburg Fortress Publications, 1994).

Josh McDowell's One Year Book of Family Devotions, Josh McDowell and Bob Hostetler (Wheaton, Ill.: Tyndale House, 1997).

Family Walk: Love, Anger, Courage and 49 Other Weekly Readings for Your Family Devotions, Bruce Wilkinson (Grand Rapids, Mich.: Zondervan Publishing, 1991).

Family Traditions That Last a Lifetime, Karen M. Ball and Karen L. Tornberg (Wheaton, Ill.: Tyndale House Publishers, Inc., 1993).

Some points to remember are:

- Make a rock solid commitment to your family time. Be creative as you work around your challenges. Don't let illness or fatigue keep you from Family Night.

- Keep it light-hearted and fun for at least 75% of the time. Start with the fun stuff.
- Use variety in the places you eat (backyard, living room, out to eat, bedroom, by the fireplace—if you have one).
- If the kids suggest something unique for Family Night, let them lead. Go along with their plan if at all feasible.
- Get each of your children their own copy of the Bible and get the same version for everyone in the family.
- Form a circle with the family when it's time to share and talk about spiritual things. Each person needs to be able to see the others.
- Keep a folder in the file cabinet or on the computer for Family Night ideas. Keep your eyes open to new ideas. These will come at odd moments, so have a place to store them for future reference. You may find some great stories in Christian magazines that would be good openers for family discussions.
- Name your family devotions. Ours was called "Family Night." You might name yours something else. But it needs designation. When the name is mentioned, it should evoke memories in each family member's mind. Have a theme song. We had several. They were "Open Our Eyes, Lord," "This Little Light of Mine," and "Jesus, I Adore You." We sang them for years as a family. I still get misty when I hear them because I envision three little girls' faces shining in candlelight, sweetly singing the melodies.
- Family time is a way to communicate to our children, "We belong to one another. We're in this together. We can face anything if we face it as a united group. You are a part of something special."[1]

DAY 1

Seated

BEGIN WITH PRAYER

Since the Lord is standing at the door of your heart knocking,
answer the "door" by asking Him to come into every room in your heart today.

THE PARADE

It has been said that there once was a little boy who wanted to see the parade but he was too short. He found a knothole in the fence and put one eye up to it so he could see. He began to complain to his mother. There were not any clowns. Everyone told him there would be clowns and there weren't any!

Even though the mother assured the little boy that the clowns would be along later in the parade, he wouldn't believe her. All he could see were floats. To him that's all there was. The mother looked over the fence and said, "I see the clowns. They are way at the back of the parade route. Just wait. They'll come." But the boy still cried and would not believe.

The mother had an idea. She grabbed the boy's hand. Behind them was a two-story house. She took the boy to the door and requested permission of the family living there to take her son to the upstairs balcony.

From that vantage point, the boy's eyes began to open wide. There before him was the entire parade. What he had seen from the knothole was only a tiny glimpse of the truth about the parade. There were the clowns and horses and cars and floats. He could see from the beginning of the parade all the way to the end.

THE PRINCIPLE OF THE FRUIT: THE ASCENSION PRINCIPLE

We have studied the principle of the shears—the crucifixion principle, and the principle of the bud—the resurrection principle. Now we are ready for the next step. It's time to study the principle of the fruit—the ascension principle.

Let's review briefly. When you accepted Christ, your old sinful nature died and was buried with Him. That is what happened in the past. Now, in the present, you are daily learning to take your flesh to the cross. That is the crucifixion principle.

When you accepted Christ, your new righteous nature was created and you were born all over again as a new creation. You have a new inner self. This is the real you. This is who you are. This is your identity. In your daily living, after a flesh area has been taken to the cross, you experience new life, Jesus' life, in that area. You have freedom where once you were in bondage. That is the resurrection principle.

When you accepted Christ, you were seated with Him in heavenly places where your real self resides. This is *where* you are.

In your daily life, you can maintain freedom and victory over the flesh by realizing your heavenly position. Because you are in Christ, you know that you are in a position of authority over Satan and his dominion. You can live a life of victory over the flesh, Satan, and the world. As a joint-heir of Jesus Christ, seated with Him in heavenly places, your work as a Christian is prayer that involves praise, sacrifices of thanksgiving, and spiritual warfare. Your life is to flow with the fruit of the Spirit because of your union with Christ. That is the ascension principle.

Let's review what we've learned.

PAST: Concerning my spirit	PRESENT: Concerning my soul	FUTURE: Concerning my body
PRINCIPLE OF THE SHEARS: CRUCIFIXION PRINCIPLE		
At the time of salvation, our "old inner man" in Adam was crucified and died.	I "die daily" as I take my flesh to the cross where I crucify it, putting it to death.	Someday I will die physically.

PAST:	PRESENT:	FUTURE:
Concerning my spirit	**Concerning my soul**	**Concerning my body**

PRINCIPLE OF THE BUD: RESURRECTION PRINCIPLE

At the time of salvation, my brand new "inner man" was created. I am a new creature in Christ. I am deeply loved by God.	After an area of flesh has been put to death, I begin to change as my mind is reprogrammed. I experience new life and freedom where once I was in bondage.	Someday my body will rise from the dead to be with Jesus Christ.

PRINCIPLE OF THE FRUIT: ASCENSION PRINCIPLE

At the time of salvation, I was seated with Christ in heavenly places far above all of Satan's dominion and power. All of the fruit of the Spirit is available to me because of Christ's life in me.	I can walk in freedom and victory over flesh, Satan, and the pull of the world by realizing my victorious position in Christ. As I allow Jesus to live His life in me, I exhibit the fruit of the Spirit.	Someday in my resurrected body, as the bride of Christ, I will rule and reign with Jesus for eternity.

You may be saying, "Denise, what in the world are you talking about? Have you lost your mind? What is this about the ascension principle? I'm very much right here on earth, thank you very much. My kids are whining, supper's burning, the phone is ringing, and my husband's coming home any minute. It doesn't feel like I'm seated with Christ in heavenly places."

I know how you feel. Been there. Done that. But I want you to look carefully at Scripture. Knowing not only who you are in Christ but also where you are in Christ can make a huge difference in living the Christian life victoriously or in constant defeat.

Do you battle with your body in over-eating or anorexia? Are you often in a "flesh war" with your husband about finances? Are your children constantly in trouble? Do you struggle with keeping your teens from being sucked in by the pull of the "world"? Are you ready for some biblical answers?

Read Ephesians 2:5–6.

What are the three things Christ did for us according to these verses?

1._____

2._____

3._____

How many times do you see the words "with Him" or "with Christ"?

_____

Read Colossians 3:1–4.

Where is Christ according to verse 1?

_____

Where are you according to verse 3?

_____

When Christ is revealed, who is going to be with Him?

_____

Where is He going to be?

_____

We know that Jesus is in heaven right now with His Father. He is sitting on His throne at the right hand of God. If you are in Christ, you are there, too. Are we talking about your earthly body? No. We are talking about your newly created spirit; your "inner being" who is that deep, personal you. How can you be in two places at the same time—both on earth and in heaven? Your spirit is eternal and it isn't limited to space and time. Earthly bodies are stuck with calendars and watches and maps so they know where and when they are. Our spirits aren't so limited.

Okay, so what if this is really true. What difference does it make when you've got a job to do, kids to carpool, supper to cook, homework to supervise, and errands to run?

Knowing where you are in Christ gives you a different vantage point in two critical areas.

First, it gives you a different perspective from which to view the daily events of your life. Remember the little boy at the parade? We need to learn (or if you already know this, be reminded) that we live on a plane above our earthly circumstances. We are not just flesh and blood limited to an earthly point of view, we are spirit beings recreated in Christ who at the moment live on earth in bodies.

We are seated with Christ in heavenly places, and the stuff of this earth—both the irritating stuff and the fun stuff—is temporary and passing. Most of it doesn't have an eternal significance. We need to focus on the eternal and let most of the rest slide off our backs.

Do you see how this could affect you when the baby's sick and you miss your meeting? Or your child's team loses the ball game because of the referee? Or your husband's late and doesn't see the kids before they go to bed? Or your teenager wrecks the family car?

If you are only here to be comfortable on earth, those things are really going to get to you. You will get irritable and cranky at best or blow up in a rage at worst. But if you know that you are seated with Christ in heaven and at the same time inhabiting a body for the purpose of bringing His kingdom and His will to the earth, you will see each of those scenarios as an opportunity to be an open channel for Jesus to bring His kingdom rule to earth.

When the baby's sick and you miss your meeting, you will let go of your agenda and listen to what the Father wants to tell you in the quiet day at home. When your child loses the ball game, you will look to see what God is working into your child's life (and yours) with the frustration. Is it kindness and goodness in the face of oppostion?

When your husband is late and misses seeing the children before they go to bed, you will recognize that God is calling you to exercise the grace of forgiveness and unconditional love when you think it might not be deserved. When your teenager wrecks the family car, you'll know the confidence of expressing patience and wisdom in dealing with the crisis.

The second benefit to knowing who and where you are in Christ is that it gives you a different perspective on your position of authority over Satan and his dominion. Since you are seated with Christ in heaven where He has been exalted and has completely defeated Satan, you no longer have to be defeated by the deception and undermining work of the devil. You can confidently go to battle for yourself, your husband, and your children knowing that you are an overcomer because you are in Christ.

Read 2 Corinthians 4:7–18.

What are some of the difficult things that can happen to Christians according to verses 7–9?

_____

_____

What evidence of the crucifixion and resurrection principles do you find in verses 10–14? Copy the phrases here.

_____

_____

What's happening to your "outer man"—your body?

_____

What's happening to your "inner man"—the real you, your spirit?

_____

Why shouldn't we focus on the irritations of daily life, according to verse 17?

_____

To keep from focusing on the daily small stuff, what are we supposed to do according to verse 18?

_____

Now is it beginning to make sense? When we know who we are and where we are, we can put the events of our daily lives and the lives of our children and grandchildren into proper perspective. We can see them as events that God uses to produce character in us. He is training us—His body, His bride—to rule and reign with Him forever. Our time on earth is the schoolroom for our training and development.

Read Ephesians 1:20–23.

How high is Jesus' throne?

_____

_____

Jesus' throne in heaven is far above all the satanic rulers and powers. They are all in subjection to Him. The language of the Bible is that they are "under His feet." You can picture Jesus with His foot on Satan's neck! What is under His feet?

_____

What is the organic relationship between Jesus and the church?

_____

Our organic relationship with Jesus is that He is the Head of the church and we are the body. It is not just an agreeable relationship, it is organic and vital to life. Neither can function without the other. They are one.

Because we are one with Christ and part of His actual body, we have authority over Satan through Christ. We are heirs with Christ. We do not have to stand for Satan's harassment and oppression. The devil does not rule over us. We are more than conquerors over him through Jesus Christ.

Read Romans 8:37.

How do we conquer?

_____

Reread Romans 8:31–39.

I want to revisit this passage in light of your mothering. Paul asks, "Who will bring a charge against you? Who is the one who condemns? Who will separate us from the love of Christ?"

Satan loves to harrass mothers with these three questions. It is so easy to be made to feel guilty about our mothering. His charge against you will sound something like, "You are a lousy mother. You always scream at your kids. You never discipline them correctly. You are a failure."

In answer to that charge, Paul says, "It is God who justifies." In other words, the truth is, you may have raised your voice in anger at your children today. You may have sinned against them. But one incident doesn't make you a lousy mother. Your behavior does not make you a success or failure. If you are in Christ, you are totally accepted by God and a valuable person regardless of your behavior. You are justified.

Of course you need to confess your sin to God and to your children, repenting and asking for forgiveness. But that one behavior does not determine who you are. Satan's charge of "lousy mother" is a lie. If you are in Christ, you are the body and bride of the Lord Jesus Christ. You are a mother full of the virtues of Jesus Christ.

Satan's attacks usually give you a vague over-all feeling of depression, despair, and of being a failure. But when the Holy Spirit convicts you of something, it is specific and clear. He will shine His holy light on a particular area of sin and flesh in your life that needs confession and cleansing.

The second question Paul asks is, "Who is the one who condemns?" Satan would surely like to try. He may condemn you with, "You let your child down on one of the biggest days of her life. How could you do such a thing? What a terrible mother you are."

Paul's answer is in essence, "Your sin that deserved the death penalty got what it deserved! It has been paid for! Christ Jesus died for it. But now He has conquered sin and the death penalty each sin deserves. He has risen. He is at the right hand of God. He is there praying for you."

The reason Satan can get to us, is that the lie he is whispering in our ear is a half-truth. We did mess up. We did let our child down and we know it. If we allow him to, however, Satan will use that sliver of truth to paralyze us. We can get stuck in either a self-condemning, self-torturous mode, or in a self-protective cover-up. Neither leads to freedom. Both lead to bondage.

The path of freedom is open to us if we openly confess to our Father when we sin and walk in the flesh. Openly admit that you *are* a failure as a mother in your own strength. But your own strength is not the power source of your life. The truth about who you are in Christ is that you have been crucified with Christ and it is no longer you who are living, but Christ who lives His life in you. The temporary flesh setback was a behavioral problem, a sin, which is not the essence of who you are—your identity.

If Satan can't defeat you with the first two questions, he may try the third, "Who will separate us from the love of Christ?" Satan's attack may come as a whiny little voice that goes like this: "Have you noticed how you give and give and give and nobody gives back? You do all the loving and caring in your home, and no one returns it. You cook and wash and clean and work. You dry tears and wipe up blood and give a listening ear. You coddle and love all day long, but there isn't anyone loving you. You need to do something for yourself for a change. You need to take charge of your life. Maybe you should just leave them and get your own life."

If you fall for that line, you will end up either in a major pity party or angry and defiant. You might even leave the very ones God has called you to serve. Or maybe you're the type of person who doesn't get mad, you just get even.

Will feeling sorry for ourselves or vengeance or independence solve the problem? Will everyone drop what they are doing and start filling your love bucket? I seriously doubt it. Will a new, independent lifestyle meet all your needs? Most who've tried it have lived to regret it.

So what is Paul's answer? Read Romans 8:35–39. Copy verses 38–39 here.

_____

_____

_____

_____

Paul reminds Christians that we are not going to live in a bed of roses. We will encounter tribulation, distress, persecution, famine, nakedness, peril, and maybe even a sword. In fact, he says we are "put to death all day long like sheep waiting to be slaughtered." Then he almost screams the answer!

IN ALL THESE THINGS WE OVERWHELMINGLY CONQUER! How? Through the love of our Jesus. Absolutely nothing that our families or the world or Satan can throw at us will separate us from Christ's love. Nothing. Nada.

We are loved to our absolute toenails. We are loved from the tip of our heads to the bottoms of our feet. It doesn't depend on perfect performance on our part. It depends on Jesus.

Can you see how these truths impact your mothering?

If you are a guilt-ridden, defeated, depressed, dejected mom, how are you going to rear healthy, strong children? You can't! The sins of the fathers (and mothers) will be passed on from generation to generation. But you can stop that cycle. You can be the first generation who knows who you are, where you are, why you are, and teaches those truths to your children!

Read John 16:33.

Since we have a heavenly position in Christ, did He promise us a trouble-free life?

_____

Read 1 Corinthians 15:57.

What do we have because of Christ?

_____

Read Revelation 1:5 and 17:14.

What are Jesus' titles?

_____

Who is with Jesus in the battle?

_____

Now we are getting somewhere! Do you see, Mom, that you have an incredibly important role to fulfill? You are a warrior with Jesus in doing spiritual battle.

Every Christian mother should know that Satan has an agenda against her child. It is outlined in John 10:10. He comes to steal, kill, and destroy. We don't have to be afraid of a "devil behind every bush," but we also don't want to lose our children to Satan's schemes.

Because of our position in Christ, we can pray from a heavenly perspective for our children and our husbands. We can pray a hedge of protection around them. We can pray that God's will be done and His kingdom's rule be established in their lives. We can bind them to Christ and loose them from satanic influences, from their own fleshy attitudes and actions, and from the world's pull on their lives. We can pray that the blood of Jesus, the name of Jesus, and the Word of God will save them, protect them, and anoint them.

For the rest of this week, we will study prayer. We will examine prayer from the perspective of the ascension principle. In other words, we'll look at it from a heavenly perspective.

I'm praying for you as you study this unit. David and I have prayed that every woman who picks up this book will have the eyes of her heart flooded with light so that she can know the truth and that the truth will set her free. I have no illusions that my words will change your life and make you a better mother. But I have complete faith in my Jesus Who will bring the work He has begun in your life to full completion.

Prayer

Lord, enable me to grasp my position with You in the heavenly places.

Open my heart to the truth. Show me this week what a difference this truth will make in my mothering.

I pray this in Jesus' name. Amen.

Mothering Tip

If your child plays sports, is in a club, or just attends class, he eventually will be hurt emotionally or wronged by a teacher, coach, or student. When that happens, practice the principle you learned today. Stop, pray, and ask God for a heavenly perspective before you say even one word. More often than not, you should remain quiet and allow your child to learn character-building life lessons: forgiveness, humility, etc. The big picture of his life is so much more important than the little stuff. Spend much time in prayer, and get the counsel of your husband before you consider going to the school to protect your child.

I want to share some stories from our three children. Each of them went through a very difficult situation at school that tempted me to run to protect them.

Danielle was in eighth grade when her school took the students on an out-of-town field trip. A few days before they left, each student was given the opportunity to write down three names of people they wanted for a roommate. Not one child in the whole grade level wrote Danielle's name. Somehow, she found out about it. When she came home and told me, she was sobbing so hard her face was swollen. Of course, I cried along with her. I didn't say much, I just hugged her and stroked her hair and told her I was sorry it happened.

Of course, inside, I wanted to choke every girl in her class, but I kept quiet. I wanted to go to the school to fix it, but knew it was the wrong thing to do.

Danielle and I prayed daily that God would show her what to do and that He would be very near her during this hurtful time.

She did get paired with some girls for the trip and when she came home, she told me the most amazing thing. She said, "Mom, Jesus taught me something on this trip I could not have learned any other way. He taught me that people will always let me down, but He never will. He will never leave me alone."

It cost us all dearly, but we saw Danielle take a giant step spiritually that day. If I had "corrected" the problem, she would have missed the powerful truth about Himself that God was trying to teach her.

Stephanie was a junior in high school when she tried out for the yearly musical. It was important to her to get a good part. She had been in the show year after year and really thought it was her turn for a special role. But when she came home from school the day the cast list was posted, her face was ashen. She had lost the running for a major part. In fact, it was a musical where most of the girls got to wear cute little costumes, and her part was to wear a below-the-knees matronly suit and an unflattering hat. I had never seen her so hurt and angry.

Again, I wept with my daughter over her grief. I told her I was sorry and how much I loved her. Mostly I just let her vent "steam." Of course I wanted to talk to someone at the school just to let them know how hurt she was, but it would have been the wrong thing to do. It was tempting to tell her she didn't have to be in the play. She could just quit and not have to face the pain and embarrassment every day. But that also would have been wrong.

I watched Stephanie humble herself and go to rehearsal with a sweet spirit every day. When performance time came, she wore that costume and smiled. Stephanie learned humility and grace in a lesson plan I would never have chosen for her. But in God's plan, it was the exact thing that challenged her character and her faith.

Brittany's turn at character-building came her junior year in high school also. She had played volleyball since seventh grade, eagerly awaiting the day when she would play on varsity. As most-valuable player her freshman year, she thought being on varsity her junior year was a shoe in. Not so. She was placed on junior varsity for a second year.

When she came to tell me, I thought I was going to have to bury her. The mixture of hurt, humiliation, anger, and grief was almost overwhelming. It was so hard to see my baby hurt like that. Every "tiger mama" gene inside me wanted to rush into the coach's office and demand the reason. But I knew it would have been wrong. God had a huge lesson in humility to teach my daughter and I knew I must not get in the way.

Did that mean I preached the girls a good long sermon in the middle of their grief and set them straight? No! I'm their mom, not their Holy Spirit. I was there to cry with them and to wipe up their tears. But in those cases, it would have been wrong to stop the pain for immediate relief.

Your situations will be different, and yes, there are times to go to the school. Situations that are dangerous to your child's mind or body must be dealt with decisively. But tread carefully, Mom, when the hurt is your child's feelings. See if God has an unexpected lesson plan for your child's character.

DAY 2

Seeking and Setting

BEGIN WITH PRAYER

Be still and know that He is God.
It is He that has made you, and not you yourself.
Acknowledge that you are a sheep in His pasture.

Reread Colossians 3:1–4.

How often do you need to seek the Lord?

_____

Verse 2 tells us how to seek Him. Copy that verse here.

_____

_____

Picture yourself in a chair watching television. You have a remote control in your hand flipping through the channels.

Something comes on that you know a Christian should not watch. Using Colossians 3:1–4, what should you do and why?

_____

_____

_____

Setting your mind is a choice. You can choose to set your mind on your mind. If you do that you will go over and over a disturbing event and try to "fix it" in your mind. You may get involved in morbid introspection searching your mind for your own faults. Setting your mind on your mind is one version of setting your mind on the flesh.

You might set your mind on your feelings. If you do, you will have out your radar for every possible offense coming your way and you may react violently. If someone hurts your feelings it will consume you. You may sulk or lash back after every episode. Or you may feel inadequate because you have not performed perfectly. If you have your mind set on your feelings, you will probably waste untold hours beating yourself or being upset with others for hurting you. Setting your mind on your feelings is another version of setting your mind on the flesh.

Or you could set your mind on your own will. You may be convinced that you are right and you are never

UNIT 9

wrong and that no one will ever be able to change your mind. You may be so dogmatic in your "rightness" that your pride and stubbornness offends everyone around you. You may become rebellious against any authority that crosses your will if you have your mind set on your own will. Setting your mind on your own will is a third version of setting your mind on the flesh.

Read Romans 8:5–6. What is the principle given in these verses for the setting of our minds?

_____

_____

The principle is clear. We are to set our minds on the things of the Spirit, not on the flesh. We are chosen people who are seated with Christ in heavenly places. We have our minds set on things above.

Do you remember that in your childbirth classes they told you to get a focal point? You were instructed to get a picture or object on which you could focus your attention during delivery. They knew that if you could focus on something outside yourself, it would enable you to overcome the pain going on in your body.

This is a little of what it's like to focus your attention on the heavenly agenda instead of earth's. If you focus your eyes on Jesus' face, the difficult circumstances of earth will grow dim.

Read Matthew 16:21–23.

What was Jesus' strong rebuke to Peter about his mind?

_____

Read Matthew 4:10.

How had Jesus overcome this same temptation?

_____

Peter was doing what came naturally. His friend and teacher was talking about His impending death, and Peter was trying to make things easier on Jesus. He was being protective and comforting. But he had his mind set on an earthly channel, not on a heavenly one. It completely ruined his perspective.

Jesus rebuked Peter for thinking in terms of the present, earthly moment instead of the eternal perspective of heaven. Oh, Mother! I wonder how often we protect and comfort our children away from God's great plan for their lives. We must begin to live from an ascension perspective. We must set our minds on things above, not on things on the earth.

Read Philippians 3:16–4:1.

List the attributes of the enemies of the cross of Christ.

_____

_____

_____

Did you catch the last one? Their minds are set on earthly things. Paul summarizes their offenses in that sentence. Their god is their appetite and their glory is their shame.

Take a moment to take stock of your wish list. What does it include?

_____

_____

_____

Is your list made up of earth stuff? Are you investing in the heavenly places?

Look at what Paul says in verse 20 about our citizenship. Where is home for us?

_____

Copy Matthew 6:33 here.

_____

_____

Read Matthew 6:25-33.

What are the earthly things we are tempted to dwell on?

_____

_____

What is Jesus' solution to that problem?

_____

_____

How much do you think Jesus worried about what He ate?

_____

_____

How much do you think Jesus worried about His clothes?

_____

_____

I cannot imagine Jesus worrying about His diet or His couture. I believe He was obedient in the way He ate and the way He dressed. I think His mind was on the kingdom work He had to do. He knew where He came from and where He was going and why. That enabled Him to stay focused and stay on task.

What practical way would help you start the process of setting your mind on the kingdom agenda?

_____

_____

_____

Prayer

Lord Jesus, I choose this day to seek You with all my heart and to set my mind on You.
Show me the starting place. Pierce my heart when I lose my focus. I am seated with You in heavenly places.
Never let me forget that truth! In Jesus' name. Amen.

Mothering Tip

The setting of your mind is a choice just like the radio or TV dial. To keep your mind fixed on heavenly things try one of the following:

Record the whole book of Philippians or Colossians or Romans 6–8 on a cassette tape and play it back while you are walking, driving your car, etc. You will memorize the whole book before you know it! This is an excellent way to set your mind on things above.

DAY 3

Standing

BEGIN WITH PRAYER

Ask God to put a hedge of protection around you as you study today.
Ask Him to lead you into all truth as you are diligent to study His Word.

As I was doing the research for this unit of study on the ascension principle, I began to see the direction the Scriptures were headed and I began to get uncomfortable. It seemed that the teaching on being seated with Christ in heavenly places, that encouraging and uplifting truth, was almost always accompanied by a discussion of victory over our enemy, Satan.

I thought to myself, "Oh, no, Lord. I just don't want to go there. There is so much division in Christianity over spiritual warfare and I'm not going to get into that. This is MotherWise and I don't want to scare the moms. Let's just keep it simple and sweet. Besides that, people who write about spiritual warfare become targets of Satan, and I'm not ready for that!"

I had been worried that I was falling behind schedule with the writing, so skimming over the top of the ascension principle seemed the way to hurry the process. I decided we'd just stick with the beautiful truth of our position in Christ and how we should keep our minds on Him. That would conclude our study of the ascension principle.

As I tried to continue writing after that little chat with God, I hit "writer's wall." I could barely remember my name! I had absolutely nothing to write about. It was like a thick, black velvet curtain fell in front of me.

I finally knelt down beside my chair in the study and got serious with my Lord. "Okay, Lord. I get it. Have it your way. I will begin the research into spiritual warfare." Thirty minutes after that prayer, the phone rang. It was the MotherWise Ministries office notifying me that I had been given an extension on my deadline! Now I had time to dive into the study of warfare to see how it applied to moms.

Within the first few minutes of my study, I had to stop and take a deep breath. It hit me that there is probably no group on the planet who needs to know how to stand against the schemes of Satan like mothers. We moms need a solid biblical understanding of our enemy and the enemy of our children in order to walk in victory. We do not have to watch helplessly as Satan devours our young! I became excited to learn how to fight for my children and how to teach you to fight for yours!

Read Ephesians 6:10–12.

Who is scheming against you?

_____

What are the four descriptive words of those who war against us?

1._____

2._____

3._____

4._____

At the end of verse 12 we are told where this battle is taking place. Where is it?

_____

Did you know you were on the front line of a battle? Because you belong to Christ Jesus and are seated with Him in heavenly places, you are involved in spiritual warfare whether you want to or whether you know it or not. If Satan can keep you ignorant of it, you will be easily defeated. If you are fearful of it, you will be ineffective at gaining victory. We've all got to take our heads out of the sand, Moms. Our children are worth it!

- Have your children been captured by the "world" and you don't seem to have any way to get them back?
- Do you have constant doubts about your salvation even though you've come to Christ many times asking for it?
- Have you ever been under a cloud of depression and you just couldn't seem to shake it?
- Do feelings of worthlessness and inadequacy overwhelm you?
- Are you often reminded of your past sins even though you've confessed them?
- Do wicked thoughts bombard your mind?
- Do you and your husband have a huge fight just before an opportunity of ministry?
- Have you ever thought of taking your life?
- Have you remembered that Satan has targeted your Christian family for destruction, while he leaves the non-Christians alone?[2]

Mother, is it becoming clearer that we have an enemy who is seeking whom he may devour? We need to take up the battle. We need to study God's Word.

Read Ephesians 6:13–18.

How can you resist Satan?

_____

What phrase does Paul repeat in verses 13 and 14?

_____

List the six things Paul tells us to do to stand firm.

1._____

2._____

3._____

4._____

5._____

6._____

To resist Satan we are to stand firm by strapping on the belt of truth. Where do we find truth? We find it in God's Word. Each day spend time drinking in the words of Scripture. It will enable you to stand against the enemy of your heart and your home.

Then we are to put on the breastplate of righteousness. If you are a believer in Jesus Christ, you have His righteousness covering your heart. You need to walk in His righteousness on a continual basis, obeying His Word. You are to put on the shoes He gives you—the shoes of the gospel of peace. You are to hold up your faith shield to quench the darts of the evil one. Your head is to be covered with the helmet of salvation and the sword of the Spirit is to be in your hand. Then you are to pray at all times with perseverance.

Read Ephesians 1:19–23.

What force raised Christ from the dead, seated Him in heavenly places above all rule and authority, and caused all things to be under Christ's feet?

_____

In what verse do you see the resurrection principle? When you find it, copy it here.

_____

_____

_____

_____

Compare Ephesians 1:21 with 6:12. What words do these verses have in common?

_____

In Ephesians 1:21 we might not realize who these rulers and powers were that are now in subjection under Christ's feet. But Paul explains in 6:12 that these are the demonic henchmen of Satan.

Knowing your enemy is the first step in gaining victory. So let's see what God's Word teaches us about Satan so we won't be ignorant of his schemes.

Read Genesis 3.

What is the descriptive word concerning Satan in verse 1?

_____

What did Satan cause Eve to doubt in verse 1?

_____

How well did Eve quote God's word? See a comparison of Genesis 3:2–3 and Genesis 2:16–17.

_____

What sin did Satan, disguised as the serpent, commit in verse 4?

_____

What did Satan cause Eve to doubt in verse 5?

_____

Satan is described as a crafty serpent. In the King James version, the phrase reads, "Now the serpent was more subtil than any beast of the field…" Our enemy is crafty and subtle. He is clever and sharp and deceptive. Satan caused Eve to doubt God's Word and God's character. He is a liar.

See John 8:44 to see how Jesus described Satan. Summarize it here.

_____

_____

To get an even more detailed picture of Satan's identity, look up the following Scriptures and write down a description of the enemy:

Job 1:7; 2:2 _____

1 Chronicles 21: _____

Matthew 13:19 _____

Luke 13:16 _____

Luke 22:31 _____

Acts 5:3 _____

Acts 10:38 _____

2 Corinthians 4:4 _____

2 Corinthians 11:14–15 _____

Ephesians 6:12 _____

1 Timothy 3:7 _____

1 Timothy 4:1 _____

2 Timothy 2:26 _____

1 Thessalonians 2:18; 3:5 _____

2 Thessalonians 2:9 _____

1 Peter 5:6–11 _____

Revelation 12:7 _____

Revelation 12:9 _____

The Hebrew word for *Satan* is spelled exactly like the English word. In Hebrew it means "opponent, the arch-enemy of good, adversary."[3] The word *devil* in Greek is "diabolos" and means "false accuser, devil, slanderer."[4] Are you beginning to get the picture of your enemy? His agenda is to blind you to the truth, to make you doubt God's Word, to deceive you, to plant lies in your head. If He can get you to believe a lie, He doesn't have to fool with you anymore. You will self-destruct eventually. Your false thoughts will become bad behaviors that will lead to destructive habits and you are trapped. Do you see why we must fight for ourselves and our families?

But don't you be afraid of Satan. Jesus absolutely overthrew all his power and authority when He went to the cross. Satan has no power over you because you are in Christ. You are God's own child. You are a kingdom woman. Don't let Satan mess with you!

Although it may seem that Satan has frightening power, read Job 1 and 2. According to Job 1:12 and 2:6, what is the limitation on Satan's power?

_____

_____

Study carefully and diligently this week. To stand firm against Satan, you must know who you are (God's child), where you are (seated with Christ in heavenly places), and why you are (an agent to bring God's kingdom onto the earth through faith, obedience, and prayer).

Prayer

Lord, You have Your foot on Satan's neck.
You have complete dominion and power over Satan's rulers, powers, authorities, and dominions.
You are King of kings and Lord of lords and my life is wrapped up in the bundle of Your life.
I am seated with Christ in heavenly places far over and above all these rulers and authorities.
You are my refuge and my rock. My God, in You will I trust. In Jesus' precious name I pray. Amen.

$\mathcal{M}$OTHERING $\mathcal{T}$IP

Twelve Scriptural Prayers to Pray for Your Children:

1. That they will know Christ as Savior early in life. (Psalm 63; 2 Timothy 3:15)

2. That they will have a hatred for sin. (Psalm 97:10)

3. That they will be caught when guilty. (Psalm 119:71)

4. That they will be protected from the evil one in each area of their lives: spiritual, emotional, and physical. (John 17:15)

5. That they will have a responsible attitude in all their interpersonal relationships. (Daniel 6:3)

6. That they will respect those in authority over them. (Romans 13:1)

7. That they will desire the right kind of friends and be protected from the wrong friends. (Proverbs 1:10–11)

8. That they will be protected from the wrong mate and saved for the right one. (2 Corinthians 6:14–17)

9. That they, as well as those they marry, will be kept pure until marriage. (1 Corinthians 6:18–20)

10. That they will learn to totally submit to God and actively resist Satan in all circumstances. (James 4:7)

11. That they will be single-hearted, willing to be sold out to Jesus Christ. (Romans 12:1–2)

12. That they will be hedged in so they cannot find their way to wrong people or wrong places and that the wrong people cannot find their way to them. (Hosea 2:6)[5]

DAY 4

Submit

BEGIN WITH PRAYER

Ask the Lord Jesus to put a hedge of protection around your heart and mind today.

Focus for a few moments on where you are seated with Christ in heavenly places.

Enjoy His presence.

Some of you may have skipped over yesterday's lesson because you are afraid. You don't want to read what the Bible says about Satan. It scares you and you don't want to be spooked. I can really relate.

But, Mom, that's your first clue that Satan is working on you. He is saying "boo" to scare you out of victory. He wants to keep you from knowing the real truth about him. He knows he is powerless over you, but if he can keep you frightened into running away from the truth about him, he can defeat you with your own fear.

Don't buy it. Study God's Word today. Allow the powerful, awesome, victorious Jesus Christ to lead you into balanced, pure truth that will lead you and your family to walk in freedom and victory.

Yesterday we looked at the identity of our enemy. That study should have opened your eyes to begin recognizing how your enemy works. Today I want you to begin by reading a passage from Isaiah that describes Satan's descent from heaven to hell (Sheol) after he sinned against God. I want you to especially pay attention to what Satan said about himself.

Read Isaiah 14:3–15.

In verses 13 and 14, what are the five things Satan claimed he would do?

1._____

2._____

3._____

4._____

5._____

What are the first two words of each of Satan's claims?

_____

Read Proverbs 16:18 and compare this verse with the five "I will's" of Satan. What was Satan's ultimate sin?

_____

List the words in verses 13 and 14 that describe *high* and *lofty*.

_____

_____

Satan's sin was pride. He wanted not only to ascend to God's throne, he wanted to usurp it! He wanted to go higher than God. He wanted to be on top of the heap. It was the sin of pride that caused his fall from heaven.

Read verse 15 and document God's penalty for his sin.

_____

_____

Would you stop in your study today to ask God an honest question? "Lord, is there a prideful attitude in me? Is there a pattern of thinking in my mind that is rooted in pride?" Then I challenge you to be very still in God's presence and listen to Him. Don't move about. Wait for Him to speak to you in a way you can understand Him and hear Him. If (but probably when) He brings something to mind that you need to confess to Him, take the time to deal with it now. Remember, confession is not saying "I'm sorry," it is saying, "I did it." Then comes repentance, that is, turning in the opposite direction from the sin.

Journal your findings after your quiet listening time.

_____

_____

_____

_____

Mom, the power to have a victorious life does not have its source on the inside of you. Remember, He is the vine—the source of all life—and you are the branch, a receptacle of that life. The power for life is only on the inside of you if it comes from Christ and Christ alone. The way, the truth, and the life has its root source in Christ and not some inner sense inside of you.

If someone tells you, "Find the truth within," they are repeating Satan's lie. No, the truth is not found within. The truth is on the outside of you and it has a name. Truth's name is Jesus. Isn't that comforting? You don't have to try to be God, knowing all. What a burden to think I have to be smart enough to know everything about everything so that everything will work out all right for everyone! I can't handle that! I am sure to make a mistake somewhere! Praise God, we have a God. He is all-wise, all-knowing, and everywhere present—all at the same time. Take a load off your back. Humble yourself and let God be God.

Read Isaiah 57:15 and copy it here.

_____

_____

_____

Where are the two places God dwells?

1._____

2._____

Read Matthew 18:4; 23:12; James 4:10; 1 Peter 5:5–6.

What is the common theme of these verses?

_____

Read 1 Peter 5:7–9.

Peter warns us to humble ourselves because _____

_____

Do you see the connection between our pride and our vulnerability to Satan's schemes? How do you think Peter knew this truth? (If you need help to answer, read Mark 14:27–31, 43–46, 54, 66–72.)

_____

_____

So today we have learned a valuable strategy against the enemy. We need to humble ourselves! If we harden our hearts and exalt ourselves, becoming "gods," we are an easy target for Satan. We have invited an attack. But if we humble ourselves, bowing before the throne of God and giving up all rights to ourselves and our opinions and our agenda, conceding control over our lives completely to Him, it shuts the door in Satan's face. He can't gain an easy entrance into our lives. That doesn't mean it's all over in the battle with Satan, but it is a good beginning.

One of the synonyms of *bow,* as in bow before the throne, is *submit.*[6] That's a dirty word to a lot of women. Me submit? Are you kidding? After your study today, I think you might be a little more open to reading Ephesians 5:22–33; 1 Peter 3:1–6; Colossians 3:18.

To whom is a wife to demonstrate submissiveness?

_____

Do you see any connection between Satan's sin and a wife's unsubmissive attitude toward her husband?

_____

When a wife humbles herself before God and chooses as an act of her will to submit herself to her husband, allowing him to take the leadership in the home, she has begun to defend her family against the schemes of the enemy. She has shut a major door in his face.

How do you submit? Start with asking your husband questions. The first question I asked David when I first began to learn to submit, (seven years into our very rocky marriage), was "May I call my mom long distance?" He nearly fell out of his chair! I had never asked his "permission" to do anything! That first question began a radical change in the way we related to each other.

David has assumed the responsibility for our family. I give him the leadership role and I support his leadership. I am not a dishrag, milquetoast wife. I always let him know my opinion about what we need to decide.

But he is the one who makes the final decision. It's clear-cut. It's biblical and it works.

What do you do if your husband won't take the lead? What if he likes for you to make all the decisions? If he's backed against the wall, squeeze in behind him. Tell him you want him to make the decisions and that you are going to wait for him to do so. Then be still and quiet and don't make a move until he does.

Is it always easy? Do I perfectly submit to my husband? Are you kidding? No, I certainly don't have it all down pat. I am on a journey like you are. But I know the liberating truth. My submission to God and to David is both an offensive and defensive weapon against Satan. It's offensive because it binds David and me closely together in unity and oneness. We don't have a constant civil war at our house. We can move on to other things like rearing our family and doing ministry. It is a defensive weapon because it doesn't give Satan a foothold in our lives. It is what I can do as a wife to become one with my husband and at the same time protect my family. The price is worth it.

Press on, Mother. Don't stop until you have studied God's Word so that you will know how to fully stand firm against the enemy.

Prayer

Lord, I do humble myself before Your throne. You alone are my God, my Lord,

my Master, my Savior. There is no one beside You who is perfect in power and authority. You are God and I am not.

I submit myself to my husband, Lord. I now yield to his leadership and position of authority in our home.

I make this prayer in the holy name of Jesus. Amen.

UNIT 9

Mothering Tip

This Saturday morning, watch cartoons designed for little children. Count the number of demonic, occultic, evil characters you see. Does it remind you of the Scripture in James about Satan like a roaring lion seeking his prey?

Watch a few music videos. Listen briefly to a rock radio station. Go into a toy store and count the number of toys with an evil seductive message.

Strategize on ways to protect your children. These "innocent" programs and products are targeted to kidnap your child. Stand firm against the enemy, Mom.

DAY 5

The Sword

BEGIN WITH PRAYER

Ask the Lord Jesus to teach you how to stand firm against the enemy.
Sit like a little girl at His feet today learning from Him.

We are going to finish today with our last look at Satan's tactics and then we will be ready to move on quickly to victory. I'm ready, aren't you?

Read Genesis 3:1–6 looking specifically for Satan's tactics and for Eve's response.

SATAN'S TACTIC: EVE'S RESPONSE:

_____   _____

_____   _____

_____   _____

_____   _____

_____   _____

Satan's first tactic was to speak to Eve. She responded by speaking back. First mistake, Eve! She should have refused having a conversation with him. What do we do when we are enticed by the enemy? Refuse to be entertained! If it comes in the form of a thought we know is not from God, we don't allow that thought any playing time in our minds.

When I am plagued by thoughts that are destructive, David will tell me, "You can't afford to think about that. Get your mind on something else." Often, I will turn on some praise music and start singing! We can refuse entrance to the wicked or fearful or destructive thoughts Satan hurls into our minds.

Second, Satan twisted God's words. Eve's response was an unsure, inaccurate rendering of God's words. She should have called Adam to come to her defense. He knew exactly what God had said and could have reminded her. She needed a clear, sharp, accurate articulation of God's Word. She needed her husband's authority.

If ever I find myself under a spiritual attack, I call out to David. When I can't even pray for myself, he prays for me. He helps me to get my perspective. He takes me back to God's Word. When we were first on this journey to know Christ better, he couldn't do that very well. But day by day, year by year, he has grown into his role as my spiritual leader. (By the way, my submission to his authority is what started *his* spiritual growth. I finally got out of the way so God could talk to him!)

Third, Satan's tactic to entice Eve was a direct lie mixed with a half-truth. It made it hard for Eve to know the difference. Satan said, "You surely shall not die!" That was a direct lie. Eve and her husband Adam would die—physically, spiritually, and emotionally. Then Satan said, "For God knows that in the day you eat from it your eyes will be opened, and you will be like God, knowing good and evil." Now that was a half-truth. Their eyes were opened all right. Their innocence was gone. They would now know the seamy side of life. But they would not be like God. That was the lie. He was enticing her to sin, the same sin he committed as recorded in Isaiah 14:3–15. He wanted her to sin the sin of pride.

What could Eve have done? She could have repeated the last thing God told her. The last instruction she had (through her husband) was "…from the tree of the knowledge of good and evil *you shall not* eat, for in the day that you eat from it you shall surely die" (emphasis mine). She should have quoted that over and over. And then she should have obeyed!

I wonder if Satan's last tactic was to look at the tree, licking his lips. I can just imagine his longing look at the tree and then a sly smile at Eve, another look at the tree and a raised eyebrow at her. He waited while all heaven and hell held its breath.

What could she do in that intense moment of indecision? Close her eyes! But Genesis 3:6 says she saw the tree—she looked. That was a serious mistake. By looking at the tree, the object of her temptation, she engaged her body in the path toward sin. Then the Scripture says she saw that the tree was good for food—it engaged her "thinker." I mean everyone has got to eat! It was only logical. "And a delight to the eyes" engaged her "feeler." It appealed to her aesthetic sensitivity. Now she was deeper down the path of destruction. "And desirable to make one wise" engaged her "chooser." Why wouldn't you choose to be wiser?

Now she was snared with her body, her mind, her emotions, and her will. She still had a way of escape. Close your eyes, Eve. Run, find Adam, Eve. Get out of there! But she didn't. She bit.

"She took from its fruit and ate; and she gave also to her husband with her…." When she ate the fruit in direct disobedience to God, she engaged her spirit in sin. Her spirit immediately died. Now Satan could use her as a pawn to get to the man. She was gorgeous and naked and seductively eating the fruit. She dominated Adam, leading him to his death and he followed.

Do you see the progression of Eve's sin? Did you see how many ways of escape were open to her? We do not have to be ensnared by Satan's schemes if we are believers. Jesus set the perfect example in the wilderness after His baptism.

Read Matthew 4:1–11.

Do you see the interesting paradox in verse 1? What did the Spirit do and what did the devil do?

_____

How did Jesus resist the devil according to verses 4 and 7?

_____

How did Jesus resist the devil according to verse 10?

_____

God allowed Satan to tempt Jesus in the wilderness. The devil only has the authority that God allows him to have. God is always in control. Jesus, the beautiful, strong Son of God flashed the sword of the Spirit, the Word of God, in His duel with Satan. Then, in the final blow, Jesus said, "Go, Satan!" and finished the fight with a powerful slash from the Word.

So how are you to defend yourself and your family against Satan? Do just what Jesus did. Memorize Scripture so that when you are under attack, it will spring from your heart. You'll be amazed at how the Holy Spirit can bring the right Scripture to your memory at the right time. But He can't enable you to recall what has not been filed away!

You can say, as Jesus said, "Go, Satan!" You are seated with Christ in heavenly places. It is a position of power and authority derived from your inheritance from the Father.

Read Revelation 5:9–10.

What has been done for you that gives you the authority to tell Satan, "Go!"?

_____

What did you learn today that will help you to stand firm against the enemy? What will you do to put it into practice?

_____

_____

Write out a prayer for your family that recognizes your newly discovered weapons in spiritual warfare.

_____

_____

_____

UNIT 9

Prayer

Lord, I am taking a firm stand against the enemy on behalf of my family. I ask You to shield and protect each one of us from Satan's attacks. You are our Shepherd and we shall not want for anything. You make us to lie down in green pastures and You lead us beside the still waters. You restore our souls. Guide us in the paths of righteousness for Your name's sake. Even though we walk through the valley of the shadow of death, we will fear no evil, for You are with us. Your rod and Your staff comfort us. You prepare a table before us in the presence of our enemies. You have anointed our heads with oil. Our cups overflow. Surely goodness and lovingkindness will follow us all the days of our lives and we will dwell in Your house forever. Amen.

Mothering Tip

Close the "door" to the enemy. Do not read horoscopes or astrology charts. Don't even do it for "fun." (See Deuteronomy 17:2–7.) Do not allow your children to do so. Destroy any astrology books or horoscope articles you have in the house. (See Acts 19:18–20.) Confess the sin of consulting spirits other than the one true and holy God our Father. Repent by turning away deliberately from it and turning to God.

Ask the Lord to reveal to you anything in your house that has allowed Satan to gain any access to you or your family. Remove it immediately and get rid of it permanently.

Thank God for the blood of Jesus that bought your victory in Christ. Ask the Lord Jesus to fill you and your family completely with His holy presence.

Reference

The Prayer Ministry of the Church, Watchman Nee (New York: Christian Fellowship Publishers, Inc., 1973).

UNIT

THE PRINCIPLE OF THE FRUIT: THE HARVEST

MOTERHING SKILL: MAKING MEMORABLE MOMENTS
(AND RECORDING THEM)

DAY 1
INVITATION TO LOVE

DAY 2
INSTRUCTION TO LOVE

DAY 3
INSPIRATION TO LOVE

DAY 4
INTIMATE LOVE

DAY 5
INESCAPABLE LOVE

The test of knowing if you are totally free comes when you can express unconditional love to those closest to you. That kind of love is what our families and friends need—especially when they least deserve it. In this concluding lesson, find the key to being a mom who is free to nourish her family with love.

UNIT 10
Bible Study Listening Guide

1. The object used to help me remember the lesson was:

_____

_____

2. The key Bible verse is:

_____

_____

_____

_____

3. What I personally need to remember from this lesson is:

_____

_____

_____

_____

MotherWise Group Prayer Requests

1._____

2._____

3._____

4._____

5._____

6._____

UNIT 10
MOTHERING SKILLS DISCUSSION:
Making Memorable Moments
(AND RECORDING THEM)

Challenge: To create meaningful times for our families and to document them in an easy, accessible format.

Most of us have stacks of pictures that aren't in albums and samples of our children's art wrinkled under mounds of magazines. How do we create happy "Kodak moments" for our families and then capture them for posterity? How do we handle family traditions at birthdays and holidays?

Which one memory do you want to leave with your children or grandchildren?

_____

_____

What is the best family memory from your childhood?

_____

What tradition does your family observe regularly?

_____

Which memory-making moment would mean the most to your husband and children?

_____

_____

How have you solved holiday hassles in a creative way?

_____

_____

_____

_____

UNIT 10

Tools to Meet the Challenge:

Let's Make a Memory: Great Ideas for Building Family Traditions and Togetherness, Gloria Gaither and Shirley Dobson (Dallas, Tex.: Word Books, 1994).

Let's Make a Summer Memory, Gloria Gaither and Shirley Dobson (Dallas, Tex.: Word Books, 1995).

15 Minute Family Traditions and Memories, Emilie Barnes (Eugene, Ore: Harvest House, 1995).

Memorable moments with your family can be as simple as watching a sunset and as elaborate as a long family vacation. I suggest that you ask your family what memories they have from your family get-togethers and make this a dinnertime conversation starter to see what you learn from each family member.

Then ask how each person would like to save those memories. Do they like to look at pictures? Can the family invest in a video camera? Do they want to draw pictures or write stories? Would they like to make a cassette tape of a happy memory some night at dinner?

Several companies have formed recently in the business of keeping memories in scrapbooks. Some families love to invest time and money on these kinds of projects. Others like to keep pictures in a box for simple filing. How do you like to keep memories?

_____

_____

One way our extended family created a lasting memory and recorded it was at one particular Thanksgiving holi-day. My ninety-year-old grandmother was very alert and spunky. We created a "set" with some wicker chairs and plants, gathered her great-grandchildren, turned on the video camera, and I "interviewed" her so she would start telling her stories. She had a phenomenal memory and could even remember an incident that happened when she was two years old.

She began to weave her tales of coming from Kentucky with her family of ten in a covered wagon all the way to Texas. She told us about Indians who came to their homestead and scared them to death. We all sat spellbound as she remembered events we had only read about in our history books. We will never forget that holiday. Now that she is gone, we have the videotapes to replay and pass on to our grandchildren.

DAY 1

Invitation to Love

BEGIN WITH PRAYER

Ask God to teach you something new about love this week.
Get still and quiet as you prepare for your study.

We have carefully examined the different aspects of vine life in our study of John 15. We discovered that Jesus is the vine where all the power of life resides. He is God; we are not. Then we looked at the branch, which represents us, and found that it must be empty in order to be filled. So we spent two weeks looking at our fleshy self-nature under the microscope to see what needs to be pruned out.

Just knowing what is wrong doesn't solve the problem. The problem has to be eliminated and we learned how to do that by taking our self-nature to the cross where it is not patched up, but is put to death. Once we have submitted to dying to our own way, a new, resurrected life can spring forth.

We saw that the bud of new life comes as our minds are transformed. New thought patterns replace old ones. And because new thoughts are in place, they give rise to new habits and behaviors. We change from the inside out. And then we learned how to maintain a more consistent walk with God. We learned that the first principle of the fruit is setting our minds on Him.

In this final unit of study, we will finish the section of John 15 concerning fruitfulness that is ripening to maturity and bringing forth the harvest.

Does a peach struggle and strain to become juicy and mature? No. It just stays attached to the branch where it receives a constant source of life-giving energy from the root. It abides.

In Galatians 5:22–23, we are given a specific list of the fruits of the Spirit. This list details the result of a life that is connected to the vine. A life that *receives* life instead of trying to *achieve* life.

List the nine different fruits given in Galatians 5:22–23.

1. _____

2. _____

3. _____

4. _____

5. _____

6. _____

7. _____

8. _____

9. _____

These are nine characteristics every mother wants to exhibit in her mothering. What mother doesn't want to have love, joy, peace, patience, kindness, goodness, faithfulness, gentleness, and self-control exuding from her being twenty-four hours a day, seven days a week? Of course, we do. And now we have discovered the key to mothering our children in the fruit of the Spirit. We don't work and strain and try to achieve those behaviors. We instead receive His love, joy, and peace and become so transparent that when our children see us they see Him. That is what it means to be free to be the mom God designed for us to be.

Let's look at the first "fruit" of the Spirit a little closer.

BIG RED HEART

Picture a very large, room-sized red heart on the floor. Imagine that it is the heart of God. If you step into the heart, you will be stepping into His heart of love. Have you ever thought what it would be like to immerse yourself in the Father-heart of God?

Read John 15:9.

Who started the loving?

_____

Who was the object of that original love?

_____

What two loves are compared in this verse?

_____

What is the invitation in this verse?

_____

Now we have come full circle to our love bucket. We began this series looking at our empty love buckets with dismay. Who will fill them? If we can't depend on our families to fill them, where will we go?

We go to the source. We don't scratch and claw to get our needs met, we sink ourselves down into the heart of God and draw up His love and His life into us. We now have what our hearts have so desired. We are filled with love because we are filled with Him. For us there is a steady constant source of love that never runs dry because He is love (1 John 4:8).

The fruit that is born comes from the overflow of vine-life energy. It is so full in the branch that it has no place to go but pours out in the form of fruit. The first fruit listed in Galatians is love.

Jesus said, "Just as the Father loved Me, I have loved you." Wow! How much does the Father love the Son? You cannot even imagine it. That is the same degree that the love of Jesus is poured out in you. You are loved. Stop just for a moment and drink that in.

The invitation is addressed to you. It reads, "Here is all the love you can possibly contain. Step in. Abide in my love. Immerse yourself in it."

What is your R.S.V.P. to this invitation? Will you accept?

_____

Read John 17:26.

Jesus explains how we get the great love of God into our hearts. Look at the first part of this verse. How does it happen?

_____

Now read John 17:3.

What is eternal life according to the second phrase of this verse?

_____

Now connect verse 3 with verse 26. What common key word or phrase is in both verses?

_____

That we may know God: that is the essence of eternal vine life. That is the heart of it. And what is the result of knowing God according to verse 26? That the love God uses to love Jesus would be in us and that Jesus Himself would be in us. That's how our buckets get filled. We know God. We know His name. How do we know His name? Because Jesus makes it known to us. It is not our struggling and striving and begging. We know Him and love Him because He first loved us.

Mother, are you still struggling with those unmet needs? Still aching to be filled? Then step into the loving Father's heart with Jesus. That heart is big enough and broad enough and deep enough to fill your innermost being.

Prayer

Lord, I receive Your love. I open my heart wide and take away the barriers.
Pour into my heart all the love that I can hold. I ask this in Jesus' name. Amen.

Share some love this week. Pack up the kids—of all ages—and visit a nursing home. In most cases, you don't even need an appointment. If you go around 5:00–5:30 P.M., you'll usually find the residents having dinner. Ask the supervisor's permission to go into the dining room and go from table to table just to say hi. It will only take about twenty minutes and you will be blessed as much or more than the residents.

If you have kids who play the piano, ask their teacher if a short recital could be arranged at the nursing home. There is usually a piano available and the Activities Directors I've met are delighted to accommodate.

If you have older kids who balk at this idea, go by yourself, and then come home and share with the family some of the meaningful moments of your visit. Don't make them feel guilty about not going with you. Just let them get acquainted with the idea slowly and perhaps someday they'll go with you.

If you start early, your kids will grow up with the important knowledge of how to share love with older adults.

DAY 2

Instruction to Love

BEGIN WITH PRAYER

Address God as "Daddy" today in your prayer time.
Tell Him everything that is on your heart and mind.

Read John 15:10–12.

What is the instruction in verse 10?

_____

The second fruit of the Spirit is mentioned in verse 11. What is it?

_____

In verse 12, the instruction becomes a command. Copy verse 12 here:

_____

_____

Jesus had given two commands about love earlier in His ministry. Read Mark 12:30–31.

What are the two commands in those verses?

1._____

2._____

We are commanded to love God with all our hearts and to love our neighbors as much as we love our-selves. That means we have three love interests. God, ourselves, and others. Jesus didn't suggest that we love. He commanded it.

Read 1 John 3:23–24.

What are the two commands in these verses?

_____

_____

But how do we love when we've been hurt? Wronged? Insulted? Abused? How can we keep this com-mandment to love?

FORGIVENESS

Read Matthew 5:43–48.

What two things are you to do for people who are hard to love, according to verse 44?

_____

There is an implied reward according to this passage. What behavior is rewarded?

_____

Write the initials of the person in your life who is difficult to love. Maybe there is more than one.

_____

Now fill in the blank. "I choose this day to love _____ [initials] as an act of my will and not my feelings. I have been crucified with Christ and no longer live. The love of Christ is in me and that is enough to love him/her."

Write out a prayer for this person. It might go something like this: *Lord, I ask You to pour out Your love on* _____. *I forgive them for every hurt they have caused me and I ask You to forgive them. Bless them, Father. Put Your hand of blessing on every part of their life. Show them Your love. I pray this in Jesus' name. Amen.*

_____

_____

_____

Mothering Tip

At the dinner table tonight, ask the family some of the following questions, choosing the ones that are appropriate for the ages of your children. Relate the questions and answers to Matthew 5:43–44.

"What should happen to a kid who hits other children at school? What should the kids do? What should the teacher do?"

"What do you think should happen to murderers? What should the police do? What attitude should we have toward them?"

"When is it time to punish wrongdoers and when is it time to love and pray for them?"

DAY 3

Inspiration to Love

BEGIN WITH PRAYER

Pray for all those in authority over you today:
for government leaders, for your pastor, and for your husband.

∽

There is no one on earth who has demonstrated love like the Lord Jesus Christ. His is perfect love. In His teaching on love in John 15, he gives us the secret to His love.

Read John 15:13.

Read 1 John 3:16.

What is the demonstration of ultimate love?

Now that you've been through this study, how would you tell a wife she can demonstrate love to her husband?

How can a mother demonstrate love to her children?

How does this self-sacrificial love fill her love bucket?

_____

Read the book of Ruth today. It is only four chapters and reads like a love story. But today I want you to focus on Ruth's sacrifice at the end of chapter 1.

Read Ruth 1:1–17.

What opportunity did Ruth have to avoid making a sacrifice?

_____

What did her sister-in-law do with that opportunity?

_____

Copy verses 16 and 17 here:

_____

_____

What sacrifice did Ruth choose to make?

_____

Do you see the thread that runs throughout this study? Do you see now how to be free? Free to love unconditionally? It happens when you lay down your life and choose to love. It happens when you pour yourself out, so He can pour Himself in.

Does that mean you are to be a milquetoast, weak wife whose husband bulldozes over her? No! Sometimes laying down our lives means laying down passivity.

Does "laying down our lives" mean that we are to do everything our kids want and we now don't have a life? No! Sometimes it means tough love for our children by setting the right priorities for our lives—and theirs. And that means they are not the center of the universe!

What does it mean to lay down our lives? It means giving up on having "what I want, when I want it, the way I want it, so I am satisfied." It means letting go of my "right" to my own agenda for my life. It means turning the controls over to Jesus and submitting my will to His.

If you are a mother of young children, a part of what it will mean to lay down your life will be in the physical area. You will probably give up some sleep. You'll probably have a little one banging on the door of the bathroom wanting in when you step into the shower. You may have a sore left shoulder and broken fingernails.

Then with elementary-school-aged children you'll be asked to give up much of your own schedule. Running them to lessons and games and birthday parties and church activities and scouts will take up the time you used to spend on your leisure or work.

Preteens and teenagers require everything you've got to give. You'll take your life in your hands teaching them to drive, cry with them when they lose the big game or the special friend, and agonize with them over college entrance exams. You'll sacrifice new living room furniture for college savings accounts and a new outfit for school play costumes. You'll lose sleep waiting up for them. You'll lose sleep when they need to talk, which is almost never before midnight.

Adult children and grandchildren still need you to lay down your life. This time it may mean giving up having them all home for the holidays so they can be with the "other" family. It may mean helping with the child care of a grandchild just when you were free of child-rearing duties. Or it may mean setting boundaries with your adult children forcing them into adult responsibilities by not picking up the pieces of their poor decisions. That may be the hardest sacrifice of all.

Laying down your life means being expendable in God's hand for the sake of those He's put into your life. It's signing the blank check of your life and handing it to God to let Him fill in the amount.

Are you willing to pay the price? Are you willing to lay down your life for your "friends"? Do you consider your family members to be your friends?

Describe the scenario in which you currently find yourself faced with laying down your life.

_____

_____

_____

Spend some quiet time today consciously laying down your life at the foot of the cross.

Now read Ruth 4:13–22. How did God fill the love bucket Ruth had poured out?

_____

_____

_____

UNIT 10

Prayer

Lord, I lay down my life. I lay it down in my marriage, my mothering, my work, and my ministry.
It is Yours. Take my life, Lord. I offer it to You now in Jesus' name.
I trust You to meet all my needs according to Your riches in glory in Christ Jesus. Amen.

MOTHERING TIP

Think before you speak. Follow through. Expect good behavior from your children. Say what you mean.

DAY 4

Intimate Love

BEGIN WITH PRAYER

Ask God to teach you how to nourish your family with love.

Read John 15:14–15.

What two kinds of relationships are contrasted in these verses?

_____

Jesus says you are no longer a _____

He says now you are His _____

if you do what He commands. (See verse 12.)

According to verse 15, how are slaves treated?

_____

How are friends treated?

_____

Jesus says we are no longer slaves; we are His friends. He goes on to explain the difference. Slaves don't know what their masters are doing. But as His friends, He has made known to us all the things He has heard from the Father. We are in an intimate love relationship with the Lord. He shares His heart with us.

I want you to reread John 15:9–15 now.

Can you find the "blanket" of His unconditional love? Copy the verse where you find it.

_____

_____

Can you find the "blue ribbon" of how much He values you? Copy the verse where you find it.

_____

_____

Do you see the "letter jacket" He has placed on your shoulders? Do you see how He has given you identity? Copy the verse where you find it.

_____

_____

The "blanket of His love" is found in verse 9. "Just as the Father has loved Me, I have also loved you." How much does the heavenly Father love Jesus? We know that love is fathomless and infinite. That is the same measure of love He has for us. You are wrapped in His love. You are snuggled into His arms, cradled in His care.

The "blue ribbon" of significance is found in verse 13. Jesus describes the expression of ultimate value and love of someone. "Greater love has no one than this, that one lay down his life for his friends." He laid down His life for you. He stretched out His arms and died for you because you were worth it! You are of ultimate value to the God of the universe! What anyone else says about your value is irrelevant!

The "letter jacket" of identification comes in verses 14 and 15. He says of us, "You are My friends.... No longer do I call you slaves...but I have called you friends...." "What a friend we have in Jesus" the hymn says. He is willing to be identified with little old me! The Christ, the Savior, the Redeemer Jesus the Lord is willing to call me His friend. He tells me everything He hears from the Father. He keeps no secrets from me. We are intimate friends sharing our hearts with one another. I belong to One who loves me so.

Take a few moments now to absorb the three gifts He is giving you. Take in the enormity of His love, your value in His eyes, and your identification with Him.

Write out a praise and worship prayer to Jesus. Thank Him for His gifts.

_____

_____

_____

_____

Prayer

Lord, I worship and praise Your holy name. You are awesome in power and authority.
I find it hard to believe Your love for me, the way You value me and the fact that You identify Yourself with me.
Thank You, Lord. Bless You, Lord. In Jesus' name. Amen.

Mothering Tip

All three of our children were involved in high school sports and drama. Invariably during a play-off series or during dress rehearsals leading up to opening night, my teens had trouble sleeping. Here's what I did that might get you started thinking about what you can do to love and support your teenager when they are under stress.

I first made some camomile tea. (Yes, just like Peter Rabbit's mother.) Then as they sipped the warm liquid, I would rub down their legs. That's always what seemed to ache the most. After they finished the tea, I would tuck them into bed just like a preschooler and rub their back, shoulders, and head. As I massaged the tight muscles, I sang old lullabies from their childhood. Somehow going through old familiar routines from their childhood seemed to relax them. Then I would tell them to "melt into the bed like a hot stick of butter." Finally, I finished the night with a short word of prayer as I patted their backs.

Were they spoiled? Well, my grandmother said you can't spoil a child with love; only if you don't make him mind. So I lavished on the love and support when my teens were under duress. It served to bring us closer together and to give my teens a boost just when they needed it most.

DAY 5

BEGIN WITH PRAYER

Pray for all the other moms in the MotherWise family.

Pray that they will know Christ and the power of His resurrection in their mothering.

Pray that all the fruit of the Spirit will come bursting forth from their lives.

Also pray that all the children whose mothers have been touched by this ministry will

"taste and see that the Lord is good" as they are exposed to the fruit

of the Spirit coming through their mom's lives.

On this last day of our time together, I want to leave you with the awe-inspiring words of Jesus:

Read John 15:16.

Did you choose Jesus first, or did He choose you?

_____

What else did He do for you?

_____

Why did He appoint you?

_____

What do you think it means when it says "that your fruit will remain"?

_____

THE LETTER JACKET OF IDENTIFICATION

Jesus chose you! Not only does He call you His friend, He chose you and appointed you to bear His fruit: the fruit of His Spirit. When you are in union with Jesus, abiding in Him, you bear His fruit. You have been chosen to be on His team. You are wearing the letter jacket that identifies you with Him. And He has given you the game plan. The first thing to do is to "go."

What does it mean to "go"? In the Greek New Testament, the word is *hupago* which means "depart, get hence, go away."[1] I want you to read three short stories that have the same word *hupago* or "go." See if you can find out what it means from the context of these verses.

Read Matthew 9:1–7.

The word *go* is in verse 6. Who was asked to go and why?

_____

_____

_____

Read Matthew 18:15–17.

The word *go* is in verse 15. Who was asked to go and why?

_____

_____

_____

Read Matthew 19:16–22.

The word go is in verse 21. Who was asked to go and why?

_____

_____

The paralytic who was healed, the mediator, and the rich young ruler were all instructed to take an active role. They were to move from where they were to where they needed to be to be obedient.

The paralytic had to pick up his bed and "go" home. It was time to move. The healing had taken place. Now it was time to move into God's plan for his life.

A mediator had to go to the brother who had sinned. He couldn't be passive and still be obedient. He had to move from where he was into God's plan for his life.

The rich, young ruler had to go and sell his possessions. He couldn't hang on to his old life and take hold of what Jesus held out to him. He had to move from where he was into God's plan for his life.

The paralytic chose to go. The rich young ruler did not.

Are you willing to "go" and bear fruit, fruit that will last? Will you move from where you are into God's plan for you?

Has God spoken to you during these ten weeks? Is there a specific area of your life where you will have to move from where you are to get into God's plan for your life?

Journal your thoughts.

_____

_____

_____

_____

John 15:16 says that not only are we to "go," but we are to "go and bear fruit, and that [our] fruit should remain." Mom, have you ever thought about the generations that will come after you? Just imagine for a moment the children of your children, and their children, and their children.

If you exhibit unconditional love to your children, and they in turn exhibit it to their children, can you see the godly line forming? If you love the Lord your God with all your heart and with all your soul and with all your mind, and your children see that and follow the Lord in the same way, can you see the "fruit that remains"?

Never in America's history have children been more in need of strong parenting. Never have we needed mothers to be full of the fruit of the vine life of Jesus more than we do now.

Will you rise to the challenge? Will you be a mother in this generation who commits body, soul, and spirit to being a branch hanging only onto the vine for life? Will you allow Him full access to your heart that He might fill it up until the fruit overflows?

Prayer

Lord Jesus, You have chosen me to be a receptacle of Your vine life.
I cannot even grasp the wonder of Your divine love.
Now Lord, take me, mold me, fill me, use me.
I give myself utterly into Your hands for Your purpose.
Raise up after me children and children's children who call upon Your holy name.
I make this prayer in the name of the one that is above all names.
That name is Jesus. Amen.

UNIT 10

Mothering Tip

Simplify your life. Today choose to do something to clear out clutter; say no to an unnecessary activity; or just stay very still and quiet. Remember that adding more activities, more possessions, and communicating with more people will not satisfy your needs. Have the courage to choose the simple life...simply dependent on the vine life of Jesus.

Review

To find out how much you retained of our ten-week study, let's recount the priorities of your life. Name the priority and the key words that go with that priority:

PRINCIPLE #1: _____

    Key Word: _____

    Key lessons you learned:

_____

_____

_____

PRINCIPLE #2: _____

    Key Word: _____

    Key lessons you learned:

_____

_____

_____

PRINCIPLE #3: _____

    Key Word: _____

    Key lessons you learned:

_____

_____

_____

PRINCIPLE #4: _____

Key Word: _____

Key lessons you learned:

_____

_____

_____

PRINCIPLE #5: _____

Key Word: _____

Key lessons you learned:

_____

_____

_____

Conclusion

You have completed the MotherWise *Freedom for Mothers* course! Congratulations! I am praying that you will continue to study God's Word as you grow as a woman of God, as a wife, and as a mother.

We would like for you to fill out the following evaluation form and mail it to our office. We would love to hear from you. We are always seeking to improve our program. We want your input. We would also like to hear how God has worked in your life during these ten weeks. So fill out the form and mail it in today or e-mail your answers to deniseglenn@motherwise.org.

God bless you.

Love,

Denise

Evaluation Form

Date: _____ / _____ / _____

Name: _____

Address: _____

_____

_____

Group Location: _____

1. What was your favorite part of *Freedom for Mothers?* Why?

_____

_____

_____

2. What was your greatest need that this Bible study met during the past ten weeks?

_____

_____

_____

3. Give your suggestions for improving the Bible study or mothering skills.

_____

_____

_____

_____

4. How many units did you complete at home?

_____

5. Please write out a testimony of what God has done in your life through MotherWise.

_____

_____

_____

_____

_____

_____

_____

_____

_____

_____

PLEASE RETURN THIS PAGE TO:

MotherWise

11875 W. Little York, Suite 1104

Houston, Texas 77041

or

Fax: (713) 849-5893

or

www.motherwise.org

Appendix

Materials from Jennifer Kennedy Dean, author of *Heart's Cry, Power Praying,* and *Live a Praying Life*—a thirteen-week workbook on prayer with videos and leader's guide, *Riches Stored in Secret Places, Secret Place of the Most High,* and her latest, *He Restores My Soul: A 40-Day Journey toward Personal Renewal* (due out in October, published by Broadman Holman) may be obtained by writing:

The Praying Life Foundation
P.O. Box 62
Blue Springs, MO 64013
E-mail: PrayLife@aol.com
Phone: (816) 228-8899
Or order on-line: www.prayinglife.org

Materials from Dr. Charles Solomon, author of *Handbook to Happiness* may be obtained by writing:
Solomon Publications
P.O. Box 6115
Sevierville, TN 37864
Fax: (423) 429-0144

To get info on *MOVIEGUIDE* and Ted Baehr's ministry:
The Christian Film and Television Commission
2510-G Las Posas Road #502
Camarillo, CA 93010
(800) 899-6684

Christian Music Magazine
107 Kenner Avenue
Nashville, TN 37205
(615) 386-3011
www.ccmmagazine.com

Notes

Unit 2

1. *Experiencing God*, Henry Blackaby (Nashville, Tenn: LifeWay Press, 1990), 8.

2. *World Book 1985*, Vol. G, 288–90.

3. *Handbook to Happiness*, Dr. Charles Solomon (Wheaton, Ill.: Tyndale House, 1983), 67, 69, 71.

4. *Strong's Exhaustive Concordance, Greek Dictionary of the New Testament*, Number 1411, 24.

5. Ibid., Number 4492, 63.

6. Ibid., Number 2311, 36.

7. Ibid., Number 2638, 40.

8. Ibid., Number 1097, 20.

9. Ibid., Number 4137, 58.

Unit 3

1. *Kids Online—Protecting Your Children in Cyberspace,* Donna Rice Hughes (Grand Rapids, Mich.: Fleming H. Revell, a division of Baker Book House, 1998), 47.

2. *Heart's Cry,* Jennifer Kennedy Dean (Birmingham, Ala.: New Hope Publishing, 1997), 15.

3. *Strong's Greek Dictionary* (Nashville, Tenn.: Thomas Nelson Publishers, 1984), Number 4561, 64.

Unit 4

1. *The Media-Wise Family,* Ted Baehr (Colorado Springs, Colo.: ChariotVictor Publishing, 1998), 127.

2. Ibid., 274, 275.

3. Ibid., 278, 279.

4. Ibid., 285, 286.

5. Ibid., 284.

6. Ibid., 272.

7. *Streetwise Parents, Foolproof Kids,* Dan Korem (Colorado Springs, Colo.: Navpress, 1992), 14–15.

8. *Strong's Hebrew and Chaldee Dictionary* (Nashville, Tenn.: Thomas Nelson Publishers, 1984), Number 1347, 25.

9. *Strong's Greek Dictionary,* Number 2754, 41.

10. *Strong's Hebrew and Chaldee Dictionary* (Nashville, Tenn.: Thomas Nelson Publishers, 1984) Number 4066, 62.

Unit 5

1. *What the Bible Says about Child Training,* J. Richard Fugate (Elkton, Md.: Full Quart Press, 1998), 238.

2. Taken from *Boundaries with Kids,* Dr. Henry Cloud and Dr. John Townsend, © 1998 by Henry Cloud and John Townsend. Used by permission of Zondervan Publishing House.

3. Ibid., 10.

4. *The Complete Book of Baby and Child Care*, Grace H. Ketterman, M. D. and Herbert L. Ketterman, M.D. (Grand Rapids, Mich.: Fleming H. Revell, 1982), 378–9.

5. *Discover the Master's Plan for Mastering Life*, © 1993 by the Association of Exchanged Life Ministries, Inc., Aurora, Colo., 9–10.

6. Taken from *The Marriage Builder*, Dr. Larry Crabb, © 1982 by Zondervan Publishers. Used by permission of Zondervan Publishing House.

Unit 6

1. From a story told by Bible teacher Joyce Meyer on a radio program.

2. *Discover the Master's Plan*, 29–30.

Unit 7

1. *World Book Encyclopedia*, Volume 2 (World Book Inc., 1987), 618–29.

2. Ibid.

3. Ibid.

4. Ibid.

5. *Discover the Master's Plan*, 37.

Unit 8

1. *Shattering Your Strongholds*, Liberty Savard (North Burnswick, N.J.: Bridge-Logos Publishers, 1993), 139–40.

Unit 9

1. *Together At Home*, Dean and Grace Merrill (Nashville, Tenn.: Thomas Nelson Publishers, 1985).

2. *Lord, Is It Warfare? Teach Me to Stand*, Kay Arthur (Sisters, Ore.: Multnomah Publishers, 1991), 14–16.

3. *Strong's Hebrew and Chaldee Dictionary* (Nashville, Tenn.: Thomas Nelson Publishers, 1984), Number 7853, 7854, 115.

4. *Strong's Greek Dictionary* (Nashville, Tenn.: Thomas Nelson Publishers, 1984,) Number 1228, 22.

5. From a sermon by Dr. Charles Stanley, pastor First Baptist Church, Atlanta, Georgia.

6. *Roget's College Thesaurus*, Philip D. Morehead and Andrew T. Morehead (New York: Signet Books published by New American Library, 1985), 53.

Unit 10

1. *Strong's Greek Dictionary* (Nashville, Tenn.: Thomas Nelson Publishers, 1984), Number 5217, 73.